Praise for David Kupelian *and*
HOW EVIL WORKS

"With the unapologetic outrage of a saint and the fearless fury of a General Patton, here comes David Kupelian turning a blowtorch of good upon the putrid cobwebs of evil. Do you remember removing the back of a clock to look into the workings? In *How Evil Works,* Kupelian lets us look directly into evil itself. There it is—every tick, every tock, every trick, every shock."

—Barry Farber, legendary radio talk-show host and author

"David Kupelian skillfully exposes the secular left's rotten-apple peddlers in devastating detail."

—Michelle Malkin, #1 *New York Times* bestselling author of
Culture of Corruption and Fox News contributor

"David Kupelian dares to tell the truth about the overwhelming forces in our society which take us away from our original American concept of freedom."

—Dr. Laura Schlessinger, talk-show host and
New York Times bestselling author

"David Kupelian reveals the hidden mechanisms that allow lies and deception to take root in modern America."

—Jerome R. Corsi, Ph.D.

"In years to come Americans will acknowledge a debt of gratitude to David Kupelian for his honesty, courage, and laser-like insight."

—Rabbi Daniel Lapin, author, radio talk-show host,
founder of the American Alliance of Jews & Christians

This title is also available as an eBook

HOW
EVIL
WORKS

Understanding and Overcoming the Destructive
Forces That Are Transforming America

DAVID KUPELIAN

THRESHOLD
EDITIONS

NEW YORK LONDON TORONTO SYDNEY

Threshold Editions
A Division of Simon & Schuster, Inc.
1230 Avenue of the Americas
New York, NY 10020

Copyright © 2010 by David Kupelian

First Threshold Editions trade paperback edition March 2011

THRESHOLD EDITIONS and colophon are trademarks of Simon & Schuster, Inc.

For information about special discounts for bulk purchases, please contact Simon & Schuster Special Sales at 1-866-506-1949 or business@simonandschuster.com.

The Simon & Schuster Speakers Bureau can bring authors to your live event. For more information or to book an event contact the Simon & Schuster Speakers Bureau at 1-866-248-3049 or visit our website at www.simonspeakers.com.

All Bible quotations, unless otherwise noted, are from the King James Version.

Designed by William Ruoto

Cover design by Linda Daly

Manufactured in the United States of America

10 9 8 7 6 5 4

Library of Congress Cataloging-in-Publication Data

Kupelian, David, 1949–
  How evil works / David Kupelian. — 1st Threshold Editions hardcover ed.
    p.   cm. — (Threshold nonfiction original hardcover)
  1. Good and evil.   I. Title.
BJ1401.K868 2010
170–dc22   2009032887

ISBN 978-1-4391-6819-6
ISBN 978-1-4391-6820-2 (pbk)
ISBN 978-1-4391-6864-6 (ebook)

To my father, Vahey S. Kupelian, who as a little boy survived the unthinkable evils of genocide, escaped to the promised land of America, worked really hard, and eventually became a rocket scientist dedicated to defending his adopted country

+

CONTENTS

+

INTRODUCTION

The great paradox of the human race—namely, that we're so smart we understand just about everything, except ourselves—has never been more striking, or more troubling, than right now.

Today, we understand the physics of an expanding universe and the mysterious behavior of quarks. We know how to create vaccines and custom genes, replace body parts and build space robots. Our knowledge of life and the universe continues to grow dramatically in every field imaginable. Except one.

We don't understand evil—what it is, how it works, and why it so routinely and effortlessly ruins our lives. Put another way, we don't understand ourselves. Despite the human race's extraordinary capacity for invention and progress, we clearly have a millennia-old blind spot in this one all-important area.

Consider: While living in an age of exponential growth in knowledge, 20 to 30 million Americans currently take powerful, mood-altering psychiatric drugs to deal with depression, bipolar disorder, and a slew of other "mental health" problems—despite the troubling link between those drugs and extreme violent behavior. Our relationships are increasingly fragile: We can't seem to stay married—

divorce and family breakdown are still rampant. Besides, we're not even sure what we believe anymore. Increasingly, Americans are forsaking their traditional faiths of Christianity and Judaism in favor of witchcraft and other pagan or New Age practices, while angry, in-your-face atheist manifestos top bestseller lists.

Meanwhile, today's culture of sexual anarchy manifests ever new and disturbing syndromes—same-sex marriage, people attempting to surgically morph into the opposite gender, pedophiles and polygamists striving to ride the gay-rights bandwagon to acceptance, and an epidemic of female schoolteachers sexually preying on their students. For many, Judeo-Christian morality, the foundation of Western civilization for thousands of years, has become a quaint memory.

America herself is in increasing conflict, more polarized than at any time since the Civil War. Politicians routinely tell colossal lies to advance their agendas, and regardless of who gets elected president, government just seems to grow uncontrollably, destroying the people's freedom, prosperity, and contentment. To top it off, a malignant version of a major world religion is replicating ferociously across the globe with a message of radical intolerance, terror, and domination, yet the submissive, almost apologetic response of many in the West resembles a national version of the Stockholm syndrome.

Clearly, despite our massive accumulation of knowledge, we're still missing something essential: an understanding of ourselves and the forces acting through us that mysteriously churn out deception, suffering, and, all too often, tragedy.

Most books about evil are written either by theologians, who offer doctrinal explanations of its origin and implications, or psychologists and psychiatrists, who present a more clinical perspective. I am none of these, but rather, a working journalist.

In the news business, a great deal of what we call "news" is, let's face it, *evil*. When a mother reads her children a bedtime story and tucks them into bed, it's not news. But if she drowns her five children in the bathtub, as Andrea Yates did, it's big news. When you've reported on personal, political, and cultural corruption for as many years as I have, it's only natural to want to identify underlying causes. Thus my long-term interest in this subject—rooted not only in my work as a journalist, but also perhaps in being the offspring of genocide survivors and so having been aware from an early age of "the evil that men do"—has resulted in an earlier book, *The Marketing of Evil*, and now this one.

In the present book, using today's most sensational news stories as a starting point, together we will explore, as the title says, *How Evil Works*—the actual mechanics, the inner workings, and the "operating system" of this most vexing and underexamined part of all our lives.

We'll explore such questions as these: *How does terrorism really work?* (It's intended not just to frighten and intimidate, but to reprogram our beliefs, per the Stockholm syndrome.) *Why are neopagan and New Age religions like Wicca becoming so popular?* (America's increasing disillusionment with Christianity has created a giant cultural and spiritual vacuum, into which alternative religions are being drawn.) *Why do so many entertainment celebrities who "have it all"— talent, fame, good looks, wealth, influence—end up self-destructing?* (Being worshipped like gods is similar to taking a potent, intensely pleasurable drug like cocaine—it feels good for a time, but inevitably causes tremendous problems.) *Why are big lies more believable than little ones?* (Everyone tells little white lies, but not big, bold, audacious ones, and so they assume others wouldn't, either—an assumption world-class liars use to their great advantage. More important, big lies possess an inherent power to upset us, thereby triggering a key control mechanism.) *Why are boys doing worse in school today than girls?* (As America becomes increasingly "feminized," boys, men, and masculinity are being subtly but seriously maligned.) *Why do we treat mental-emotional-spiritual problems like rage and depression with drugs?* (We've been seduced by secular medical "experts" who tell us what all egos love to hear: "It's not your fault.")

Fortunately, exposing these hidden dynamics to the light of day triggers something truly amazing: once we really understand "how

evil works"—not just in the disasters and mega-crimes that dominate the headlines, but in our own lives as well—evil actually loses
much of its power over us, and the way out becomes more clear.

Indeed, facilitating such understanding—and perhaps even some
healing, something we all desperately need—is precisely the aim of
this book.

HOW
EVIL
WORKS

CHAPTER 1

✦

IN GOVERNMENT WE TRUST

Why We Elect Liars as Leaders

Nixon: "I Wasn't Lying. I Said Things That Later On Seemed to Be Untrue"
  —*Washington Post*, NOVEMBER 29, 1978

Clinton Concedes He Lied About Affair
  —*Washington Times*, AUGUST 18, 1998

Obama Promises "Tax Cuts" to 95 Percent of Americans, Even Though 44 Percent of Filers Pay $0 in Income Taxes.
  —*Manchester Union Leader*, NOVEMBER 4, 2008

Did you ever stop to wonder why most governments—no matter where on earth you look, or what time period you consider—tend toward being tyrannical and predatory? I'm not referring just to those unfortunate nations suffering under openly brutal dictatorships. Even here in the West, where our elected governments portray themselves as benevolent and democratic, somehow they always end up taxing, legislating, and regulating us into servitude. Why?

To bring this topic into sharp focus, let's start by taking a whirlwind tour of the world's governments:

• Before America and its coalition partners invaded Iraq and deposed Saddam Hussein, giving the Iraqi people a chance to choose another destiny, here's what life was like there, according to the U.S. State Department: "In 1979, immediately upon coming to power, Saddam Hussein silenced all political opposition in Iraq and converted his one-party state into a cult of personality. Over the more than 20 years since then, his regime has systematically executed, tortured, imprisoned, raped, terrorized and repressed Iraqi people."[1] Though Iraq was once "rich in culture with a long history of intellectual and scientific achievement," Saddam "silenced its scholars and doctors, as well as its women and children" with unimaginable cruelty, the official report documents:

> Iraqi dissidents are tortured, killed or disappear in order to deter other Iraqi citizens from speaking out against the government or demanding change. A system of collective punishment tortures entire families or ethnic groups for the acts of one dissident. Women are raped and often videotaped during rape to blackmail their families. Citizens are publicly beheaded, and their families are required to display the heads of the deceased as a warning to others who might question the politics of this regime.[2]

With such unspeakable atrocities a part of daily life, why didn't more Iraqis complain publicly? Maybe because of Saddam's decree in 2000 authorizing the government to amputate the tongues of citizens who criticized him or his government.

The report also documents Saddam's use of chemical weapons (that's right, "weapons of mass destruction") against his own people, destroying more than sixty villages and 30,000 citizens—some international organizations say 60,000—with mustard gas and nerve agents.

• In North Korea, every citizen is the slave of a demented ruling family. While Kim Jong Il—or the "dear leader," as all are required to call him—lives in ostentatious regal splendor, most North Koreans endure crushing poverty. Indeed, during the 1990s as much as 10 percent of the nation's population—an estimated two and a half million people—starved to death as a result of the communist nation-cult's dysfunctional command economy.

"The unwritten and unspoken compact prior to the famine," explained Andrew S. Natsios, administrator of the U.S. Agency for International Development, in Senate testimony, "was that the people surrendered their freedom in exchange for which the state agreed to care for them, heavily tempered by political loyalty, from cradle to grave."[3]

"Cradle-to-grave security"—there's that coveted socialist holy grail we're always hearing about. But for millions of North Koreans, all they've gotten in the bargain is cradle *and* grave, with not much in between. In fact, it's impossible to adequately convey the sheer horror they endure in their day-to-day lives, but perhaps this quick story from the *Washington Post* will provide a tiny taste:

> Han, a Communist Party official in North Korea, was walking home from work when he heard he was in trouble. He had smuggled a radio back from China after an official trip. He listened to it late at night, huddled with earphones on and shades drawn, to hear music that brought him a whisper of sanity and took him away from the horrors of his day.
>
> Now, someone had found it, or someone had told.
>
> "It could have been my children who said something outside. It could have been my friend; one knew," said Han, 39, who spoke on condition he be identified only by his surname.
>
> "If a farmer or laborer had a radio, he could have been released," Han said. "But I was an official. In my case, it would have been torture and a life sentence in a political prisoners' camp."[4]

Torture and life in prison for possessing a radio? That just about sums up life in this communist "workers' paradise" that has devolved into a brutal and bizarre national cult.

• Zimbabwe, once a gleaming gem of a country in the central highlands of southern Africa, featuring the breathtakingly beautiful, mile-wide Victoria Falls, used to be a major breadbasket for the entire continent. That was when it was called Rhodesia. But once Marxist Robert Mugabe was elected prime minister in 1980, Zimbabwe gradually was transformed into yet another indescribable hell-on-earth.

Thousands of productive white-owned commercial farms have been stolen by hordes of government-sanctioned thugs, the owners brutalized, tortured, and murdered, the farms left in ruin—causing the catastrophic collapse of the nation's once-robust agricultural base. Reformers and political opponents are routinely executed and Christian churches bulldozed. As a result, Zimbabwe's formerly thriving economy has disintegrated, causing the world's highest—and frankly incomprehensible—inflation rate, over 11 million percent![5] Average life expectancy has been cut almost in half, from 57 to only 34 years for females and 37 for males—the shortest life span of any nation on earth.[6]

Yes, I know, these are some of the worst governments on earth. But in truth, a great many other nations are not much better. Burma and Sudan are ruled by brutal military dictatorships and mass slaughter and genocide are normal there. The vast Middle East is made up largely of Arab-Muslim police states, almost two dozen of them, where Islam's strict, medieval sharia law reduces everyday life to one of repression, cruelty, and paralyzing fear at best—and at worst, terrorism, "honor killings," and death by stoning for relatively minor offenses (and sometimes for *no* offense)—all sugarcoated with a stiflingly rigid and intolerant religious code.

• China, currently with about a fifth of the world's population—more than 1.3 billion souls—is still at core a ruthless and suffocating communist dictatorship, despite its prodigious economic growth. The government imprisons anyone who dares criticize it. "An estimated 500,000 people are currently enduring punitive detention without charge or trial," reveals Amnesty International, "and millions are unable to access the legal system to seek redress for their grievances. Harassment, surveillance, house arrest and imprisonment of human rights defenders are on the rise. . . ."[7]

There's no free press in China, news organizations being largely owned and run by the government, which even censors the Internet (cyber-dissidents are imprisoned for signing online petitions and calling for reform). And the government's notorious one-child policy has been heartlessly enforced via mandatory sterilization, forced abortion, and even infanticide. Chinese goods may be cheap, but life there is even cheaper.

• What about Russia? Most in the West have the impression much has improved since the bad old Soviet days, but appearances can be deceiving. According to Andrey Illarionov, former senior economic policy adviser to Vladimir Putin, freedom in Russia has *deteriorated* dramatically in recent years. Specifically, he reveals, the year 2006 "was an extraordinary one in a sense of destruction of all types and all elements of freedom. Whichever area we can look at—the political system, legal system, court system, civil society, rule of law, division of powers, freedom of expression, freedom of mass media, freedom of association—everywhere, in each area, we see tremendous backlash against the basic liberties of Russian people."[8] As this supposedly "reformed" giant of a nation, which spans eleven time zones, continues increasingly to resemble its former, malignantly aggressive "superpower" alter ego, Russia internally is in crisis. Its judicial system is almost dysfunctional, there's virtually no freedom of the press, and international human rights organizations report widespread abuses, including systematic torture of people held by police.

We could continue on with our tour, but we'd just find that most other governments, from the Far East to Africa to South America, are corrupt, predatory, and power-hungry. Each typically perfumes its tyranny with an idealistic, utopian philosophy such as communism or Islamic fundamentalism to help control the population.

Even Europe and the United Kingdom, once the crown of Western civilization, are firmly in the grip of secular (de facto atheistic) socialism, which suffocates their once-vibrant Christian culture and seduces their citizens into giving up their hard-won freedoms, independence, and wealth in exchange for "cradle-to-grave" security.

That brings us to America.

The United States of America has a transcendent heritage of liberty rooted in self-government and personal responsibility, the result of a revolutionary two-hundred-year-old "experiment" so gloriously successful it became a shining light in an otherwise mostly dark world.

Yet, in recent decades, we too have been seduced. Many of us have been taught in our universities that the "self-evident truths" the founders relied upon are just outdated and dangerous myths. The press routinely portrays values the founders considered to be evil (high taxes, unrestrained federal power, permissive sexual morals) as good, and good as evil. Same with Hollywood, which once showcased pro-American and patriotic themes but now glorifies sex, extreme violence, and total moral confusion.

With this constant cultural subversion in the background, no wonder millions of Americans have gradually been demoralized into depending on government to solve all of their problems, fueling today's uncontrolled, cancerlike growth in government.

Power-hungry demagogues have always used basically the same methods: they demonize "the rich," claiming they obtained their wealth by exploiting and stealing from the downtrodden; they stir up racial or tribal hatreds at every opportunity; they blame convenient scapegoats for problems they themselves have caused; and they promise universal peace and happiness if we'll just give them unlimited power over us.

But they win our support only by appealing to the basest part of us—hate, dissatisfaction, greed, and especially *envy*. They know instinctively that if they can stir up and ignite these dark and addictive passions in all of us, they will seduce us away from our inner dependency on God, and instead create a massive voting bloc of people dependent upon *them*. The reward for this transference of fidelity is great power for them, and confusion, demoralization, and ultimate bondage for us. In its purest form, this phenomenon is known today as Marxism, communism, socialism—the spiritual core of which is raw envy.

Communism, as we know, is atheistic—where the government is the only god, the giver of blessings, the solver of problems, the dispenser of justice and mercy, the source of civilization's progress. Unfortunately, the only "progress" it actually confers is the progression from freedom to slavery.

Yet this is exactly the appeal that more and more Americans today have been conditioned to respond to, as we have gradually fallen away from the Judeo-Christian, free market values that once animated our culture and institutions. The envy-based system Marx unleashed on the world is alive and well, and in different forms still dominates large parts of the world. In America, it has taken root in the once-noble Democratic Party, and has made significant inroads into the Republican Party as well. In the age of Obama, it is coming into full bloom.

Although Ronald Reagan admirably presided over the dismantling of the "evil empire" of the Soviet Union, freeing its many "satellite" slave states, one cannot destroy evil itself. The temptation of socialism continues to corrupt whole societies, including America.

Even the encouragement of immorality—sexual promiscuity, abortion, easy divorce—is all part and parcel of the socialist modus operandi, because dissolute, dysfunctional people who have crossed the moral line and thus become estranged from the laws of God now need the "god" of socialist government.

MONSTER.GOV

To understand how the U.S. government has become the huge, parasitical entity it is today, let's clear our minds, take a deep breath, and for just a few minutes reflect on the truly transcendent and self-evident first principles of life, liberty, and property. Then the true basis for a just government—as well as an understanding of where we've gone astray—will come into sharp focus.

The brilliant French economist, statesman, and author Frédéric Bastiat expressed it eloquently:

> We hold from God the gift which includes all others. This gift is life—physical, intellectual, and moral life.
>
> But life cannot maintain itself alone. The Creator of life has entrusted us with the responsibility of preserving, developing, and perfecting it. In order that we may accomplish this, He has provided us with a collection of marvelous faculties. And He has put us in the midst of a variety of natural resources. By the application of our faculties to these natural resources we convert them into products, and use them. This process is necessary in order that life may run its appointed course.
>
> Life, faculties, production—in other words, individuality, liberty, property—this is man. And in spite of the cunning of artful political leaders, these three gifts from God precede all human legislation, and are superior to it. Life, liberty, and property do not exist because men have made laws. On the contrary, it was the fact that life, liberty, and property existed beforehand that caused men to make laws in the first place.[9]

What is law, then? Very simply, explains Bastiat, "It is the collective organization of the individual right to lawful defense":

> Each of us has a natural right—from God—to defend his person, his liberty, and his property. These are the three basic requirements of life, and the preservation of any one of them is completely dependent upon the preservation of the other two. For what are our faculties but the extension of our

individuality? And what is property but an extension of our faculties? If every person has the right to defend—even by force—his person, his liberty, and his property, then it follows that a group of men have the right to organize and support a common force to protect these rights constantly. Thus the principle of collective right—its reason for existing, its lawfulness—is based on individual right. And the common force that protects this collective right cannot logically have any other purpose or any other mission than that for which it acts as a substitute. Thus, since an individual cannot lawfully use force against the person, liberty, or property of another individual, then the common force—for the same reason—cannot lawfully be used to destroy the person, liberty, or property of individuals or groups.[10]

Nothing could be clearer than these basic, commonsense principles of fairness that any child could understand. Yet, over time, American government has abandoned its original principles, and the Constitution has become merely a venerated relic, with little deference paid to the founders' intent or vision. Indeed, ever since the Civil War (when the federal government, by force, imposed its authority on the individual nation-states to keep the union intact), government has grown steadily—and has almost never stopped growing. Today it is a virtual cancer, drawing much of the life and productive capability out of the nation, while feeding its own uncontrolled growth.

For example, here's how scientist and energy expert Arthur Robinson, Ph.D., explains America's scandalous inability to provide for its own energy needs:

> The reason is simple. Americans no longer possess the freedom to produce the goods and services required to maintain their former standard of living. Taxation—both direct and indirect through currency inflation—runaway government

regulation and government-sponsored-and-encouraged litigation have reduced the productivity of Americans below that required to maintain their way of life. This tyranny—this economic slavery—has been produced entirely by the federal and state governments of the United States.

There are no resource limitations, technological limitations, or geopolitical reasons for the current energy shortages and high prices. These shortages and prices are solely the result of taxation, regulation, and litigation that have stifled American energy-producing industries.[11]

More fundamentally, government has robbed Americans of their very substance by corrupting their money system. Congress created the Federal Reserve System in 1913, handing over to a private banking cartel the crucial responsibility for the nation's money supply, a responsibility that the founders had specifically vested in Congress in Article 1, Section 8 of the Constitution. Since then, Americans have seen the value of their money lose *95 percent* of its purchasing power[12] (a clandestine form of grand theft) and their economy continually destabilized by the Fed's artificial manipulation of interest rates and the money supply—all of which serve to cripple the free market. As Texas congressman and money expert Ron Paul puts it, "Every economic downturn suffered by the country over the last 80 years can be traced to Federal Reserve policy."[13]

If you reflect on what money really represents—it is your life and substance, literally stored energy—you'll see that life itself is being robbed by government.

As citizens struggle to earn enough to support their families and pay their mortgages, the government literally throws their money away. Yes—*throws it away.* The watchdog group Citizens Against Government Waste annually issues its famed *Pig Book*, which details the preceding year's wasteful spending by the federal government. You know, such as $1 million for the "Waterfree Urinal Conservation Initiative" or $50 million for an "indoor rainforest" in Coralville, Iowa.[14] Such spending has gone into overdrive under Barack Obama, with *twenty thousand* taxpayer-funded "stimulus" projects, including $3.4 million for an "eco-passage" in Florida to protect turtles from being run over by cars, $2.2 million for skylights in Montana's state-run liquor warehouse,[15] $1 million to pay for the removal of crickets in Utah, $200,000 for gang tattoo removal in Southern California, and almost $2 million for "swine odor research" in Iowa. And that's only a few projects—there are thousands of others.[16]

The level of squandering of taxpayers' substance is a wonder. One audit showed the U.S. Defense Department wasted $100 million on unused commercial airline tickets it had purchased, never bothering to collect refunds even though the tickets were returnable and refundable.[17]

And government doesn't just *waste* your money—it sometimes uses it to *fund evil*. Not too many years back, the public was less than thrilled to learn that the federal government was funneling their hard-earned tax dollars into support for obscene, perverse, and blasphemous "art." There was the "homoerotic photography" of Robert Mapplethorpe, featuring images too repugnant to be described here. Then there was Andres Serrano's *Piss Christ*, consisting of a crucifix submerged in the artist's urine (as well as *Piss Pope*, with the image of the pope in urine). And of course there was David Wojnarowicz's *Tongues of Flame*, depicting Jesus shooting up heroin. All funded by you.[18]

It's not just obscene art we've paid for; it's obscene politicians, too. We have a never-ending stream of sexually promiscuous "public servants": President Bill Clinton had a predatory sexual relationship with a White House intern barely older than his daughter. Then there was New Jersey governor James McGreevey, who held a press conference, wife stoically at his side, to announce he was coming out as a "gay American," and New York governor Eliot Spitzer, who frequented high-priced prostitutes, and presidential candidate John Edwards, who cheated on his cancer-stricken wife while accepting the "Father of the Year" award,[19] and Nevada senator John Ensign, a high-ranking, profamily Republican who cheated on his wife with a married female staffer. Even South Carolina governor Mark Sanford, once a top GOP presidential hopeful, confessed to an extramarital affair. The revelations are endless—our leaders frequenting prostitutes, preying on teenage congressional page boys, and betraying their sacred marriage vows.

In the current era, the socialistic transformation of America has accelerated at a truly frightening and unprecedented rate, with the expenditure of sums of money not comprehensible by mortal man, the nationalization of entire industries, and—less obvious to the public—the growing corruption of government itself. As Pulitzer-winning journalist George Will wrote in the *Washington Post,* "The [Obama] administration's central activity—the political allocation of wealth and opportunity—is not merely susceptible to corruption, it *is* corruption."[20]

But all this corruption and outrageous behavior shouldn't really be surprising. Why? For starters, it's very common for human beings, in or out of government, to lack strong moral principles—leaving them free to lie, manipulate, and steal in a multitude of obvious and subtle ways. Since virtually everyone is beset by typical human flaws such as egotism, greed, lust, envy, anger, and so on, how on earth do we expect the same flawed individuals suddenly to manifest great selflessness and nobility when they get into government? Doesn't make much sense, does it? That's precisely why our founders wisely created a national government with very limited powers and lots of internal checks and balances.

What we need to understand is that it's not just deranged psychopaths like Saddam Hussein and Robert Mugabe who give us tyrannical government; regular politicians and bureaucrats do it, too. As long as they're unprincipled and self-serving, more inclined to preserve their job, personal advantage, power, wealth, and comfort than to risk it all by championing the public good, the state will grow ever more tyrannical.

I know this sounds pretty negative, but we really need to understand why it is that governments just about always end up playing God and controlling our lives. Only then will the way out become clear.

Therefore let's pause, take a breath, and briefly reflect on the bottom-line reality of our lives on this earth. Though widely ignored, it's a fundamental truth almost everybody knows deep down:

There *really is* an all-knowing God. He *really does* create human beings whose true purpose is to discover ultimate fulfillment through obedience to Him in all things. And our life goes badly—and is *supposed to go badly*—if we defy His laws, which besides being written in the Bible are also "written" clearly inside each of us. (That is, we know it's wrong to steal from our neighbor, not just because Scripture says so, but because it's *obvious*—or as Jefferson put it, "self-evident" truth.)

If we fail to find this inner fidelity to God, then we *automatically* designate someone or something else to fill that necessary role: we will worship another "god." Moreover, when we are in rebellion against the true God, we *need* lies and deception to maintain our illusions—and people who love power are all too eager to step up and play that role for us.

That's right: we elect liars as leaders because we actually *need* lies if we're avoiding inner Truth. So, for example, let's say you've had an abortion but are in denial over the fact that you ended a life; you'd be attracted by the lies of an eloquent pro-choice politician defending abortion as a cherished constitutional right. Or say you foolishly took out a huge subprime home loan beyond your ability to repay; you'd probably support the politician who blames it all on greedy lenders and promises to force other taxpayers to bail you out. For those living in denial, lies do a great job of excusing their failings and validating their illusions.

Since bad government relies so totally on persuasive lying, let's take a closer look at that phenomenon. There's much more to it than you might think.

WHY POLITICIANS LIE,
AND WHY WE BELIEVE THEM

In *The Marketing of Evil*, I explore many powerful manipulation techniques used to alter Americans' attitudes toward everything from abortion to divorce to homosexuality. But there's one technique that reigns supreme as the king of all propaganda weapons—lying. To make evil look good, and good appear to be evil, you have to lie.

The power of lies is not so much in the little "white lies" that are part of the fabric of most of our lives. It's in the big lies. It's paradoxical, but we're more likely to believe big lies than small ones.

How can this be? Wouldn't the big, outrageous lie be more easily discerned and resisted than the small, less consequential lie? You'd think so, but you'd be wrong.

There's dark magic in boldly lying, in telling a "big lie"— repeatedly, with a straight face, and with confidence and authority.

One of the greatest liars of the last century, Adolf Hitler, taught that the bigger the lie, the more believable it was.

During World War II, the U.S. government's Office of Strategic Services, a precursor to today's CIA, assessed Hitler's methods this way:

> His primary rules were: never allow the public to cool off; never admit a fault or wrong; never concede that there may be some good in your enemy; never leave room for alternatives; never accept blame; concentrate on one enemy at a time and blame him for everything that goes wrong; people will believe a big lie sooner than a little one; and if you repeat it frequently enough people will sooner or later believe it.[21]

Hitler himself, in his 1925 autobiography, *Mein Kampf*, explained with eerie insight the fantastic power of lying:

> [I]n the big lie there is always a certain force of credibility; because the broad masses of a nation are always more easily

corrupted in the deeper strata of their emotional nature than consciously or voluntarily; and thus in the primitive simplicity of their minds they more readily fall victims to the big lie than the small lie, since they themselves often tell small lies in little matters but would be ashamed to resort to large-scale falsehoods. It would never come into their heads to fabricate colossal untruths, and they would not believe that others could have the impudence to distort the truth so infamously. Even though the facts which prove this to be so may be brought clearly to their minds, they will still doubt and waver and will continue to think that there may be some other explanation. For the grossly impudent lie always leaves traces behind it, even after it has been nailed down, a fact which is known to all expert liars in this world and to all who conspire together in the art of lying. These people know only too well how to use falsehood for the basest purposes. . . .[22]

Truly the words of an evil genius. But let's bring this explanation down to earth: Suppose, just prior to election day, a candidate accuses his opponent of immoral or illegal behavior. Even if the charges are totally false, and even if the accused candidate answers the charges credibly and effectively, "the grossly impudent lie always leaves traces behind it." In plain English, no matter how effectively the accused answers the charges, some people will still believe he's guilty, and many others will still retain varying degrees of doubt and uncertainty regarding the accused, who may well lose the election due to the cloud hanging over his head. This, as Hitler said, is the magic of lying that "is known to all expert liars in this world."

The "doubt-inducing" quality inherent in a "big lie" is actually more powerful even than Hitler explained in *Mein Kampf*. Let's say someone tells you a real whopper—for example, "Your husband/wife is cheating on you. I saw it with my own eyes." Although it's *totally untrue,* the big lie has the ability to upset you in a way the little, everyday white lie doesn't. And when you get upset over anything, guess what? You feel a little bit of guilt for becoming upset, a little angry, a little confused, perhaps a little fearful—and bingo, all those conflicting emotions cause you to be unable to think straight, and can easily result in your compulsively *believing* the lie. To put it another way: when you're upset, the lie takes on a mysterious quality of attraction and believability, as though a protective force field has temporarily been disabled, allowing the lie to enter your mental inner sanctum.

Hitler's principle is exactly what lying, ruthless leaders everywhere bank on to get their way with the public. Believe me, they understand all this—which is why we need to also.

USING LIES TO CREATE A CRISIS

One of the most creative uses of lying—and a key tactic for bending a population to your will—is the creation of a crisis. Now, anyone even superficially familiar with the history of the political left has heard references to the strategy of creating crises as a means of transforming society. You've probably heard of the "Hegelian dialectic," a key Marxist technique whereby an idea ("We need more gun control laws!") generates its opposite ("No, we don't need more gun laws, we just need tougher sentencing of criminals!"), which leads to a reconciliation of opposites, or synthesis ("Okay, we'll compromise by passing new gun control laws, but watering them down somewhat"). Likewise, maybe you've heard of the "Cloward-Piven Strategy"— inspired by left-wing radical organizer Saul Alinsky, whose methods Barack Obama adopted—which openly advocates the *creation of crises* to destroy capitalist society.[23] This is how socialist progress is achieved "peacefully": through conflict or crisis, which always is resolved in the direction of greater socialism.

The problem is, this "crisis creation" talk just sounds so crazy, so foreign to us, that it's hard to believe our fellow human beings, no matter how confused or deluded, could actually engage in such a practice. But it's not only true, it's actually a common part of everyday life.

Consider this nonpolitical example and note how it illustrates the power of a crisis to mold people to the deceiver's will: In one child abduction case, a little girl was approached after school by a man she didn't know. He claimed her house was burning down, that her parents were busy putting out the fire, and that he was a friend of the parents, who had asked him to pick up their daughter and take her to them. The crisis—and the emotional upset the girl experienced over the thought of her house being on fire and her parents in danger—drowned out her normal caution about getting into a car with a stranger. You guessed it: the stranger was a predator who had concocted the lie for the sole purpose of upsetting and thereby tricking the girl into going with him so he could brutalize and murder her.

This tragic story makes an important point: a crisis throws us off our guard, upsets us, and inclines us to make decisions and accept "solutions" we normally would reject.

Politically, the strategy is to create a crisis, or exploit a real one, by throwing people into a mode where they can be redirected toward a predetermined "solution"—whether it's imposing "carbon penalties" on businesses in response to fears of global warming, or a trillion-dollar taxpayer-funded corporate bailout in response to a dire "financial crisis," or draconian gun control laws in response to a rash of school shootings. We're talking about solutions that people would normally reject, but now in a crisis *accept,* and that establish as a result a new baseline of what is *normal*—which becomes the starting point for pushing the nation still further leftward in response to the next "crisis."

Let's look at a few examples of fake "crises." They're all around us:

• Small towns and cities across America pull a certain stunt with depressing regularity around election time. They claim that if taxpayers don't vote in favor of a new tax levy, they'll be forced to eliminate or drastically cut back police and fire protection—two of the few services the people actually want from their government. I once lived in a town where the city council and city manager decided the way to force voters to approve their new tax levy would be to threaten to completely eliminate police protection within the city limits between midnight and 8 A.M. No joke. This was a crisis of their own creation and for their own obvious purposes. After all, the city council members and their budget committee could have reprioritized their budget to cut back on street sweeping, park maintenance, library hours, raises and benefits for city employees, or other things less crucial to the public safety and welfare, and gotten by on the existing tax base without leaving the citizens vulnerable to criminals every night. As I said, this is a common tactic in cities and towns up and down the turnpike.

• The radical environmental movement's primary modus operandi is the creation of crises where none exist. The "spotted owl" crisis in my home state of Oregon is a great example. Environmentalists claimed the northern spotted owl was dying out because of commercial logging of old-growth forests where the birds nested. So in 1991 a compliant judge halted logging in Oregon's national forests, causing the loss of about thirty thousand jobs, an 80 percent reduction in timber harvesting, a consequent decrease in the supply of lumber, and sky-high prices. I remember—I was there. However, it wasn't owls that environmentalists were in love with; they were in love with stopping loggers from harvesting any trees in Oregon's old-growth forests. The owls just provided the needed "crisis."

Here's the rest of the story. Long after Oregon's timber-based economy was decimated by the court-ordered logging ban, the northern spotted owl population inexplicably continued to decline. Surprise! New research showed logging in old-growth forests wasn't the problem at all. The real problem, it turned out, was competition from another larger and more aggressive species of owl that liked the same habitat and food as the spotted owl.

The truth is, ever since "socialism" lost its luster as the salvation of mankind (because it has never actually worked as promised anywhere), the environmental movement has become one of the most powerful, modern battering rams of the left for advancing the same socialist agenda. And of course, the biggest environmental cause of all is global warming.

• Today, a generation of children worldwide is being brainwashed into believing they face imminent doom—monster hurricanes and tornadoes, polar ice melting and raising ocean levels, leading to catastrophic flooding, tidal waves, and other cataclysmic events. Many have been forced to sit in classrooms and watch Al Gore's film, *An Inconvenient Truth,* in which he claims the oceans may rise by twenty feet, leading to worldwide devastation. Not to be outdone, NBC reporter Meredith Vieira warned on national TV of the oceans rising— are you ready?—*two hundred feet.*[24] Thus, while the kids suffer from doomsday nightmares, grown-ups respond to the "crisis" by clamoring for "solutions" offered by the environmentalist crisis creators.

And yet, not only is there no scientific basis for either NBC's two hundred feet or Gore's twenty-feet figure, in reality *tens of thousands* of scientists have gone on record stating their belief that man-caused global warming is a fake crisis. Indeed, as of this writing, more than 30,000 American scientists, including over 9,000 with Ph.D.s, have signed a petition stating: "There is no convincing scientific evidence that human release of carbon dioxide, methane, or other greenhouse gases is causing or will, in the foreseeable future, cause catastrophic heating of the Earth's atmosphere and disruption of the Earth's climate."[25] And yet this "crisis," based on increasingly dubious science, has become the U.S. government's pretext for imposing truly draconian policy initiatives that many fear will cripple the nation's economy.

• Another legacy of phony environmental crises is our fear of nuclear power. In truth, nuclear energy is clean, homegrown, and abundant, and its safety record is extremely good. Many other nations—including France, Russia, and Japan—have long taken advantage of this amazing power source. But irrational fear, in response to an environmentalist-created "crisis" mentality, has gripped the American consciousness for decades and contributed greatly to our dangerous national dependence on foreign energy sources.

• The "Fairness Doctrine" is a freedom-destroying solution to a crisis that doesn't exist. With the exception of talk radio and certain online and cable TV news offerings, virtually the entire news media establishment is overwhelmingly left of center. Yet some congressmen and senators claim there's an unfair *conservative* bias in the media (talk radio) that demands "balance" by legally forcing radio stations to provide airtime to "opposing views"—that is, to the left-leaning views that utterly dominate the rest of the information media.

• Racism is largely a manufactured crisis in America today. So-called black leaders such as Reverends Jesse Jackson and Al Sharpton are longtime professional race-baiters who thrive on stirring up racial suspicions and hatreds. In reality, America is probably the least racist nation in the world. Yes, we had slavery, but that ceased a century and a half ago when we sacrificed more than six hundred thousand American lives in the Civil War (more than in all other American wars combined) to exorcise it from our nation. Yes, we had segregation—but we long ago repented of this and made it illegal. Since the civil rights movement of the 1960s, led by Reverend Martin Luther King, Jr., the vast majority of Americans—hundreds of millions of normal, middle-class citizens—believe deeply and wholeheartedly in the color-blind America that King envisioned. If the election of a black president in 2008 doesn't prove this, nothing will.

Yet Sharpton, Jackson, and others have thrived for decades on literally creating the perception of racism where none existed—for their own benefit. From the fake rape claims of Tawana Brawley to the fake rape claims against the Duke lacrosse team members, the false accusation of racism remains a powerful weapon of the left.

• Similarly, charges of rampant anti-Muslim bigotry and hate crimes in the United States, leveled by groups such as the Council on American-Islamic Relations and the American Civil Liberties Union, constitute a totally fake crisis. Actually, Americans have demonstrated extraordinary restraint and magnanimity toward Muslims since the September 11, 2001, terror attacks and the subsequent revelations of widespread Islamist antipathy toward America. In fact, according to the FBI's own statistics, in the five years following 9/11, anti-Islamic hate crimes in the United States *decreased* by 68 percent![26]

We could go on and on—fake crises are everywhere. In fact, crisis is the central operating principle of the Obama presidency. Everything is a crisis, an emergency, and has to be fixed *right now*—all for the purpose of vastly increasing government power and control over citizens' wealth, behavior, their very lives.

Here's the key point: people who want to manipulate and remold us are always creating crises, small or large, real or imagined, to use as leverage. That leverage, to be precise, is our emotional upset and our resulting inability to think straight and make sensible decisions. Repeat: just upsetting us through any means whatsoever constitutes a mini-crisis—by means of which we can be manipulated. Although being upset by some injustice or cruelty seems like a "small" crisis in the scheme of things, it is the basis for all other crises, even the largest.

If you think about it, this process of remolding us through crises is a perversion of what God does with His children. He "creates a crisis"—or perhaps more accurately, *allows* a crisis to develop in our lives because of our ignorance of His laws, which cries out for resolution. Our marriage and family are in crisis, or our health is in crisis, or our finances are in crisis, yet if we are sincere, truth-loving souls, that crisis mysteriously has a way of maturing and changing us, and we end up growing in *His* direction.

You might well wonder what kind of person could be so deranged that he or she would create a phony crisis for the purpose of exercising power over others. But this shouldn't be hard to comprehend. For one thing, lots of us are so troubled and insecure that we develop an unhealthy need to be needed by others. It's a very common syndrome. Consciously or unconsciously, we tempt or corrupt people into becoming dependent on us, so as to fulfill our unhealthy need to be needed.

Moreover, consider that if you are consumed by pride—in other words, if you're a big egomaniac—you actually have a subconscious need or desire for other people to fail. Why? Because your own sense of worth is based on comparing yourself with other people, and particularly with cultivating others to look up to you. Unfortunately, a politician's need for adulation can be fulfilled only if he weakens and fools other people into depending on him for their sustenance and happiness.

So, if you're a dishonest, ambitious, and manipulating politician like so many, even though you haven't murdered anyone, haven't committed genocide, haven't put people feet-first through a plastic-shredder like Saddam Hussein, you're still spreading evil and misery throughout the land.

If this syndrome describes you (whether in politics or in your marriage or at your workplace), you may not be aware of the forces working through you. Oh, you may occasionally catch a fleeting glimpse of it, but you quickly escape from this painful, humiliating realization. For a fraction of a second you see it, but then it's gone.

But let me ask anyway: Have you ever seen another person lose his temper, or fail in some other way—and felt a very slight, perverse sense of satisfaction? Or, when someone has done really well and received credit for it, or made a lot of money, or just expressed a brilliant idea, have you ever noticed a subtle feeling of envy rearing its head inside you?

It's okay. Most everyone has experienced feelings like this at some point—perhaps often. But if you're a sincere soul and are willing to observe these base feelings emanating from the dark side, and if deep down you really don't agree with those feelings, then in a very real sense those feelings are not you. You could say there are two of you: with the *real* you being the observer who is chagrined over the dark thoughts and feelings rising from the deep. Watching those thoughts and feelings honestly leads to repentance and real change.

However, many people are not sincere. And these types of thoughts, and the dark forces behind them, come to dominate their lives, albeit unconsciously. And that is why, without being a Saddam Hussein, but just being a prideful, selfish, denial-based person, you can do terrible things to other human beings—deceive them, betray them, enslave them. You can destroy lives and civilizations.

This, then, is exactly why we have limited government in America: because power corrupts, and now we know why.

By the way, what we're talking about here—the tendency for government to be dishonest and predatory—didn't start with Karl Marx. It has ever been with the human race. More than two thousand years ago, the great orator and statesman Marcus Tullius Cicero is said to have foretold the decline and fall of the Roman Empire with these words, which exquisitely described the ravages wrought by lying politicians:

A nation can survive its fools, and even the ambitious. But it cannot survive treason from within. An enemy at the gates is less formidable, for he is known and carries his banner openly. But the traitor moves amongst those within the gate freely, his sly whispers rustling through all the alleys, heard in the very halls of government itself. For the traitor appears not a traitor; he speaks in accents familiar to his victims, and he wears their face and their arguments, he appeals to the baseness that lies deep in the hearts of all men. He rots the soul of a nation, he works secretly and unknown in the night to undermine the pillars of the city, he infects the body politic so that it can no longer resist. A murderer is less to fear.

When all is said and done, we elect liars as leaders because we *need* lies. And we need lies because we're running from truth.

Lies that fulfill us in a wrong way are offered to us constantly, in every area of life. If our marriage is in trouble, there's always "the other woman" or "the other man" who will embrace and reassure us that we're great people and that our spouse is the problem. But their lying "solution" only makes things immeasurably worse. If we're depressed or full of rage, but not really interested in understanding ourselves, we have experts eager to prescribe drugs to mask our symptoms—a false "solution" without hope of real change. Or we can bypass the doctor and go straight to the liquor store or criminal drug dealer to procure another wrong "solution."

William Penn said it all: "If man is not governed by God, he will be ruled by tyrants." Freedom apart from God is just an illusion of pride. This is because when we are at war with our conscience, something has to sustain our denial, our secret war against the still, small voice of Truth within—hence our need for lies. And government, in the form of other prideful human beings, is only too happy to oblige.

John Adams, a principal crafter of the Constitution and later our second president, understood this very well, writing: "Our Constitution was made only for a moral and religious people. It is wholly inadequate to the government of any other."

Benjamin Franklin expressed the same vital reality this way: "Only a virtuous people are capable of freedom. As nations become corrupt and vicious, they have more need of masters."

But the Bible puts it most eloquently and succinctly of all: "Where the Spirit of the Lord is, there is Liberty" (2 Corinthians 3:17).

CHAPTER 2

+

SEXUAL ANARCHY

What's Behind Today's Epidemic
of Teacher-Student Sex?

*Dozens of Arizona Teachers Accused of Having Inappropriate or Illegal
Relationships with Students*
  —CBS AFFILIATE KPHO.COM, MAY 21, 2009

*Outrage Follows Ruling that Teachers Can Have Sex with 18-Year-Old
Students*
  —FoxNews.com, JANUARY 15, 2009

Coroner: Teacher in Student-Sex Case Kills Self
  —NBC AFFILIATE WYFF.COM, MARCH 21, 2009

For centuries, we considered sex to be sacred. It was to be reserved
exclusively for a man and a woman joined permanently by marriage
vows, and all other forms and circumstances of sexual expression
were forbidden—locked away, as it were, in a sort of Pandora's box,
heavily guarded by the sentinels of Judeo-Christian civilization.
Confining sex to marriage was universally seen as essential to strong
marital unions and secure families, and thus to the very fabric of
civilization itself.

Then, with stunning rapidity, all that unraveled.

The change first emerged into public view during the heady and intoxicating 1960s under the banner of "sexual liberation." While the public was distracted by colorful spectacles of youthful rebellion, psychedelic drug use, and the rock "invasion," behind the scenes a full-bore assault on Western institutions and values—particularly traditional sexual morality—was taking place.

Today, a half century later, what began then has evolved to heights and depths of sexual anarchy simply unimaginable to previous generations. It's as though some of us sneaked up to Pandora's box, killed or seduced the guards, broke the locks, opened the box wide, and blew up the lid. And the sexual genie, once restrained but now liberated, has penetrated virtually all areas of life and conjured up an ongoing societal transformation.

We've progressed way beyond free sex. News reports today showcase homosexual marriages, teen "sexting," and middle school hookups, transgenders marching in parades proudly displaying their surgically mutilated bodies, and ever-increasing tolerance of adult-child sex.

But perhaps no story better exemplifies today's catastrophic confusion about sex, or more poignantly illustrates how normal people can morph into sexual predators and destroy their own lives and others', than the bizarre epidemic of female schoolteachers victimizing their students.

The case of Pamela Diehl-Moore is typical enough. The popular middle school teacher, then forty-three, had been charged with having sex with a child—a thirteen-year-old male student who had just completed seventh grade. Now, in an emotional and bizarre courtroom scene, she stood before a Hackensack, New Jersey, judge awaiting sentencing, having tearfully pleaded guilty.

And what would that sentence be? Considering all the intense media coverage of male sexual predators victimizing female children, one might expect a stiff prison term accompanied by a withering rebuke.

But when New Jersey Superior Court judge Bruce A. Gaeta opened his mouth, the words that came out did not express criticism of the teacher, nor acknowledge any damage she had done to her victim.

"I really don't see the harm that was done here," the judge announced, "and certainly society doesn't need to be worried. I do not believe she is a sexual predator. It's just something between two people that clicked beyond the teacher-student relationship."

"Clicked"? With a thirteen-year-old?

"Maybe it was a way for him, once this happened, to satisfy his sexual needs," the judge added. "People mature at different rates." Gee thanks, Judge.

According to court transcripts, Gaeta summed up his shocking judicial leniency this way: "I don't see anything here that shows this young man has been psychologically damaged by her actions. And don't forget, this was mutual consent. Now certainly under the law, he is too young to legally consent, but that's what the law says. Some of the legislators should remember when they were that age. Maybe these ages have to be changed a little bit." [1]

Translation: The forty-three-year-old teacher didn't really do anything wrong in having sex with a schoolboy, the kid wanted it, statutory rape laws are unrealistic, and the age of consent should be lowered.

The sentence? Five years probation—no jail time.

In yet another court case, U.S. district court judge J. Thomas Marten in Kansas also questioned whether sex with kids was really bad. "Where is the clear, credible evidence that underage sex is always injurious? If you tell me because it is illegal, I reject that," Marten said, according to the Associated Press. [2]

Although most judges don't publicly sing the praises of statutory rape as these two did—indeed, Judge Gaeta later was investigated and reprimanded by the New Jersey Supreme Court—many regular Americans apparently agree with them. A lot of us just don't seem to think there's much of a problem when female teachers have sex with their male students.

"What is the deal lately with hot female teachers seducing their

13- to 16-year-old students?!" asked one blogger expressing the prevalent "what's-the-problem?" attitude: "I think the woman is getting off on the social taboo factor more than anything else. At least, that's what the expert psychologists say. I just wish I had a teacher stupid enough and bored enough in my grade school to make my pubescent dreams come true. If it wasn't illegal and there were no jilted husbands, it's almost a victimless crime."

And Bob Shoop, a Kansas State University education professor and expert witness in thirty court cases involving sexual abuse in schools, summed it up this way: "I think our society sort of says to the boy: 'Congratulations, that's great. Everybody fantasizes about having a sexual relationship with an older woman.'"[3]

As for the perpetrators themselves, often they just think they're expressing love.

One of the most famous cases of a teacher-student sexual relationship is that of Mary Kay Letourneau, who, unlike Diehl-Moore, served seven years in prison for the statutory rape—or "child rape" as it is called in Washington—of a thirteen-year-old boy at the school where she taught. Four months after her 1997 arrest, Letourneau, thirty-four at the time and married with four children, gave birth to a daughter fathered by the boy, Vili Fualaau. Pleading guilty, she was sentenced to eighty-nine months in prison, but her term was suspended except for six months in jail—and the requirement that she stay away from Vili after her release.

But no sooner was she let out—early, for good behavior—than Letourneau was discovered in a car with Fualaau and re-arrested. Incensed, the judge sent her straight to prison to serve out the rest of her seven-and-a-half-year sentence.

While Letourneau was behind bars, however, in March 1998 prison officials discovered that she was pregnant with another child by Fualaau. Before long, she and the boy coauthored a book—released in France, but not the United States—titled *Un Seul Crime, L'amour* ("Only One Crime, Love"), for which her attorney reportedly brokered Letourneau a two-hundred-thousand-dollar advance. Then 2000 saw the release of her movie, *All-American Girl: The Mary Kay Letourneau Story.* Not surprisingly, she and husband Steve got divorced during all this.[4]

When Letourneau was finally paroled on August 4, 2004, Fualaau, then twenty-one, successfully petitioned the court to lift its no-contact order and the couple married on May 20, 2005, with high-dollar tabloid TV cameras rolling.

The wedding invitations read: "Please join Mary and Vili for their special day. They hope to make this the best wedding experience for you. A luxurious touring bus will whisk you away to their wedding destination. Food and refreshments will be available for your bus ride. Please respect the need for privacy and know that pictures from the wedding will be available for the guests at a later date."

In other words, leave your cameras at home, because we're cashing in on our controversial wedding by selling exclusive video rights for a *lot* of money.

The two hundred to three hundred wedding guests reportedly went through identity checks and metal detectors, and signed secrecy and release-of-privacy statements due to the TV videotaping. The couple's two daughters were the flower girls.

Entertainment Tonight and *The Insider* had exclusive rights to the wedding, with Seattle's KING 5 News reporting the couple would earn around $750,000 for their wedding footage.

The couple, along with their two daughters, reportedly live off the high-six-figure paycheck they received for selling their wedding video and reside in a beachfront home in a Seattle suburb.[5]

"JUST BEING REBELLIOUS"

Sensational news stories of schoolteachers like Letourneau preying on students become a little more understandable when you realize the 1960s sexual revolution has advanced to the point that sex and school seem to go together these days.

Here's what the *Washington Post* found when it interviewed high school students in and around the nation's capital:

Two students were discovered recently having sex in an Anne Arundel County high school gym. Four students at Col. Zadok Magruder High in Rockville were arrested in June after performing sex acts in the school parking lot. A boy and a girl at Springbrook High in Silver Spring were caught "touching inappropriately" in a school bathroom. Last year, three teenage boys at Mount Hebron High in Howard County were arrested after a student accused them of sexually assaulting her in a school restroom, but charges were dropped after the boys said the sex was consensual and the girl recanted.

"Students would have intercourse on the stairwells, locked classrooms, in the locker rooms," said Ihsan Musawwir, 18, a recent graduate of Dunbar Senior High School in the District. "It was embarrassing for me to walk in on it."

Jessica Miller, 19, who graduated in June from T.C. Williams High School in Alexandria, said that for some students there, sex on campus is a popular fantasy—and sometimes a reality—particularly in the auditorium.

"It's so big, it's so dark," Miller said. "There's a lot more places to find privacy—behind the stage and on the catwalk."

But what's the appeal? "Just being rebellious," she said. "Coming back to class and saying, 'Ooh, guess what I just did? I just had sex in the auditorium.'" . . .

Cpl. Michael Rudinski, president of the Maryland Association of School Resource Officers, said teenagers do whatever they think their peers are doing, whether they are or not. "The thing about young people is when they see things in the mass media and they think it's going on, they start doing it."[6]

WORSE THAN THE CATHOLIC
CLERGY ABUSE SCANDAL?

In today's sexually permissive school environment, just how prevalent is the teacher-student sex problem?

Get ready for a shock. According to a major study commissioned by the U.S. Department of Education, the most in-depth investigation to date, nearly 10 percent of U.S. public school students have been targeted with unwanted sexual attention by school employees.

Titled "Educator Sexual Misconduct: A Synthesis of Existing Literature," the report says the mistreatment of students ranges from sexual comments to rape. In fact, says the study's author, Charol Shakeshaft, professor of educational administration at Hofstra University, in Hempstead, New York, the scope of the school sex problem appears to far exceed the clergy abuse scandal that has rocked the Roman Catholic Church.[7]

Comparing the incidence of sexual misconduct in schools with the Catholic Church scandal, Shakeshaft notes that a study by the U.S. Conference of Catholic Bishops concluded 10,667 young people were sexually mistreated by priests between 1950 and 2002.[8]

In contrast, she extrapolates from a national survey conducted for the American Association of University Women Educational Foundation in 2000 that roughly 290,000 students experienced some sort of physical sexual abuse by a public school employee between 1991 and 2000.

The figures suggest "the physical sexual abuse of students in schools is likely more than 100 times the abuse by priests," said Shakeshaft, according to *Education Week*. Indeed, more than 4.5 million students are subject to sexual misconduct by an employee of a school sometime between kindergarten and twelfth grade, says the report.

The National Education Association disputes Shakshaft's conclusion, calling it "a misuse of the data to imply that public schools and the Catholic Church have experienced the same level of abuse cases." "I take great umbrage at that suggestion," said NEA spokes-woman Kathleen Lyons, according to *Education Week*. "That just seems like someone is reaching conclusions based on half the data that's needed."[9]

Shakeshaft acknowledges that many factors could alter the anal-ysis, including undercounting of youth abused by priests, but she argues this simply provides impetus for better research. "Educator sexual misconduct is woefully understudied," she says in her report. "We have scant data on incidence and even less on descriptions of predators and targets. There are many questions that call for an-swers."[10]

GROOMING

Like all sexual predators, "sexual abusers in schools use various strate-gies to trap students," explains Shakeshaft. "They lie to them, isolate them, make them feel complicit, and manipulate them into sexual contact. Often teachers target vulnerable or marginal students who are grateful for the attention."

The report draws a clear distinction between true pedophiles—that is, adults who target prepubescent children—and those who criminally seduce pubescent but underage youngsters. "The abusers of children younger than seventh grade have different patterns than those who abuse older children," she says, making a disturbing but familiar point about pedophiles' modus operandi:

> The educators who target elementary school children are often professionally accomplished and even celebrated. Par-ticularly compared to their non-abusing counterparts, they hold a disproportionate number of awards. It is common to find that educators who have been sexually abusing children are also the same educators who display on their walls a com-munity "Excellence in Teaching" award or a "Teacher of the

Year" certificate. This popularity confounds district officials and community members and prompts them to ignore allegations on the belief that "outstanding teachers" cannot be abusers. Many educators who abuse work at being recognized as good professionals in order to be able to sexually abuse children. For them, being a good educator is the path to children, especially those who abuse elementary and younger middle school students.

In contrast, she notes:

> At the late middle and high school level, educator abusers may or may not be outstanding practitioners. At this level, the initial acts are somewhat less premeditated and planned and more often opportunistic, a result of bad judgment or a misplaced sense of privilege.

Shakeshaft gives a chilling description of the various techniques of "grooming"—a practice common to virtually all child molesters. Grooming, she explains, is a process whereby

> an abuser selects a student, gives the student attention and rewards, provides the student with support and understanding, all the while slowly increasing the amount of touch or other sexual behavior. The purpose of grooming is to test the child's ability to maintain secrecy, to desensitize the child through progressive sexual behaviors, to provide the child with experiences that are valuable and that the child won't want to lose, to learn information that will discredit the child, and to gain approval from parents.
>
> Grooming allows the abuser to test the student's silence at each step. It also serves to implicate the student, resulting in children believing that they are responsible for their own abuse because "I never said stop."

Grooming often takes place in the context of providing a child with extras like additional help learning a musical instrument, advisement on a science project, or opportunities for camping and outdoor activity. These opportunities not only create a special relationship with students, they are also ones for which parents are usually appreciative.[11]

Most sexual molesters work very hard to keep their victims from telling others. This is not as hard for the perpetrator to accomplish as it may seem. For one thing, children who are sexually abused by teachers often don't recognize what is happening as abuse. "In many cases," says the report, "they are told that what is happening is love. Many abusers of children at all ages couch what they are doing to the children as love, both romantic and parental."

Other techniques for keeping children quiet, says Shakeshaft, are "intimidation and threats (if you tell, I'll fail you)," "exploiting the power structure (if you tell, no one will believe you)," and "manipulating the child's affections (if you tell, I'll get in trouble; if you tell, I won't be able to be your friend anymore)." Since kids typically get something out of the relationship—everything from attention and gifts to physical pleasure and a feeling of belonging—they can easily be made to feel responsible, something offenders use to their advantage.

But what happens when, despite the powerful manipulation of their minds and feelings by the sexual predator, children actually do go to authorities?

In many cases, says the federally funded report, they are just not believed: "Because of the power differential, the reputation difference between the educator and the child, or the mindset that children are untruthful, many reports by children are ignored or given minimal attention."

Several studies estimate that only about 6 percent of all children report sexual abuse by an adult to someone who can do something about it. Indeed, fear of not being believed is the number-one reason kids don't report their sexual victimization at the hands of adults.

Shakeshaft cites the case of one teacher, Kenneth DeLuca, who was convicted of sexually abusing thirteen students between the ages of ten and eighteen over a period of twenty-one years. Although nearly all the students reported the abuse at the time it was occurring, school officials ignored the accusations. "Overwhelmingly, the girls experienced a disastrous response when they told about DeLuca's behavior," said the report. "Many were disbelieved, some were told to leave schools, parents were allegedly threatened with lawsuits."

Even more shocking, Shakeshaft's report documents that offending teachers have frequently gotten off virtually scot-free even when their sexual misdeeds are exposed to school administrators.

• In one study of 225 cases of teacher sex abuse in New York State, although all the accused had admitted to sexually abusing a student, not one was reported to the police and only 1 percent lost their license to teach.

• Another study reports that 159 Washington State coaches were "reprimanded, warned, or let go in the past decade because of sexual misconduct"—yet "at least 98 of them continued coaching or teaching afterward."

• Still another study reports that many school districts make confidential agreements with abusers, essentially trading a positive recommendation for a resignation. In one case, a Seattle educator named Luke Markishtum "had two decades of complaints of sex with students and providing alcohol and marijuana to students prior to his arrest for smuggling six tons of marijuana into the state. The district paid Markishtum the remainder of his salary that year, agreed to keep the record secret, and gave him an additional $69,000." [12]

"LUCKY DAY"

In recent years, there has been a seeming explosion in a special type of teacher sexual abuse—female teachers having sex with underage teenage boys, who as a rule are willing participants in the sex.

"Generally the male doesn't feel victimized," said Steven B. Blum, a consulting psychologist to a sex offender program in Nebraska. "A lot of teenage boys would see that as their lucky day," he told the *Los Angeles Times*.[13]

Lucky day? What about the next day, and the next year and beyond? Experts say sexually victimized boys experience later difficulty in developing age-appropriate relationships and gravitate toward pornography and one-night stands. They are also more likely as adults to suffer depression, anxiety, and drug addiction.

The sixteen-year-old victim of Margaret De Barraicua, a thirty-year-old California teacher who pleaded guilty to four counts of statutory rape, did *not* consider it his "lucky day." "I'm not the same boy," he said in a letter read in court in Sacramento. "At school I became the center of attention. Everyone knew my name." But the boy was so traumatized, his mother wrote in a letter read in court, that "his hair is falling out."[14] And the father of a Colorado boy molested by Silvia Johnson—who held drug, alcohol, and sex parties at her home with teenage schoolboys to be "cool"—told the court the forty-year-old woman "took away my best friend, my hunting buddy. I can't have him back now. He is gone."[15]

Many theories and factors are advanced to explain the major upsurge in illegal teacher-student sexual relationships, including:

- Two-breadwinner families mean children have more unsupervised time to be preyed upon.
- Cell phone technology, text messaging, and e-mail afford opportunities for teachers and students to communicate privately that didn't exist a generation ago.

- The explosion of hard-core pornography, especially online, has resulted in the exposure of children to graphic sexual images to a far greater degree than at any time in history.

But overshadowing virtually all explanations for adult-child sex is the simple fact that the perpetrators—and in the case of female offenders having sex with underage boys, the victims as well—often don't think there is anything wrong with what they are doing. Essentially, the rationale is: Consensual sex doesn't kill, injure, or rob anyone, so where's the victim? Why is "love" (remember Letourneau's book, *Only One Crime, Love*) even a crime at all?

How did we get to the point that so many of us, including even some of our judges, just don't see anything wrong with adults having "consensual" sex with children? To truly answer that question, we're going to have to venture beyond the boundaries of conventional journalism—beyond the presentation of facts, examples, studies, statistics, theories, and comments from experts. Journalism can do an excellent job of describing the symptoms of this problem, but can never arrive at its cause, or cure.

Are you ready for a ride into new territory?

AWAKENING

"You don't have a soul. You are a soul. You have a body."
  —C. S. Lewis

In *Prince Caspian*, C. S. Lewis's second *Narnia* book (released as a feature film in 2008, following the roaring success of *The Lion, the Witch, and the Wardrobe*), the story unfolds in a latter-day secular time, much like our own today.

In that story's "modern" era, most, though definitely not all, of the people had forgotten about the magic, miracles, and mirth that were ever present during Narnia's golden age, forgotten about the existence of the talking animals, indeed forgotten about Aslan the king himself.

The contemporary elite came to regard the beliefs and loyalties that once had been the very heartbeat of Narnian existence as nothing more than pernicious fables clung to by their ignorant, superstitious ancestors. Even the mention of the sacred things of the past was now forbidden by the murderous usurper, King Miraz, since merely speaking of such powerful truths posed a grave threat to his rule.

That is America today. In what was once the finest and most robust expression of Western Judeo-Christian civilization and the core values underlying it, most of us, too, have forgotten.

Forgotten the founding spiritual and moral values of our nation and culture.

Forgotten the simple, intuitive understanding of right and wrong that we grasped effortlessly when we were innocent children, but which we were later intimidated or seduced into doubting—and abandoning.

Forgotten the core truth about man's condition—that he is in reality a "fallen" being, "born in sin," and that his sexual urges must be channeled into marriage.

Freeze. Notice how, for some readers at least, that last sentence made you wince, if not recoil in horror. *"Fallen being"? "Born in sin"? Man, where's this guy coming from? Does he really believe that ancient religious mumbo jumbo?*

That, my friends, is exactly the "forgetfulness" of self-evident "truth we all once knew" that I'm talking about.

This basic truth that human beings are fallen and corruptible—a reality not only spelled out in the Bible from Genesis to Revelation, but also clearly evident from observing everyday life—this understanding of man's condition that is at the core of our legal system and the very reason for limited government ("Power corrupts, and absolute power corrupts absolutely"), is now embarrassing to us.

For many people alive today, this Christian worldview, which animated Christopher Columbus, the Pilgrims, and the Founding Fathers in the most profound possible way, is just a fairy tale, an embarrassing anachronism, perhaps even "the source of most of humankind's strife and war."

We're living in latter-day Narnia, where we mock and deny the "old truths" that, unbeknownst to us, still form the very substance of everything valuable we possess today.

Very simply, we've forgotten what we as human beings actually are, and why we have been put here on this beautiful blue globe we call Earth. We've forgotten that we're here to serve a much higher purpose than just fulfilling our own desires.

We've become like Martians who, arriving on Earth for the first time, encounter a Ford Mustang convertible. Not having any idea what it is or its maker's intended use, the Martians mistakenly conclude it must be a hot tub and proceed to fill it with water and bathe in it. And then, when you come along and tell them they're ruining this valuable car by their misuse of it, they become angry and accuse you of attempting to deny them their rightful pleasure.

What does this have to do with sex? Without the understanding of our spiritual origin and destiny—of who we are and what purpose our maker intended for us—we can't possibly understand sex and its intended role in our lives. Instead, all we have driving us are the desires, the physical and emotional "needs," cravings, and compulsions we find welling up from within us.

Sometimes these desires are normal, the kind of sexual attraction to the opposite gender that God ordained, leading to bonding and marriage and children. But for some of us, our sexual cravings are rooted in trauma, that is, generated from our emotional reactions to the cruelty, confusion, and seduction we've experienced along the path of life. Remember, pain causes us to seek the relief of pleasure.

For example, let's take Mary Kay Letourneau's sexual attraction to a thirteen-year-old boy. What could have caused it?

Do you suppose it could have anything to do with her husband, Steve, allegedly being a serial cheater? Or that her father, ultraconservative U.S. congressman John Schmitz, was exposed for having a secret affair with a former student?[16] Do you think a young girl's deep resentment over both a hypocritical and cheating father, and later on, over an angry, adulterous husband, could possibly give rise to a forbidden attraction? An attraction based not only on sex, but also on her being worshipped and idolized by a young, relatively innocent, nonthreatening male (after years of betrayal by "adult" males). No doubt all this was intoxicating to Mary Kay. Intoxicating and toxic.

In a world with a little more understanding and real love in it, a person like Mary Kay could perhaps be helped. But in our secular, mechanistic world, there is precious little real understanding of what makes people tick and thus not much help for troubled people like this.

Yet an even more important factor in this sexual-predator epidemic is the fact that "right" and "wrong" just aren't real to most of us anymore. Even if Letourneau was attracted sexually to a child, for whatever reasons, it's still *wrong* to have sex with a thirteen-year-old. And knowing something is wrong is enough reason not to do it—even if part of us wants to.

After all, most people have strong drives and urges. Even normal, red-blooded men, loyal to their wives and children, have powerful sexual drives that, if followed down the rabbit hole without regard to right and wrong, could easily turn them into adulterers.

The problem is, having turned our backs on Judeo-Christian morality and the inner conscience that testifies to it, many of us rely on emotional feelings alone to guide our way through life. So, if childhood problems cause us to grow up feeling uncomfortable as a man (or a woman), instead of looking within for understanding and healing, we undergo barbaric sex change operations and "hormone therapy" and pretend we're the opposite gender for the rest of our lives. If we feel sexually attracted to the same gender, we convince ourselves this uprush of inner feeling—often rooted in something gone wrong in our formative years—is actually genetic, or God-ordained, or the expression of who we "really" are. If we feel badly about having an unintended child growing inside us, instead of looking for a moral and life-affirming solution, we kill the child.

Of course, choosing what's principled and perhaps self-sacrificial over our selfish feelings—that is, preferring something noble and higher over something ignoble and lower—implies there is a God, the source of the higher, as well as evil, the source of the lower.

But according to today's secular, de facto atheistic worldview, there is no good or evil, no heaven or hell—we're all just highly evolved animals. If that's true, however, there is just no logical reason adults shouldn't be able to have sex with children or whomever or whatever else they please.

To illustrate the difference between humans and animals, let me mention that my children raise goats as a hobby. They have a male goat to breed with the various females. Although the buck is just a few months old, it readily mates with the various females—old, young, big, small, it doesn't matter. They come into heat, and he does his job. Everything's as it should be.

Now, if that is all humans are—animals—then we too should all be able to walk around having sex with anyone we want, just like goats. In fact, why can't we roam around naked—like goats? Can you imagine what would happen if we all went to work, school, and the supermarket stark naked?

Some people, wrongly believing mankind's universal embarrassment over their private parts (yes, "universal"—even in darkest Africa the natives wear loincloths) represents an unhealthy shame toward their own bodies, embrace nudity as a philosophy and lifestyle. But they have misinterpreted the embarrassment and abandoned a core truth: the fact that humans have embarrassment over sex and need to keep themselves covered all the time is *not* some repressive Victorian hang-up over sex. Rather, it is evidence—a very important and powerful clue, and one we better interpret correctly— that our sexual nature somehow is tied in with our—gasp!—fallen "animal" self.

You see, the truth is, we're not just animals, like goats. We have two natures: an animal nature that eats and procreates, and a spiritual, eternal soul that survives this life.

If we were only animals, then this chapter would be pointless and all the concerns expressed earlier about sexual predators would be wrongheaded, the prosecutions unjust, the incarcerations cruel, the stigma undeserved. If we are only animals, there is simply nothing at all wrong with forty-three-year-old schoolteachers having sex with their thirteen-year-old students, as long as it is "consensual."

Moreover, if we are just animals, then *all* consensual sexual activity—any place, any time, any type—is fine, just like with my children's goats.

In that case, of course, when we die we just get buried in the ground and that's the end of us. No afterlife, no soul or consciousness surviving the dissolution of our bodies, no ultimate standard of right and wrong, and no ultimate accountability before the Creator for the way we've lived our lives. Just a nice meal for worms.

Is that what you believe? Many people do. That's what ex-Beatle John Lennon was preaching in his New Age anthem: "Imagine there's no heaven, It's easy if you try, No hell below us, Above us only sky."

For many, this all-consuming obsession with denying God, Judeo-Christian values, and our own immortal souls centers on one thing only. Do you know what it is? Do you know what the source is for most of the hostility we see toward Christianity in today's culture? It doesn't have to do with Jesus Christ's admonition that we must love one another, feed the poor, or comfort the sick. No one is threatened by those things. Rather, at the root of so much loathing toward Christianity and the Bible is what they have to say about *sex*.

The Old Testament book of Leviticus, for instance, is full of detailed laws and prohibitions regarding sexuality and sexual behavior. Why is this so? What on earth did sexual behavior have to do with

God's setting the House of Israel apart from the rest of the pagan world so it could be worthy of His special blessing and destiny?

"Why can't we all just be nice to each other," you might wonder, "and have as much sex as we want, with whomever we want, whenever and however we want, as long as it's consensual? And why can't we call that good, righteous, and loving?"

Very simply, how do we know sex outside of marriage—whether adultery or premarital sex or homosexual sex or teachers seducing kids—is wrong, a sin before God and an offense to our fellow human beings?

It happens that God has provided some major clues for us, the obvious implications of which we somehow manage to ignore—just like the elephant in the parlor.

For some, the most persuasive clues are in the Bible. Both the Old Testament and the New Testament are unequivocal in their condemnation of homosexual sex, of fornication (a term rarely used anymore), of adultery. Jesus raises the bar the highest when He says: "Ye have heard that it was said by them of old time, Thou shalt not commit adultery: But I say unto you, That whosoever looketh on a woman to lust after her hath committed adultery with her already in his heart" (Matthew 5:27–28).

But the Bible is far from the only clue. Biblical truths are reflected in everyday life. So, stealing and murder and lying aren't wrong just because the Bible says so. Rather, the Bible says stealing and murder and lying are wrong because they *are* wrong. They were always wrong, and the Bible testifies to that timeless Truth that predates the Bible itself. (Remember, in Abraham, Isaac, and Jacob's time there was no Bible.)

Thus the wrongness of sexual immorality should also be as self-evident as the wrongness of stealing or murder.

What? You say you can see that stealing, lying, and murder are wrong because they result in victims, but you can't see that premarital or homosexual sex is wrong, because you can't see the victim?

Let's look at a few more clues.

Here's a stunningly obvious one: sex has the potential to produce offspring. And since the evidence is irrefutable that children need both a *father* and a *mother*, as well as a stable, long-term, loving home life, this one clue alone leads inexorably to the conclusion that sex is meant only for a committed heterosexual marriage.

Another clue: a ghoulish smorgasbord of sexually transmitted diseases—many incurable, such as AIDS, herpes, and human papillomavirus (thought to be one of the main causes of cervical cancer), as well as hepatitis, syphilis, chlamydia, gonorrhea, and a host of others—is a pretty powerful indicator that we weren't meant to have wanton, rampant sex.

Still another clue: hundreds of millions of babies aborted worldwide—over a million per year just in America. The horror of this is truly beyond imagining, our minds incapable of digesting the reality of it. But try one tiny slice: news reports document that in Zimbabwe, *newborn babies* clog up the sewers in the capital of Harare, because so many are flushed down toilets and dumped in drains—about twenty per week.[17] Very simply, millions of us are killing our offspring.

Let's stop for a minute and ask: Just how obvious do clues need to be before we figure out the message? Horrible plagues and millions of unwanted babies seem like pretty good indicators that we were not intended to use our bodies the way many of us do. Yet in our cleverness we find ways to circumvent these divine roadblocks by way of artificial birth control, abortion, alternative sexual acts, and so on. But we're still just making an absurd end run around God's obvious decree that sex, very simply, is sacred.

Another way we know extramarital sex is wrong is simply that it's pure selfishness and self-gratification. In marriage, there is life-long commitment, as well as the deep respect for one's spouse that can germinate and grow only in the soil of lifelong commitment. In nonmarried sex there is nothing but exploitation—using the other person in an attempt to fulfill ourselves. Without commitment, it's impossible for there to be love—since love *is* commitment. Sorry, the truth hurts.

The Bible admonishes us mortals to choose sides, between life and death, between good and evil. Most often, that choice takes the form of choosing to side with our higher nature against our own lower nature. Satanism and other worldviews based on deception and seduction have always taught the opposite: side with your lower nature against your higher nature, a conflict Satanists (and yes, they do exist) blame on a vengeful, capricious, and cruel God ("Why did he create us with all these powerful urges and drives, only to forbid their expression?").

In our culture today, just as in latter-day Narnia, the prevailing mind-set is, increasingly, to mock and demonize those who rebuke our growing infatuation with our lower nature.

At the center of this struggle is sex, one of the greatest mysteries of life. If we never understand sex, we never understand life. For many of us, unfortunately, our understanding has been hijacked by the 1960s cultural and sexual revolution, which was based on lies.

Yes, lies. The sexual revolution glorified the destruction of Judeo-Christian civilization and the morality at its core. Like all revolutions, it seemed sweet at the time. Do you remember?

It seemed so promising, so genuine, so liberating. Boomers will remember 1967's "Summer of Love" in San Francisco's Haight-Ashbury district. A hundred thousand young "flower people" flocked to the West Coast mecca of the hippie revolution. Scott McKenzie sang, "If you're going to San Francisco, Be sure to wear some flowers in your hair. If you're going to San Francisco, You're gonna meet some gentle people there." Free love and expanded consciousness (with the help of marijuana and LSD) would save our nation from the ravages of war and the greedy materialism that led to conflict. It was beautiful, otherworldly—or so it seemed.

But somehow, just a few short years later, the flowers had faded and Haight-Ashbury was transformed into a scene of crazed, meth-addicted hippies and runaways with human degradation, venereal disease, and crime everywhere. Already, the toxicity of the '60s revolution was becoming apparent. Today, that cancer has metastasized throughout our culture to the point that lost children have sex in the school auditorium.

Funny thing about lie-based revolutions: they all turn out bad. Communist revolutions promise freedom and equality, but deliver despotism, misery, and death. In the same way, the sexual liberation movement, which offered freedom, equality, self-fulfillment, and unlimited pleasure, has just about destroyed America.

It's not too late. There's hope for us yet. But we absolutely must realize that if we just keep going along with whatever compulsions and drives we see rising up in us, and wallow in them, and justify them, and condemn anybody who dares ask the tough questions, we're living as animals, not humans.

And believe me, that's not truly living. Unless, of course, you're a goat.

CHAPTER 3

+

HOW TERRORISM REALLY WORKS

The Ultimate Stockholm Syndrome

A Ghastly Act Leaves Hundreds of Children Dead
—*Akron Beacon Journal*, SEPTEMBER 8, 2004

Al-Qaeda Planned to Bomb 12 Planes with Liquid in Carry-on Luggage
—*Toronto Globe and Mail*, (CANADA) AUGUST 11, 2006

Palestinians Use Booby-Trapped Horses in Terror Attack
—HOT AIR, JUNE 8, 2009

I'm looking at a photograph of a beautiful young Christian girl who has just been beheaded by a gang of six rampaging, machete-wielding Muslim men.

Her bloody body is lying on an autopsy table. A few inches to the left of her torso lies her severed head, nestled in a bunched-up black plastic trash bag. Delicate features, lovely dark hair matted with blood, eyes closed, her face appears sad and almost serene—an eerie contrast to the incomprehensible terror and brutality she had just endured.

Two other teenage girls, both Christian, were also decapitated during the same massacre on the Indonesian island of Sulawesi. The young Muslims, all clothed in black, savagely attacked the sixteen- to nineteen-year-old girls with machetes as they walked across a cocoa plantation on their way to the private Christian school they attended. Their heads were found some distance from the bodies; one girl's was discarded mockingly in front of a church.

Islamist attacks on Christians, including one a few months earlier in the nearby, predominantly Christian town of Tentena that killed twenty-two and injured over thirty, are common in this area, with more than forty local attacks in a two-and-a-half-year period.[1]

Indeed, in one of our era's most alarming trends, such brutal jihadist violence has been duplicated all over the world in recent years, from Israel to India, from Russia to the Philippines, from Sudan to the Balkans, and right on into the heart of Europe with massive Muslim rioting in France and the terrorist train bombing in Spain, plus the subway bombings in London—and of course the 9/11 attacks in America that killed almost three thousand. Violent Islamic jihadism, in remission for centuries, is once again growing and metastasizing worldwide.

Islam has pursued global domination before. In past centuries it conquered not only Arabia, Persia, Syria, and Egypt, but major parts of Africa, Asia, and Europe, until it was ultimately defeated and lost its will to conquer—for a time.

For Americans, largely ignorant of world history, Islamic radicalism sprang mysteriously to life on their television screens for the first time on the morning of September 11, 2001, and has dominated our national security concerns ever since. But those familiar with the major tides of world events recognize the violent spread of Islam as one of the most malignant geopolitical forces during the last fourteen centuries, one that has touched billions of lives.

I personally lost dozens of family members—perhaps more than one hundred—in the genocide of the Christian Armenians by the Muslim Turks in the early twentieth century. In *The Marketing of Evil* I tell the story of my grandfather's murder by the Turks, and how my grandmother Mary Kupelian and dad, Vahey (then a little boy), made a harrowing escape on horseback, avoiding torture and death, and ultimately found their way to a new life in the greatest country on earth: America.

But on my mother's side of the family, the sword of Muhammad was even more merciless. My great-grandfather, a Protestant minister named Steelianos Leondiades, was confronted with a terrible life-or-death choice when he traveled to the major Turkish city of Adana to attend a pastors' conference in 1908. Here's how his daughter, my grandmother Anna Paulson, told the story: "Some of the Turkish officers came to the conference room and told all these ministers—there were seventy of them, ministers and laymen and a few wives: 'If you embrace the Islamic religion you will all be saved. If you don't, you will all be killed.'"

My great-grandfather, acting as a spokesman for the ministers' group, asked the Turks for fifteen minutes so they could make their decision, according to my grandmother's account. During that time the ministers and their companions talked, read the Bible to each other, and prayed. In the end, none of them would renounce their Christian faith and convert to Islam.

"And then," Anna recalled, "they were all killed.

"They were not even buried. They were all thrown down the ravine."

The only reason we know any details of this massacre—one of many during that hellish period when 1.5 million Armenians were exterminated—is that one victim survived the ordeal. "One man woke up; he wasn't dead," my grandmother said. "He woke up and got up and said, 'Brethren, brethren, is there anybody alive here? I'm alive, come on, let's go out together.'" Had it not been for that survivor's account, no one would have known about this modern-day martyrdom. (Coincidentally, details of the appalling decapitations of the three Christian girls in Indonesia also emerged thanks to a lone survivor—a fourth student who was also attacked and severely injured, but who somehow miraculously survived to tell authorities about the deadly rampage.)

My great-grandfather and his fellow ministers in that conference room were martyrs, real ones. But today, we most often hear the word *martyr* used to describe Islamic radicals who commit unspeakable mass atrocities against innocent people while dementedly chanting "Allahu Akhbar, Allahu Akhbar, Allahu Akhbar" ("Allah is greatest") to drown out what little is left of their conscience.

That's not martyrdom. It's terrorism—and it's about time we understood what terrorism is really all about.

HOW IT WORKS

On one level, terrorism works by simply causing us so much pain, suffering, emotional turmoil, and fear of future attacks that we give in to the terrorists' demands. This much we all understand.

But the ultimate goal of terrorism is to capture our hearts and minds—to convert as many of us as possible.

What? How can terrorizing us transform our attitudes in *favor* of the terrorists' viewpoint? Wouldn't we recoil in horror and, if anything, move further away from empathy for the perpetrators? Not necessarily.

Remember, for centuries militant Muslims have converted "infidels" to their religion by threat of death (just as Islam's legal system, sharia, to this day prescribes death as the penalty for leaving Islam). This forced conversion and retention process, so alien and repugnant to us in the West, where religious liberty is enshrined, really does work, and not just on individuals but on entire societies.

Stop and consider what happens when we're powerfully intimidated and frightened by anything, including terrorism. Wonder of wonders, some of us start to side with the intimidator/terrorist. Of course, part of this is the survival instinct of siding with our enemy so he won't hurt us. But there's much more to it: when we're confronted with serious intimidation, most of us become very upset emotionally, angry, fearful, confused. The problem is, extreme emotion like this throws our minds into "program mode," so to speak. That's the state of mind and emotion in which we are vulnerable to being converted "at the point of a sword."

It's no exaggeration to say that intense emotion can open the door of your mind to total paradigm change, to seeing good as evil and up as down. After all, that's the political left in a nutshell—a topsy-turvy worldview that emanates primarily from deep and abiding anger.

Remember "peace mom" Cindy Sheehan? After losing her soldier son in Iraq, she was lionized by America's establishment press as the courageous public face of the antiwar movement. But she saw evil as good and enemies as friends—referring to terrorists flocking to Iraq to kill American soldiers as "freedom fighters." And calling President George W. Bush—who, by taking the fight to the enemy in Afghanistan and Iraq after 9/11, amazingly kept America safe from another terrorist attack for the remaining seven years of his presidency—a "lying bastard," a "jerk," an "evil maniac," a "gangster," a "war criminal," a "murderous thug," and, of course, a "terrorist."[2]

Or what about Ramsey Clark, former U.S. attorney general during Lyndon Johnson's presidency? After serving as America's chief law enforcement official, Clark emerged as the radical, America-hating leftist he always was, traveling to Hanoi to support America's enemies during the Vietnam War, meeting Iran's Ayatollah Khomeini in 1979 while condemning the "crimes of America," accusing President George H. W. Bush of "genocide" and "crimes against humanity" for the 1991 Gulf War, and defending the terrorists who bombed the World Trade Center in 1993. After the 9/11 attacks, Clark predictably opposed any retaliation against Afghanistan or al-Qaeda. Most recently, he served as chief defense counsel for Saddam Hussein in the Iraqi special tribunal's trial of the former dictator, referring to Saddam respectfully as a "commander . . . courageous enough to fight more powerful countries."[3] After Clark complained that the tribunal, which ultimately convicted and sentenced Saddam for war crimes, was "a mockery of justice," the Iraqi judge threw Clark out of the courtroom, declaring in Arabic, "No, *you* are the mockery . . . get him out, *out*!"[4]

Somehow, no matter how malevolent the enemy, no matter how insane, widespread, and vicious his deeds, some of us mysteriously come around to siding with him. Why?

Of course there's more than one answer to that question. Some people are just plain rotten, and so they quite naturally sympathize, openly or secretly, with the evil in others (which they view as good). There's not too much we can do about that, except expose it. However, there's another reason more and more people—many of them decent souls—are coming around to siding with evil. And this is something we really do need to understand, or else we're in danger of falling victim to it ourselves.

SYMPATHY FOR THE DEVIL

Let's take a quick trip back in time, to 1973. On August 23 of that year, at 10:15 A.M., a submachine-gun-toting escaped convict named Jan-Erik Olsson attempted to rob a bank in Stockholm, Sweden, and in the process took four hostages.

During their five-and-a-half-day captivity, the hostages—three women and one man—were locked in a bank vault, threatened repeatedly at gunpoint, strapped with dynamite, and had nooses attached to their necks so they'd be strangled to death if police attempted to rescue them by means of a gas attack.

Yet, incredibly, while they were thus held captive, the hostages developed a strong and lasting emotional bond with Olsson and another ex-con who had joined him. They came to sympathize with and support the criminals holding them hostage and threatening their lives, while fearing and disparaging the police who were risking their own lives trying to save them! In fact, some of the captives later testified in court on behalf of their captors, refusing to give evidence against them—and even raised money for their tormentors' legal defense.

This phenomenon of captives bonding emotionally and siding with their captors, dubbed the "Stockholm syndrome" after the bank hostage case, has been observed in similar hostage situations over the years, and has also shed light on other seemingly inexplicable behaviors.

Indeed, as clinical psychologist Joseph M. Carver points out, "law enforcement personnel have long recognized this syndrome, with battered women who fail to press charges, bail their battering husband/boyfriend out of jail, and even physically attack police officers when they arrive to rescue them from a violent assault."[5]

All those unfortunate enough to be caught up in a powerfully intimidating relationship—hostages, abused women or children, cult members, prisoners of war, concentration camp inmates, victims of incest—are considered vulnerable to the Stockholm syndrome, whose clinical characteristics include the following:

1. The captives start to identify with their captors, at first as a means of survival, calculating that the captor won't hurt them if they are cooperative and supportive.
2. The captives realize a rescue attempt is dangerous and could result in their being hurt or even killed, and so they come to fear and oppose efforts to rescue them.
3. Longer-term captivity (here's where it gets really weird) fosters an emotional attachment to the captor, as the victims learn of the captor's problems and grievances, as well as his hopes and aspirations. In some cases, the captives come to identify with and believe in the justness of the captor's "cause," effectively joining his side.

To make this dry symptom picture come alive, let's briefly explore a sensational example everyone remembers.

Patricia Hearst, granddaughter of legendary newspaper publisher William Randolph Hearst, was kidnapped at gunpoint in 1974 by three people identifying themselves as soldiers in the "Symbionese Liberation Army."

A privileged, sheltered nineteen-year-old, Patty was thrust into utter chaos and terror. Following her violent abduction, she was locked in the trunk of a car and transported to the group's head-quarters, where she was kept blindfolded for two months, forced to live in a closet, physically and sexually abused by various group members, threatened with death, lied to constantly, and forced to tape-record messages condemning her family and loved ones.

The group's deranged leader, Donald DeFreeze—a black escaped convict who liked to call himself "Field Marshal Cinque Mtume"—demanded utter obedience, and like Charles Manson half a decade earlier was intent on igniting a "people's rebellion" against the gov-ernment and corporate America. (The SLA's charming slogan was "Death to the fascist insect that preys upon the life of the people.")

The whole nation was shocked when, two months after her ab-duction, a gun-toting Patty Hearst was seen on surveillance video helping the SLA pull off an armed robbery of the Hibernia Bank in the Sunset district of San Francisco. Stealing more than ten thou-sand dollars, the robbers wounded two bystanders and took off in a getaway car.

"Tanya," as the new Patty defiantly renamed herself (after the girlfriend of communist revolutionary Che Guevera), now claimed via tape recordings released to the public that she had joined the SLA and was dedicated to its revolutionary cause. "I am a soldier of the people's army," she announced, boasting of her willing participa-tion in the bank robbery and calling her parents "pigs."

Finally, in September 1975, nineteen months after her ordeal began, the FBI rescued the kidnapped newspaper heiress. But in-stead of taking her home, reuniting her with her family, and help-ing her get therapy and perhaps a good deprogrammer, they arrested her and charged her with bank robbery! Incredibly, then–attorney general William Saxbe brazenly declared that Hearst "was not a reluctant participant" in the bank robbery and was just "a common criminal," a widely discredited charge he still stubbornly clung to a quarter century later in his autobiography.[6]

During Patty Hearst's thirty-nine-day trial, defense experts explained to the jury about brainwashing, describing techniques that, if capable of breaking a tough U.S. soldier trained to withstand powerful mind-control pressures, could certainly succeed in messing up the mind of an emotionally distraught and traumatized nineteen-year-old girl.

Key to the defense was Dr. Robert Jay Lifton, a professor of psychiatry and psychology and world-renowned expert on Chinese brainwashing or "thought reform" methods. He made a persuasive case that the way the SLA treated Patty Hearst paralleled *exactly* the carefully worked out brainwashing techniques the Chinese communists had developed—each resulting in dramatic personality and worldview changes.[7]

And yet, on March 20, 1976, after deliberating twelve hours, the jury returned a verdict of guilty and Patty was given the maximum possible sentence: thirty-five years in prison—twenty-five for the robbery plus ten more on a related firearms charge. Although a subsequent judicial review shortened her sentence to seven years, Patricia Hearst was shipped off to the federal correctional institute in Pleasanton, California, where she served twenty-one months behind bars. Fortunately for her, President Jimmy Carter commuted her sentence in 1979 and she was released from prison.

Big question: Since Patty Hearst was clearly kidnapped, traumatized, and brainwashed, how on earth could a jury convict her and send her off to prison? How could a clueless attorney general view the bank's surveillance video and conclude beyond any doubt that she's just "a common criminal"? Are we really that ignorant of how our own thoughts and feelings, loyalties and allegiances, can be ruthlessly manipulated by others given the right circumstances? Are we that out of touch with how evil works?

Yes, we sure are.

There are of course many such examples of the Stockholm syndrome that crop up in the news cycle. Remember Elizabeth Smart, the fourteen-year-old girl who was kidnapped from her Salt Lake City home in 2002 by two members of a polygamist cult? After two months of captivity, the teen "willingly" accompanied her captors wherever they went and made no attempts to escape, and in fact grew increasingly attached to them. When Utah law enforcement finally caught up with her nine months after her abduction, she was wearing a gray wig and large sunglasses and claimed she was eighteen and not Elizabeth Smart. Asked by investigators why she was wearing a wig, she insisted it was her real hair. In other words, the fourteen-year-old's mind had been seriously tampered with. Only when police showed her a pre-abduction photograph of herself did the spell break, as tears came to her eyes and she admitted she was indeed Elizabeth Smart.[8]

Then there's Yvonne Ridley, the British journalist who in 2001 was captured by the Taliban in Afghanistan while disguised in a burka. Held captive and interrogated for ten days, she later confided to the BBC: "I was horrible to my captors. I spat at them and was rude and refused to eat."[9] Figuring she'd be either gang-raped or stoned to death, she told another U.K. newspaper, "I wondered how much pain I could take and prayed that, whatever happened, I would die quickly."[10]

But Yvonne wasn't raped or otherwise physically abused, and in fact claimed she was treated rather decently—at least compared to the treatment she had feared. (Psychologists say Stockholm syndrome victims fearful for their lives regard *not being killed* by their captors as an act of kindness.) Eventually she was released, after promising her captors she would study the Quran if they let her go. Amazingly, a couple of years later Ridley left the Church of England and converted to Islam, quitting her journalist position at the *Sun-*

day Express, leaving her only child behind in Britain, and moving to Qatar.[11]

The question is, how might Patricia Hearst's captivity and torment at the hands of her captors, and Elizabeth Smart's and Yvonne Ridley's, have led to their "conversion" to the worldview of their captors?

Here's a key principle of how evil works: hate can easily morph into "love." Not real love, of course, but rather an emotional identification and bonding many of us mistakenly think of as love. These victims were obviously angry, emotional, and fearful during their ordeals—totally understandable considering their circumstances. But do we also understand that being in an extremely upset state, with all the confusion, doubt, and turmoil that accompany such strong emotion, also renders us suggestible, malleable, vulnerable to being influenced and even reprogrammed?

This is the operative mechanism of the Stockholm syndrome: it isn't just being close to hostage takers and learning about their problems and aspirations that cause conversion to their viewpoint. What causes the "mind meld" to occur is the intense emotion—the terror the hostages feel when their very lives are being threatened, and the rage that underlies the fear. That emotional climate has a way of wiping their mind's hard drive clean and allowing for new programming. This is brainwashing at its most elemental level.

"UNDER CHRONIC SIEGE"

Clearly, individuals can have their brains scrambled when subjected to great stress and cruelty. But what about entire societies? If, as psychologists say, the abused bond to and identify with their abusers as a means of enduring or avoiding violence, is it possible the same holds true for nations similarly threatened?

If there's one country that has long existed in a state of siege, it is Israel. Surrounded by Arab states sworn to destroy it, Israel has been subjected to repeated wars of intended annihilation since its 1948 founding. After six decades of such chaos, a significant number of Israel's leaders and citizens have embraced appeasement of their Arab victimizers.

It wasn't always so. When I was growing up, Israel set the worldwide standard for dealing with aggressors. A tiny country the size of New Jersey, it defeated the combined armies of Egypt, Syria, and Jordan in 1967 in the Six-Day War, destroying Egypt's Soviet-supplied air force preemptively before a single MiG could get off the ground. Likewise with Israel's surprise hostage-liberating raid on Uganda's Entebbe Airport in 1976, which made good men and women the world over shout for joy. A few years later, Israeli warplanes' under-the-radar bombing of Iraq's Osirak reactor kept Saddam Hussein's nuclear ambitions in check.

With its legendary military, its refusal to negotiate with terrorists, and of course its secret arsenal of nuclear weapons as "peacekeepers," Israel was the world's undisputed expert at dealing with bad guys.

Former Israeli prime minister Ariel Sharon described the necessary mind-set in his autobiography, *Warrior,* recalling his years as a military leader fighting for his nation's survival. In dealing with Israel's Arab attackers, Sharon said he "came to view the objective not simply as retaliation, or even deterrence in the usual sense. It was to create in the Arabs a psychology of defeat, to beat them every time and to beat them so decisively that they would develop the conviction they could never win." [12] He had it exactly right.

Remember, jihadists' modus operandi is extreme intimidation. To neutralize this crazed mind-set, the only language they understand is shock-and-awe strength, which has the proven potential to counterintimidate them into submission. This, however, is where narcissistic leaders like Jimmy Carter and Barack Obama go astray, vainly imagining they can sit down with people totally possessed by evil and charm them with their empathy, superior intellect, and sheer personal magnetism—and negotiate peace. In reality, anything short of overwhelming, paralyzing, courage-destroying strength is perceived by terrorists and tyrants as pathetic weakness and an engraved invitation to commit more atrocities.

Unfortunately in recent years, despite the passionate protest of many stouthearted Israelis, much of the nation's leadership and intelligentsia have led the Jewish state down a path of near self-destruction, making concession after concession to its enemies, retreat after retreat, in the vain hope that peace would somehow result.

But rather than peace, their Arab neighbors—including Hamas and Hezbollah—have just been encouraged to engage in ever more attacks until they've "liberated" all of Israel, which they call Palestine.

In his book *The Oslo Syndrome: Delusions of a People under Siege*, Dr. Kenneth Levin, a clinical instructor of psychiatry at Harvard Medical School and a Princeton-trained historian, explores what has happened to Israel. Many Jews today, says Levin, living "under chronic siege" for all these years, have "deluded themselves into believing they could win peace through embracing the indictments of their enemies and seeking to appease them":

> Segments of populations under chronic siege commonly embrace the indictments of the besiegers, however bigoted and outrageous. They hope that by doing so and reforming accordingly they can assuage the hostility of their tormenters and win relief.[13]

Noting that this self-blame or self-hatred "has been an element of the Jewish response to anti-Semitism" throughout history, Levin compares today's Israeli response to constant "besiegement" with "the psychodynamics of abused children, who almost invariably blame themselves for their predicament, ascribe it to their being 'bad,' and nurture fantasies that by becoming 'good' they can mollify their abusers and end their torment."

Exhibit A for Levin's case is the Israeli peace movement, whose "distortions of Arab aims and actions, and its indictments of Israel likewise reflected the psychological impact of chronic besiegement." Writes Levin:

> The Peace Movement had argued that Israel's refusal to acknowledge previous wrongdoing and make sufficient amends and concessions was what perpetuated the Arab-Israeli conflict. Hence, the rationale of Oslo was that Israel would now win peace by providing such concessions to the PLO. Israel pursued this path even as the Palestinian leadership continued to tell its constituency that its goal remained Israel's destruction and continued to collude in a terror campaign against Israel.[14]

Many other commentators echo Levin's analysis, including celebrated Israeli novelist and essayist Aharon Megged, who writes: "We have witnessed . . . an emotional and moral identification by the majority of Israel's intelligentsia, and its print and electronic media, with people committed to our annihilation." [15]

Clearly, as Levin demonstrates, the "corrosive impact of besiegement" can lead both individuals and nations down a self-destructive course if they're not careful.

THE SYNDROME SPREADS

If the scrappiest kid on the block, Israel, can fall prey to the Stockholm syndrome, where constant besiegement and fear mysteriously give birth to widespread sympathy with jihadists threatening the Jewish state's very existence, might this same dynamic also help illuminate the way radical Islam is currently affecting the rest of the world?

Europe is already well in the syndrome's grip. Although Britain has exploded with more extremist Islamist activity (including the gruesome London bombings) and active terror cells than almost anywhere else in the Western world, most Brits express a chipper view of the Muslims in their midst, according to a poll by the Pew Research Center. Almost two out of three Britons—63 percent—claimed a favorable opinion of Muslims.[16]

But this love is unrequited. The level of raw hatred British Muslims have for non-Muslim Brits is higher than anywhere on the Continent. "Across the board, Muslim attitudes in Britain more resembled public opinion in Islamic countries in the Middle East and Asia than elsewhere in Europe," summarized London's *Guardian* newspaper.[17] And in July 2008, the "most comprehensive survey ever undertaken of Muslim student opinion in the UK" showed an astonishing "60 percent of active members of campus Islamic societies said killing in the name of religion can be justified." [18]

Is it just possible that the extreme "tolerance" Brits display toward the militant jihadists in their midst is nothing more than weakness—a timid, smiling attempt to pacify the bully in the vain hope he won't hurt them anymore?

Meanwhile, across the channel, in France, Muslims rioted for weeks in and around Paris in late 2005, burning over one thousand cars, rampaging through three hundred towns shooting at police and firemen—and yet the press barely mentioned that the rioters were Muslims. (The media typically used code words and phrases to communicate who the demonstrators were, without having to actually use the words "Muslim" or "Islamic," saying things such as "Many of the demonstrators were second-generation immigrants from northern Africa.") Though Muslims represent no more than 10 percent of France's population, the nation is scared to death of this ever-growing, unassimilated minority, and even the police fear entering Muslim areas. Furthermore, in this once-Christian nation, an estimated 200,000 to 400,000 of France's 5 million Muslims live in polygamous households, despite the fact that plural marriage is officially outlawed in France.[19]

Here's the bottom line: many people are so intimidated by radical Islam, so fearful of becoming victims themselves, that their fear is *unconsciously transformed* into a strange sympathy and support for the terrorists, or at least for their worldview. The key word here is *unconsciously*. We're not talking about merely "playing along" as a survival strategy; we're talking about actual change, conversion, paradigm shift.

But then, isn't this exactly how forced conversion to Islam "at the point of a sword" has always worked throughout the centuries? And isn't this what's really behind the absurd, bending-over-backward political correctness we see in America and Europe today with regard to Islam? Just consider:

- In 2008, a British government-backed awards event banned "The Three Little Pigs" from consideration because the presence of pigs in the classic children's story might offend Muslims.[20]
- In 2007, Muslim convicts incarcerated in Britain's high-security Leeds Prison were outraged that the prison mistakenly posted a menu offering ham sandwiches as one of three Ramadan food choices, and a few claimed they were actually served ham. Indignant Muslim prisoners sued the prison for $20 million.[21]
- The U.S. government, not wanting to offend Muslim sensitivities, rarely uses the words *Muslim* or *Islamic* when describing Islamic terrorism. For instance, when a massive jihadist plot to blow up ten airliners over the Atlantic and kill thousands was foiled in 2006, then-chief of homeland security Michael Chertoff briefed his agency using only the word *extremists* to describe the plotters—no mention of Islam. All of the two dozen would-be terrorists were Muslims.[22]

As long as the West becomes continually weaker and more contemptible in its attempts to placate Islam, the conflict will just intensify. In fact, believe it or not, it is our weakness that is actually fueling the growth of Islamofascism. That's right: When you behold the ever-increasing radicalization, arrogance, and fury of today's jihadists, realize that we are literally feeding it. We're nurturing it. We're rocking the cradle.

It's similar to the syndrome of a teenage boy with an explosive anger problem. He's totally out of control, a danger to himself and others, and everyone around him is trying to be ever so nice, to placate him and keep him from getting angry again. Yet paradoxically, the more they walk on eggshells around him, the more his contempt and rage toward them is enflamed. So now the "well-meaning grown-ups" just don't know what to do. Since they don't comprehend that they're fueling the problem, everything they do to "help" just makes him worse and brings on ever-bigger tantrums.

And make no mistake, radical Islam in the world today has become a religion of tantrums:

- In 2002, before the Miss World beauty pageant was to start in Nigeria, a local newspaper columnist named Isioma Daniel wrote the following in praise of the contestants' beauty: "What would Muhammad think? In all honesty, he would probably have chosen a wife from among them." In response to this "dishonoring" of the Prophet Muhammad, Muslims went utterly insane with rioting, killing at least 205 people with machetes, or by beating them to death or burning them alive. Another five hundred were hospitalized and three thousand made homeless. Churches, newspaper offices, and hotels were burned to the ground by Muslim mobs enraged by one sentence in a newspaper column.[23]
- In 2005, *Newsweek* reported—falsely—that an American interrogator at the U.S. prison at Guantánamo Bay, Cuba, had flushed a Quran down a toilet, which led to angry protests throughout the Muslim world and at least fifteen deaths.[24]

- In 2006, a Danish newspaper published twelve cartoons depicting the Prophet Muhammad, and in response imams incited Muslim riots, leading to over fifty deaths.[25]
- Later in 2006, Pope Benedict XVI quoted a Byzantine emperor's centuries-old negative comment about Islam, prompting the firebombing of churches and the murder of several Christians, not to mention calls from radical Muslims for the pope's execution.[26]

And our response to these and other murderous tantrums? We ban "The Three Little Pigs" to demonstrate our religious "sensitivity."

Do we dare look unflinchingly at the West's inordinate fear of Islam—and the resulting absurd deference that fear has morphed into? If so, we will discover a large-scale Stockholm syndrome conditioning process that's been infecting us for years.

Put even more plainly, millions of us are secretly intimidated by Islam, and that intimidation has a way of metamorphosing within us into sympathy, respect, and even identification with Islam.

Look at it on a personal level: If I were to make you really upset and fearful of me, your behavior and attitude toward me would change profoundly. And I don't just mean you'd be really resentful toward me. With some people, at least, your upset and fear could be psychologically flipped into "love" and "loyalty."

Haven't you ever wondered how entire populations comprising millions of people—for example, Mao Zedong's China or Pol Pot's Cambodia—could so easily and quickly be converted from relative freedom to a toxic and destructive worldview like Marxism? That process is exactly what we're talking about here.

WHAT WOULD THE
"GREATEST GENERATION" DO?

Is there a cure for this terrible syndrome? Yes, and since Americans have a history of vanquishing tyrants, even in recent decades, let's explore the powerful lessons they've bequeathed to us.

First, let's look at how the "Greatest Generation" managed to triumph over major evil "isms," namely, Nazism and Japanese imperialism.

To understand how the World War II generation was able to deal so effectively with monstrous totalitarian movements, it's essential to realize the fundamental difference between America then and now. For all our problems back then, America had tremendous national unity and a strong sense of identity. Judeo-Christian values were still paramount in work, play, and everyday life—they made up the cultural "air" we all breathed. We weren't yet crippled by national guilt, self-doubt, and self-hatred as we are today. There's no way we could have been bamboozled into thinking same-sex marriage is perfectly normal, or that slaughtering innocent babies in the womb is moral and constitutional, or that posting the Ten Commandments on a courthouse wall somehow violates the First Amendment.

In other words, we were not corrupted with the antibiblical philosophies and utter confusion that have suffocated our modern era and robbed it of genuine moral strength. Back then, the unified national character and confidence of the Greatest Generation allowed us to make the tough decisions that were necessary to preserve our nation, rescue our allies, and end a terrible war.

Perhaps the most controversial action in U.S. military history was dropping atomic bombs on Hiroshima and Nagasaki to break the will of the maniacal Japanese war effort. Decades later, arguments still abound both for and against this use of the A-bomb. But whatever you may think in retrospect about the destruction of those two Japanese cities, what is undeniable is that doing so accomplished more than end the war with Japan. It *broke* Japan. It confronted the "evil spirit" that had possessed that nation—a totalitarian, emperor-worshipping military cult obsessed with expansion—and violently exorcized it. Having neutralized the evil that had captivated Japan, America became that nation's friend and helped massively reconstruct it, ultimately turning Japan into the civilized, successful, First World economic power it is today. Think how utterly amazing that is.

For that matter, after the Allies annihilated Hitler's war machine and along with it the German capacity and will to conquer its neighbors, the United States also helped a newly sober Germany become a great Western power. Our enemies, Japan and Germany, became our friends.

No, I'm not saying "Nuke Mecca." I am simply affirming what Ariel Sharon said years ago: we must create in the enemy "a psychology of defeat, to beat them every time and to beat them so decisively that they would develop the conviction they could never win."

Remember, moral weakness—appeasement—whether in individuals or nation-states, always encourages violence. Just as with communists and Nazis, today's Islamofascists regard goodwill gestures and concessions as contemptible weakness and an irresistible invitation to take advantage. Hitler, shortly after the appeasing Neville Chamberlain arrived home proudly displaying his worthless "peace" agreement, turned around and attacked Britain.

So, what would the U.S. Congress of that era do today about frequent threats by radical Islamists to commit further terror on the U.S. homeland? The Greatest Generation's lawmakers would probably—after making a brief apology to all law-abiding Muslims living here—announce immediate and severe restrictions on immigration into the United States from Muslim countries. No more Muslim chaplains in our prisons to act as recruiters. No more Saudi-funded, anti-American Islamic schools here. If a mosque in the United States is proven to have been used for storing terror weapons and fomenting revolution, it gets bulldozed—immediately. You get the idea. We're at war.

These are the kinds of measures the World War II generation would have implemented, at least for starters. Call it tough love on a national scale. But that in turn requires two things in short supply today: courage and moral clarity.

WHAT WOULD REAGAN DO?

Fast-forward a couple decades beyond the World War II generation and its battle with Nazism and fascism. One of the best examples of courage and moral clarity in dealing with totalitarian evil was Ronald Reagan and his forty-year war against communism.

First and foremost, recognize that, like Winston Churchill and other prominent nonappeasing leaders, Reagan was widely reviled in his day. America's establishment elite had nothing but contempt for him.

As Peter Schweizer, author of *Reagan's War: The Epic Story of His Forty-Year Struggle and Final Triumph Over Communism*, recalls:

> Historian Edmund Morris, in his 874-page authorized biography, concludes that Reagan is simply incomprehensible, an airhead who has lived a charmed life. Diplomat Clark Clifford has called him an "amiable dunce," and Nicholas von Hoffman said it was "humiliating to think of this unlettered, self-assured bumpkin being our president." Tip O'Neill flat out said in public, "He knows less than any president I've every known." Anthony Lewis of the New York Times claimed he had only a "seven-minute attention span." Author Gail Sheehy declared he was "half asleep" while he was president.[27]

That's how the Washington and New York elite regarded Ronald Reagan, and many of them still do.

Now consider the villain: communism, the utopian supercancer that seduced and enslaved large parts of the world. More than 100 million people were killed during the last century because of this Marxist fantasy enforced by guns, gulags, and nuclear-armed ICBMs.

Reagan, from his acting days, when he stood up to the communist takeover of Hollywood, through his years as California's governor and later as president, remained steadfast in his mission. That's "moral clarity."

Setting the stage for Reagan's presidency was Jimmy Carter, one of America's weakest and most overtly appeasing presidents, more interested in being loved as a great peacemaker and winning Nobel Prizes than in effectively confronting evil. His term as commander in chief greatly encouraged Soviet expansionism around the globe, from Afghanistan to Central America.

Once elected, however, Reagan spearheaded a comprehensive plan to win the Cold War, while gracefully bearing the insults and mockery of know-nothing Beltway critics.

Ignoring the advice of "experts" even in his own administration, Reagan personally mapped out a four-part plan—not just military, but economic, political, and psychological—to crush the Soviet Union. This will be news to many people, who have been indoctrinated by public education and the news media to believe that Reagan, the "amiable dunce," the "cowboy actor" with the "million-dollar smile," just happened to be in the right place at the right time, and reaped undeserved credit for winning the Cold War.

I remember when I first realized Ronald Reagan was doing something extraordinary. It was March 23, 1983. I happened to be in Kmart's electronics section, in front of a whole bank of televisions, all tuned to the same channel. While I stood there, on came Ronald Reagan, who proceeded to deliver his historic speech announcing for the very first time his plan to build the Strategic Defense Initiative (SDI).

I couldn't believe my ears. Here was a president who, for the first time in decades, talked about actually *defending* America—protecting it from a Soviet nuclear first strike. At that moment, hope for America was reborn in me, and in millions of others.

Reagan had kept Congress in the dark about SDI and gone directly to the American people, and Congress never forgave him for that. SDI was immediately derided as "Star Wars" by Teddy Kennedy, and the rest of the establishment elite picked up that label, using it to this day to mock the idea of missile defenses.

Yet history has shown it was Reagan's "Star Wars" that broke the back of the Soviet empire. When Reagan and his Soviet counterpart Mikhail Gorbachev were on the world stage at the 1986 Reykjavik summit, the Soviet leader offered to help eliminate *all nuclear weapons from the earth* within ten years—if only Reagan would give up SDI. When Reagan said no and ended the summit, the media and the mainstream political establishment howled at this stupid, warmongering cowboy actor who blew the once-in-a-lifetime opportunity to rid the world of nuclear weapons. "Reyjkavik Summit Ends in Failure," blared headlines the world over.

But Reagan, guided by courage and moral clarity the rest lacked, knew exactly what he was doing.

Three years later, we all turned on our TV sets to watch the evening news and witnessed something unimaginably wonderful. The Berlin Wall, the hated symbol of totalitarian brutality Reagan had visited more than any other president, came tumbling down. Not only the Berlin Wall, but the entire Soviet Union was tumbling down! Nation after nation was set free from the Evil Empire, which was self-destructing before our eyes.

"Today," notes Schweizer, "it is fashionable to explain that victory in the Cold War was a group effort, including every American president from Truman to Reagan. Former President Gerald Ford says the credit doesn't belong to any one leader but to the American people, as if who happened to be in charge really didn't matter. Others, such as former Secretary of State Madeleine Albright, contend that it was the ultimate team effort. 'There were the communists and there were us; the good guys and the bad guys . . . it was fairly easy to understand.' If Reagan did anything, says [historian Robert] Dallek, it was simply to stand on the shoulders of every other Cold War president before him." [28]

Despite the denigration of Reagan by small, envious, inconsequential people, he presided over the defeat of the greatest evil of the twentieth century. But then, Reagan didn't really care what others said—and that was his secret and his strength. (He kept a plaque on his Oval Office desk that read: "There is no limit to what a man can do or where he can go if he doesn't mind who gets the credit.") [29]

"While others were distracted by short-term considerations," said former British prime minister Margaret Thatcher, "President Reagan single-mindedly pursued his vast strategic goals—and he succeeded." Lech Walesa, the heroic former president of Poland, said: "Ronald Reagan played an invaluable role in bringing about the fall of communism and ending the Cold War without resorting to military solutions. This is not something easily found in the world of politics." [30]

And when Reagan visited newly freed Poland shortly after the end of his presidency, Walesa's parish priest presented him with a sword. "I am giving you the saber," said the priest, "for helping us to chop off the head of communism." [31]

So, what can today's leaders learn from Reagan that would guide them in winning the war against Islamofascism? How do those great-sounding words *courage* and *moral clarity* translate into action?

The first prerequisite of a great president, indeed, the first prerequisite of any truly consequential person, is that he must be able to stand alone. At almost every point on the long road to defeating the Soviet Union, Reagan had to endure not just his critics, but his friends and advisers. When he spoke out against martial law in Poland in 1981, virtually every leader except Lady Thatcher opposed him. When he wanted to fight the Soviets in Afghanistan, European leaders balked. When he insisted on raising America's depleted defense budget, most of his own cabinet said no. Before he delivered his speech announcing SDI, senior Pentagon advisers were opposed. In every instance, Reagan gracefully overruled them and forged ahead.

"How remarkable it is to contemplate that if Reagan had paid too much attention to the polls, his advisers, or the allies, many of his most critical Cold War–winning policies never would have been enacted," concludes Schweizer. "Indeed, the Cold War might not have ended when it did, or at all."[32]

What if Reagan were president today? "He would insist that America stay on the offensive," said Schweizer, "recognizing that it is the nature of extremist Islam that is the real problem. Terrorism is but a grisly symptom. Until the totalitarian nature of this ideology is destroyed, terrorism is inevitable; peaceful coexistence is simply not an option."[33]

Somehow, a prescription like this—"stay on the offensive," "the totalitarian nature of this ideology [must be] destroyed," "peaceful coexistence is simply not an option"—doesn't quite resonate with today's seemingly more enlightened, multicultural sensibilities. And although history will likely judge George W. Bush's aggressive military response to the 9/11 attacks, both in Afghanistan and Iraq, as having been just wars led by an unfairly demonized president, his much weaker successor, Barack Obama, has canceled the "Global War on Terror" by rebranding it under the muddled name "Overseas Contingency Operations." Once again, the denial and deference we display toward forces intent on destroying us is actually great weakness—evidence of our loss of courage and moral clarity—disguised as virtue.

If we can embrace the reality that radical Islam needs to be met with overwhelming, unapologetic firmness at every turn, the question emerges: What about efforts to influence the hearts and minds of the larger Muslim world—to nudge it toward moderation and away from radicalism and violence?

Such efforts are essential to prevailing long term in the current clash of civilizations, a war that rages not just between Islam and the West, but between radical Islam and that religion's more moderate, modern elements, who just want to live and let live. The great majority of Muslims worldwide, even those somewhat sympathetic to militant Islam, might actually be susceptible to moving toward a more moderate worldview. But one thing is required.

Whatever outreach the West employs to champion the virtues of freedom and tolerance—and likewise, whatever appeals moderate Muslims make to their more radical brothers and sisters—are useless and doomed to failure if we appease, rather than effectively confront and neutralize, the violent jihad movement.

Worldwide totalitarian movements—the terrible isms of communism, fascism, Nazism, and Islamism, which have seduced millions with insane ideologies wedded to great hatred—have something in common: they share the will to utterly dominate other human beings and enslave nations, to impose their rule indiscriminately, to subjugate, and to do so through utter ruthlessness. Human life means nothing. Hundreds or even millions can be sacrificed to further the particular totalitarian ism.

What counterforce, then, can effectively oppose such a soulless, destructive power? Only men and women with great courage and moral clarity—and a calm, fearless determination to do what's right no matter what. Reagan had it. In the sphere of everyday life, it's called grace under pressure, and it's the antiterror (and anti-intimidation) antidote we're all looking for: the ability to withstand cruelty and craziness without becoming twisted up emotionally inside. Strength *and* patience—a rare combination of qualities that emanates from genuine faith—impel us to "hate the sin," so to speak, "but *not* the sinner." When we discover how to do that, we are immune to the Stockholm syndrome and to a great deal of other evil in this world.

CHAPTER 4

+

THE SECRET CURSE OF CELEBRITY

Understanding Today's Rampant Narcissism

Celeb Antics a Mental Disorder
—*New York Post*, MARCH 19, 2009

Some Estimate Hollywood Divorce Rate at Close to 80 Percent
—MSNBC, NOVEMBER 27, 2002

Narcissism Epidemic: Why There Are So Many Narcissists Now
—*U.S. News & World Report*, APRIL 21, 2009

As a young boy growing up in the suburbs during the relatively in-nocent 1950s, I always relished the annual television rebroadcast of *The Wizard of Oz.* Like all kids, I was transfixed by the tornado whipping Dorothy's house up into the sky and plopping it down in Munchkin Land, her adventures with the Scarecrow, Tin Man, and Cowardly Lion, the scary (but fake) wizard, and of course the maniacal Wicked Witch of the West ("I'm melting! I'm melting! Ohhhhh . . . What a world! What a world!").

In the lead role was sixteen-year-old Judy Garland, whose soul-ful acting and classic rendition of "Somewhere Over the Rainbow" touched millions. Garland was so talented and beautiful that regular American kids could only wonder what it must be like to be her, a real movie star, playing exciting roles while getting rich and being loved by everyone. What a life she must have had!

That's why I remember the shock I felt when my parents told me this gifted young actress had lived a miserable life and had died of a sleeping pill overdose. Indeed, when she left this world at the much-too-early age of forty-seven, Judy Garland had struggled for two decades with drug and alcohol addiction, had been married five times, was plagued with self-doubt, and had made several suicide attempts.

She's far from alone. There have been many such tragic celebrity deaths over the years. Marilyn Monroe was idolized in her day as America's reigning "sex goddess." Yet inwardly she grew increasingly depressed and dependent on alcohol and prescription drugs, finally dying at thirty-six, also from a sleeping pill overdose. The 2007 "drug intoxication" death of Monroe wannabe Anna Nicole Smith was eerily reminiscent of her idol's tragic demise.

Elvis Presley was probably the most worshipped man on earth and possessed wealth beyond imagining. Yet at age forty-two, full of inner conflict—evident in his drug addiction, weight gain, and increasing isolation—his legendary drug use finally caught up with him. In fact, during the year prior to Presley's 1977 death, one physician alone reportedly prescribed ten thousand hits of amphetamines, barbiturates, narcotics, tranquilizers, sleeping pills, laxatives, and hormones for "the King."

Elvis's successor as "the King of Pop," Michael Jackson, the most celebrated music entertainer of the modern era, also had a severe, long-term dependency on prescription painkillers. In mid-2009, the fifty-year-old superstar died from a massive drug overdose ("acute propofol intoxication") administered by his personal physician. Ironically, Michael Jackson had been married briefly to Elvis's daughter, Lisa Marie Presley. The day after Jackson died, Lisa Marie blogged about a conversation she had with Michael years before regarding Elvis's death, during which Michael confided to her: "I am afraid that I am going to end up like him, the way he did." [1]

Of course, many other rock music superstars have met early

deaths from drug-related causes, including guitarist Jimi Hendrix, the Doors' Jim Morrison, singer Janis Joplin, the Who's John Entwistle and Keith Moon, Beatles' manager Brian Epstein, Nirvana's Kurt Cobain, Led Zeppelin's John Bonham, guitarist Mike Bloomfield, blues musician Paul Butterfield, and dozens of others.

But Hollywood actors and actresses, who presumably lead a somewhat more disciplined life than the superheated, temptation-rich nightlife of rock stars, are also plagued by the same demons. Actor and comedian John Belushi died at thirty-three of a heroin and cocaine ("speedball") overdose. Same with comedian Chris Farley, another *Saturday Night Live* alumnus, dead also at thirty-three. And acclaimed child actor River Phoenix died at just twenty-three— like Belushi and Farley, of a "speedball" overdose.

More recently, twenty-eight-year-old Australian-born actor Heath Ledger—on the heels of his portrayal of "the Joker," an irredeemably evil psychopath in the ultradark Batman blockbuster *The Dark Knight*—was found dead in his Manhattan apartment. The New York medical examiner determined Ledger had died of an apparently accidental overdose of powerful painkillers, sleeping pills, anti-anxiety medications, and other prescription drugs—*six* in all.[2]

These sad headline stories are only the barest tip of the iceberg. For every self-destructive celebrity who dies such a tragic, early death, there are literally hundreds of their peers who live profoundly dysfunctional, conflict-ridden lives. Drug and alcohol abuse and sexual promiscuity are routine, and divorce virtually the norm.

More than ever, the public is inundated with never-ending news of outrageous behavior—from cocaine use to drunk driving to high-profile sexual flings—on the part of troubled young "superstar" performers like Nicole Richie, Lindsay Lohan, and Britney Spears. Sometimes there's outright criminality, as seen in the shoplifting arrest of actress Winona Ryder, or Robert Downey, Jr.'s imprisonment for serial drug abuse ("It's like I have a loaded gun in my mouth and my finger's on the trigger, and I like the taste of the gunmetal," Downey told a judge in 1999).[3] Truth is, many of the "stars" idolized by millions of Americans are, according to experts, so troubled as to border on being mentally ill.

Physician and addiction expert Drew Pinsky, M.D., of TV and radio fame, has treated many celebrities over the years. In *The Mirror Effect: How Celebrity Narcissism Is Seducing America,* he and co-author Dr. S. Mark Young claim "life-threatening eating disorders, addictions to drugs and alcohol, self-harming behaviors like cutting or overdoses, trips to rehab and public relapses, sex tapes, and outrageous diva behavior" on the part of the worshipped class are not only epidemic, but are getting more extreme[4]:

> The behavior of today's celebrities is much more dramatically dysfunctional than it was a decade ago. The personal lives of these figures—many of them young, troubled, and troubling—have become the defining story lines of our entertainment culture, played out in real time and held up for our amusement, scrutiny, and judgment. Celebrity gossip, branded as "entertainment news," details stories of excessive partying, promiscuity, diva-like tantrums, eating disorders, spectacular meltdowns, and drug and alcohol abuse, behaviors that have become more open, more dramatic, and more troubling than in previous generations.[5]

Perhaps the most perplexing part of this whole celebrity dysfunction epidemic is that it involves the very people who seem to possess everything most of us secretly covet—talent, good looks, wealth, fame, and influence.

They've got it all, right? So what goes wrong? What secret curse afflicts them?

Before we dive deep into the scary realm where real answers lurk, let's acknowledge the obvious: each case has its own unique contributing factors. As a child actress Judy Garland was routinely given amphetamines to get her going and barbiturates to help her sleep, a shockingly unenlightened management routine that undoubtedly set the stage for the addiction and tragedy that would consume her later in life. Marilyn Monroe was sexually abused as a little girl, she never knew her father, and her mother was institutionalized as a paranoid schizophrenic. No question about it: celebrities, just like the rest of us, are profoundly shaped by childhood traumas and other major life experiences.

Yet there is one powerful dynamic that is common to virtually all dysfunctional celebrities, and which does indeed become a curse to them.

In their scathing exposé *Hollywood, Interrupted,* Andrew Breitbart and Mark Ebner take a shot at answering the question of why superstars are so often full of conflict and their family lives so disastrous. "The short answer," claim the authors, "is ego. Insatiable ego. Constantly massaged ego. 24-hour-a-day concierge ego. 400-thread-count linen at the five-star luxury dog kennel ego. Trading in your pre-fame spouse for a world-class model ego."

What does it take to be a superstar? According to Breitbart and Ebner,

> Every celebrity, by design and necessity, is a narcissist. The desire to become a star requires an incredible appetite for attention and approval. To achieve fame and its accoutrements takes laser-like focus and a nearly commendable ability to stay self-centered in the service of the dream. Maintaining celebrity is a 24-hour-a-day process requiring a full-time staff to solidify the star's place at the top of the social pecking order. An impenetrable ring of "yes" creatures—including assistants, publicists, managers, agents, hair and make-up artists, stylists, lifestyle consultants, Pilates instructors, cooks, drivers, nannies, schedulers and other assorted caretakers—work round-the-clock to feed the star's absurd sense of entitlement. Celebrities focus on the minutiae of self all the time—and they make sure that no distractions like airplane reservation snafus or colicky babies interrupt this singular focus. This

often extremely lucrative self-obsession invariably becomes downright pathological. . . .

Massive ego and narcissism may be the primary ingredients for achieving and maintaining Hollywood success, but they are also the No. 1 cause of the grandiose foibles in their storied, disastrous personal lives. The full-time job of parenting requires absolute selflessness. In contrast, the full-time job of celebrity requires absolute selfishness. The two by definition do not naturally co-exist. Yet, because of their fame, money and social power, stars somehow think they can defy the odds and maintain a high level of professional success, and still raise healthy families in the process.

No wonder so much rotten fruit is hanging from the dysfunctional celebrity family tree.[6]

That's a good start, but we need to go much deeper. The closest the authors come to really pinpointing the celebrity "curse" is with this observation: "The desire to become a star requires an incredible appetite for attention and approval."

Approval, praise, applause, adulation, adoration, worship. What could be wrong with all that? After all, it makes both the "worshipper" and "worshipped" feel good—and no one's getting hurt. Or are they?

Reality check: deriving our sense of self-worth from the praise and adulation of others may feel great, but it also produces great problems. As we're about to find out, worship does extremely weird things to human beings.

Not for nothing does the Bible warn that worship is meant for God alone—in fact, it's the first of the Ten Commandments: "Thou shalt have no other gods before me" (Exodus 20:3). When humans are idolized and praised—or more precisely, when they lower themselves to *accept* that homage and bask in its warmth and glory—the idolized "star" starts to change profoundly for the worse. Let's find out why.

AMERICAN IDOLATRY

Pinsky and Young spent two years persuading two hundred entertainment celebrities to take the psychological test called the Narcissistic Personality Inventory, or NPI. The results, published in the October 2006 *Journal of Research in Personality,* confirmed their darkest suspicions: "Our work suggests that contemporary culture has become fixated on a group of stars whose narcissistic tendencies appear to be approaching personality-disorder levels."[7]

And what exactly is "narcissistic personality disorder"?

According to the Mayo Clinic, it's "a mental disorder in which people have an inflated sense of their own importance and a deep need for admiration. They believe that they're superior to others and have little regard for other people's feelings. But behind this mask of ultra-confidence lies a fragile self-esteem, vulnerable to the slightest criticism."[8]

If this description seems to fit a lot of people, that's because the modern narcissism epidemic, experts tell us, isn't confined to entertainment celebrities, but is increasingly manifesting in everyone from errant politicians to crooked bankers to wife murderers.

For instance, Keith Ablow, M.D., psychiatry correspondent for Fox News, notes "the brazenness of Illinois Governor Rod Blagojevich allegedly attempting to sell a U.S. Senate seat and securities trader Bernie Madoff allegedly bilking investors (including charities) of about $50 billion in a Ponzi scheme" has all the earmarks of serious narcissism.

Having evaluated "dozens of white-collar criminals and very violent offenders over the past decade . . . I've realized many of them share recognizable psychological characteristics with convicted murderer Scott Peterson," notes Ablow, who wrote a bestselling book on the notorious wife killer. "Like Scott Peterson, Blagojevich and Madoff (if guilty) have to possess a sense of narcissistic entitlement that allows them to feel justified in manipulating others to their ends."[9]

It gets worse. It turns out that a great deal of America is evidently suffering from this psychological malady. The "narcissist" label has even been applied—and quite frequently—to President Barack Obama. Pulitzer Prize–winning columnist and former psychiatrist Charles Krauthammer asks, "Does the narcissism of this man know no bounds?"[10] Jack Kelly, journalist and former high-ranking Reagan administration Pentagon official, says, "The most dangerous thing about having a narcissist in a position of power is his unwillingness— perhaps his inability—to ever admit error. . . . Obama acknowledged the troop surge in Iraq has produced dramatic improvements, but said he still would oppose it."[11] And radio giant Rush Limbaugh said of Obama: "He's supremely narcissistic. . . . This is all about him. This has nothing to do with the country. It has nothing to do with our way of life. Every aspect of his presidency is about building him up, making him appear to be a savior, messiah. . . ."[12]

No doubt about it. From top to bottom, "the United States is currently suffering from an epidemic of narcissism," insist Jean M. Twenge, Ph.D., and W. Keith Campbell, Ph.D., in *The Narcissism Epidemic: Living in the Age of Entitlement:*

> In data from 37,000 college students, narcissistic personal-
> ity traits rose just as fast as obesity from the 1980s to the pres-
> ent, with the shift especially pronounced for women. The rise
> in narcissism is accelerating, with scores rising faster in the
> 2000s than in previous decades. By 2006, 1 out of 4 college
> students agreed with the majority of the items on a standard
> measure of narcissistic traits. Narcissistic Personality Disorder
> (NPD), the more severe, clinically diagnosed version of the
> trait, is also far more common than once thought. Nearly 1
> out of 10 of Americans in their twenties, and 1 out of 16 of
> those of all ages, has experienced the symptoms of NPD.[13]

Lurking beneath these ominous statistics "is the narcissistic culture that has drawn in many more. The narcissism epidemic has

spread to the culture as a whole," the authors say, lamenting that "American culture's focus on self-admiration has caused a flight from reality to the land of grandiose fantasy":

> We have phony rich people (with interest-only mortgages and piles of debt), phony beauty (with plastic surgery and cosmetic procedures), phony athletes (with performance-enhancing drugs), phony celebrities (via reality TV and You-Tube), phony genius students (with grade inflation), a phony national economy (with $11 trillion of government debt), phony feelings of being special among children (with parent-ing and education focused on self-esteem), and phony friends (with the social networking explosion). All this fantasy might feel good, but, unfortunately, reality always wins. The mort-gage meltdown and the resulting financial crisis are just one demonstration of how inflated desires eventually crash to earth.[14]

"The evidence Twenge and Campbell have compiled is compel-ling and appalling," summarizes Holly Brubach in the *New York Times*. "Never mind the celebrities; their arrogance is equaled if not surpassed by the grandiosity of so-called average Americans. Like Allison, the Atlanta teenager featured on MTV's series 'My Super Sweet 16,' who wants Peachtree Street blocked off for her birthday party so that she can make a 'grand entrance.' When the planner reminds her that Peachtree is a major thoroughfare with a hospital where ambulances come and go, she replies: 'They can wait one sec-ond. Or they can just go around.' "[15]

Or the school student who, when corrected by her math teacher for writing a zero in the wrong place, responded: "Thank you, but I prefer it my way." Child psychologist Carol Craig warns that today's parents and teachers are so "obsessed with praising" children that they're literally creating a generation of disturbingly egotistical kids.[16]

If the popular diagnosis of universal "narcissism" is starting to wear a little thin for you, there may be good reason. You see, on the one hand, narcissistic personality disorder is a genuine psychiatric condition with an extensive diagnostic symptom picture that pretty much corresponds with a classic sociopath—extreme delusions of grandeur, near-total lack of empathy for others, constant demand for adulation, and so on. However, as with all such personality disorders, there are many degrees, and the lesser manifestations of narcissism are seen everywhere today in daily life. Thus, explain Twenge and Campbell, *"Narcissism* has become a popular buzzword," hurled by the popular press at every misbehaving public figure. In fact, the authors note, sometimes the "narcissists" even diagnose themselves, employing the label almost as an excuse: "Former presidential candidate John Edwards explained his extramarital affair by stating, 'In the course of several campaigns, I started to believe that I was special and became increasingly egocentric and narcissistic.' As the *New York Times* noted, narcissism 'has become the go-to diagnosis by columnists, bloggers, and television psychologists. We love to label the offensive behavior of others to separate them from us. "Narcissist" is among our current favorites.' " [17]

While "narcissism" has become a convenient, all-purpose label for the monumental egotism of other people, there's disagreement as to its causes. *The Narcissism Epidemic* authors dismantle the "prevailing myths that have made us inclined to tolerate and even encourage narcissism," says Brubach, "that it's a function of high self-esteem, that it's a function of low self-esteem, that a little narcissism is healthy, that narcissists are in fact superior, that you have to love yourself to be able to love someone else." [18] Even a top U.S. medical center begins its section on "Causes" with the statement: "It's not known what causes narcissistic personality disorder." [19]

What are we really looking at here? What is the hard-core, street-level reality behind what we superficially call today's "epidemic of narcissism"? Let's find out.

"THOSE TWO IMPOSTORS"

The longer I live, the more I realize that the most crucial, life-giving truths—those truths that would be the most valuable and whole-some in helping people find true happiness within themselves and harmony in their relationships—are virtually never talked about. And I do mean never. Not talked about in the popular culture, nor academia, nor in journalism (my field), nor in psychiatry or psychol-ogy. Even our modern churches rarely touch it.

So, why don't we take a stab at it here?

What could possibly be wrong with the good feelings we get, the ego warmth, the inner glow to our pride we derive from bask-ing in the approval and adulation of others? And is it really possible that human beings, whether celebrities or regular folk, could actu-ally overdose and self-destruct on huge quantities of the "drug" of praise?

As we begin to explore this seemingly strange question, let's set the stage by recalling Rudyard Kipling's classic poem "If," a vivid word portrait of what it means to possess genuinely noble character. As you may recall, it starts like this:

> If you can keep your head when all about you
> Are losing theirs and blaming it on you,
> If you can trust yourself when all men doubt you
> But make allowance for their doubting too . . .[20]

It goes on, verse by verse depicting a spiritually mature person's quiet inner strength, until Kipling gets to these lines:

> If you can meet with Triumph and Disaster
> And treat those two impostors just the same . . .

Impostors? How can triumph and disaster both be impostors? Hold that thought, while we skip down to the last stanza:

If you can talk with crowds and keep your virtue,
Or walk with kings—nor lose the common touch,
If neither foes nor loving friends can hurt you . . .[21]

There it is again: We know foes are bad, but how can "loving friends" possibly hurt us?

Kipling was on to something magnificent. But for us to really understand this mystery—and live it—we have to do something that may be a little scary in this modern, "narcissistic" era: we need to realize that not everything that makes us *feel* good necessarily *is* good.

After all, if we assume that what feels good *is* good, and what feels bad *is* bad, we have a huge problem, because lies often make us feel good—and so does cocaine, and so does sex with a stranger. And then of course we also have a big problem with truth, because truth often hurts.

With this basic principle in mind, then, let's revisit our clinical definition of narcissists. We're told they have "an inflated sense of their own importance and a deep need for admiration," but at the same time are "vulnerable to the slightest criticism." [22]

Addicted to praise, supersensitive to criticism? We're talking about people whose entire sense of self-worth is based on what others say to them and about them. Compliments make them "feel good" and criticism makes them "feel bad," which means *other people* are in control of how they feel. Not good.

This prompts a big-picture question: Why on earth are human beings—any of us—so insecure that we need approval and reassurance from others to maintain our sense of well-being? And why are we so adversely affected by the unkind words of others? Where does this lack of wholeness, this emptiness that craves reassurance, come from in the first place?

Furthermore, assuming we can agree that it's not ideal for us, as mature adults, to have our happiness based on the vacillating moods of other flawed people, the next unavoidable question is, If we're not meant to be rooted in the outside world, with all its confusion and outright craziness, what else is there to serve as the wellspring of our identity, confidence, contentment, and purpose, but something *inside ourselves*?

Yet what is there inside of us that could possibly fulfill such an extraordinary role, other than the direct influence of God?

Hit the pause button, please: I know everyone has a different idea of who or what God is, and that some don't believe He exists at all. So let's talk about God for a minute.

When I say "God," I'm not talking about a concept many of us quickly conjure up in our busy minds: a vague, remote, and impersonal cosmic being we've heard about, and who, although He supposedly performed miracles and was intimately involved with the human race millennia ago (as recorded in the Bible), is seemingly AWOL today, with no discernible influence on the modern world.

I'm talking about the Living God, who created the universe with its elegant solar systems and exploding fireballs larger and farther away from us than we can possibly comprehend. I'm talking about the One who fashions all matter out of miniature solar systems, each pebble, water droplet, dirt clod, and snowflake composed of trillions of tiny "moons" (electrons) orbiting tiny "planets" (atomic nuclei), and all their endless spinning powered by His never-ending delivery of energy careening through the universe. And then, in the midst of this dazzling display—between the macrocosm of unimaginably large, fiery cosmic clockwork and the microcosm of unimaginably small atomic clockwork—He creates life, blossoming in endless variation, complexity, beauty, and wonder, the crowning glory of which is man.

Evidently, God has gone to a lot of trouble creating us, so it's certainly fair to ask why He did it: What is our purpose?

Actually, we all know the answer, even though part of us reflexively doubts or denies it. We all intuitively know we're here to be obedient to our Creator, who cares enough to enfold within each of us a tiny bit of Himself, to light our way, to be a "lamp unto our feet." We're literally designed for this purpose—to discover how to follow the moment-to-moment faith impulse God imparts to us from within, in an unbroken chain of service to him. In return, He gives us direction, purpose, energy, and genuine and lasting happiness, which means, among other things, we no longer crave the vain reassurances of other troubled souls.

But of course, we humans are born somewhat separated from this paradisiacal state. (In Christian parlance it's called "original sin," but this is not a matter of religious dogma, it's the basic undeniable reality of our lives.) What's more, there's another spiritual influence drawing us in an opposite direction—downward. And the part of us that is attracted and easily pulled in this wrong direction is, for want of a better word, pride.

We're confused about pride in the modern era. It used to be universally understood to be a bad thing, but today even the word itself has evolved several contradictory meanings, some of them good. We speak of "pride of craftsmanship" (doing an expert job) and "pride of ownership" (maintaining your home and property well, rather than trashing it as renters sometimes do). Even the Marines' slogan— "The Few, the Proud, the Marines"—uses pride as a synonym for nobility and courage.

That's all fine, but what we're focused on here is the spiritual, biblical meaning of *pride,* which is nothing less than a private war with God.

And here's what this war is all about, at least as Western, Judeo-Christian culture has understood it for thousands of years: God creates man and gives him a choice between good and evil, which to us feels more like a choice between obeying our conscience even if it hurts, and rebelling against it and giving in to our lower impulses. Animals have no such choice. Sharks may be killing/eating machines, but being fearsome predators is just their nature—there's no choice involved and nothing evil about it. The only creature with a choice is man, who can basically do one of two things with that little bit of God inside him: he can appreciate the real God and learn to live in obedience to the "still, small voice" of conscience, or he can ignore his conscience and lamely attempt to be his own god—seeking those who will worship him (craving and demanding ego support), judging the unrighteous (hating and punishing anyone who offends him), and so on. It's ugly when we play god.

So, in a very tangible sense, human beings have two natures—one noble and the other very ignoble. Our conscience pulls in one direction, urging us to strive toward honesty, patience, kindness, courage, and unselfishness, while the lower nature pulls downward on the strings of our thoughts and feelings, toward anger, selfishness, lust, greed, resentment, and envy.

Which side wins? What makes the good side grow and the bad side gradually wither away, so we can develop real character like the guy in Kipling's poem?

Very simply, genuine change for the better is quite natural and effortless for the person who honestly recognizes and acknowledges his own flaws. But guess what? If we are coked up on the anesthetizing "drug" of praise, or false love, we can't see our flaws. To the contrary, we see our failings as virtues!

This may be easier to recognize if we focus momentarily on the other feel-good emotional "drug," which has the same effect of making us invulnerable to seeing our own faults. It's called hate.

For example, what allows anti-Semites to avoid introspection and maintain their self-delusions is their compulsion to blame Jews for all their problems. Their hatred acts like a narcotic drug that numbs their conscience—that is, recognition of their own faults—which would otherwise naturally tend to impress itself on their minds. They're filled instead with the ecstasy of false righteousness based on Jew hatred.

But we all know this, right? Hating can make losers "high," and blaming others "blows their mind clean" of any awareness of their own problems. Yet do we also recognize that getting high on the drug of false love has exactly the same effect?

Under the influence of either of these emotional drugs of false love or hate, we become deluded, egotistical, and very, very blind to our faults, making us blind therefore to pretty much everything else. In that condition, we get into lots of trouble.

I'll tell you how I know this so well. As a young person I was known primarily as an accomplished classical violinist. During my teen years, I was always concertmaster (first chair) in the orchestras I played with, won virtually all the competitions I entered, was the featured soloist performing concertos with various orchestras, and so on. I spent my summers at the elite upstate New York music school attended by all the top Juilliard School violinists and got to hang out with people like Itzhak Perlman and other world-class fiddlers, who were then teens like me. I *lived* for music—or more precisely, I lived for what my persona as a stand-out musician did for me. Everyone respected me for what I did, and my sense of self-worth came to be bound up in what other people said about me.

You may respond: "So what? You excelled at something, people naturally praised you for it, and you soaked it up. What's the problem?"

Here's the problem: As happens with many performers, I became accustomed to the admiration of others. But when you live for appreciation and applause, that motivation doesn't cease when you leave the stage. All of life becomes a stage, and you're constantly performing to elicit a positive response from everyone else. Although I'm using myself as an example here, truth be known, to a greater or lesser degree most of us do exactly the same thing for most of our lives. We're not whole people, and in a ceaseless attempt to fill that inner emptiness with other people's "love" and approval, we're less than honest, we calculate what we say, how we come across, how we look, all to manipulate others into seeing us in a favorable way. This was my problem as a young "performer"—both on- and offstage.

Actually, the classical music world swept me up in two ways: One was the adulation of others, which temporarily filled my emptiness—but left me more empty and hungry for approval later. The other was the fact that music itself became a whole world of fascinating, complex, and esoteric distraction into which I could escape, losing awareness of my problems, angers, insecurities, and so on. Between these two factors—the overwhelming approval of others for being a musical "star," and having my head filled nonstop with the music itself—I was pretty blind to myself as a teen.

It wasn't until I reached my early twenties and had finished seventeen years of schooling and an intense, nonstop pursuit of performance excellence that I came up for air. And when I did, when I finally put the music aside and slowed down the pace of my life, I began to discover the real me, who had been all but lost in the excitement, glory, and super-ambition of my earlier years. I found that, whereas I once craved the applause of others, now I began to thrive on an inner spiritual fulfillment that came naturally as a result of simple clean living, honest self-examination, and quiet prayers and reflection.

It was like a gradual change of life-support systems—from an outer one to an inner one. A major and necessary result of this transformation was that I discovered a lot of problems within me that I had been blind to during all the years I was "high" on the praise of others. But what a blessing—what a relief—to face those problems I'd been running from for so many years without even realizing it. Now change and real healing were possible.

So, that was the beginning of my "reborn" life as a Christian. I quietly found God, right where He'd always been: as close as a sincere, repentant heart.

"I'M SOOOOOO PROUD OF YOU"

Let's take one last pass at this difficult subject by personalizing it.

Have you ever been praised so excessively that you felt uncomfortable? You didn't know how to respond, how to act; you felt awkward. You might even have replied by saying something stupid, feeling so completely off balance. In much the same way that a cruel, thoughtless comment can affect you emotionally, so can too much praise affect you emotionally—and adversely.

This is a very confusing experience, because after all, you're not being criticized or condemned, but praised—and that's supposed to be a good thing! So why are you so uncomfortable?

Let me ask any celebrities reading this: Have you ever noticed you tend to resent or have a subtle contempt for the fan going overboard in his or her praise of you?

Maybe another personal story will shed some light on the reason for this. Many years ago I took my family out for the evening and I noticed that my young son was reluctant to walk ahead and open the building's door for his mother and sister. But isn't that just good manners? He's always been a conscientious, smart, and thoroughly decent boy. So, why the problem with opening up a door for the opposite sex? It didn't make sense.

A bit of discussion unearthed a previously unknown (to me) bit of family history: It seems on a previous occasion when I was not present, my son had quite naturally opened the door for a couple of women, but one of them praised him so lavishly for his wonderful, gentlemanly manners that he became awkward and embarrassed. He actually resented the person who overdid the praise, and to avoid a repeat occurrence of the discomfort he felt, for a time he steered clear of opening doors for women.

Silly? Don't laugh. This type of response is much more common than we might imagine. There's a violation of our spirit when someone serves up inordinate praise. No wonder celebrities get so messed up.

Hey, you're drivin' me nuts. Are you now saying we should never compliment people?

Of course not. There's a huge difference between saying, "Good job, son, that was great!" and saying, "Son, you are so awesome. And I am soooooo proud of you. You're just great, and handsome, and talented, and really, really *special*!" That kind of praise is corrupting. Because whenever we build our pride, we're growing in conflict with God.

If you glazed over that last sentence, read it again, since it capsulizes this entire chapter. It's a core truth about how evil works in our lives. If we don't understand that by feeding our prideful ego, no matter how good it feels to us, we're just increasing our inner conflict with our Creator, then we don't understand ourselves, we don't understand life, and we don't know where true happiness is.

It's possible your reaction to all this discussion about the dangers of praise is still a big "So what?" If so, remember this: if you are sensitive to people praising you—if you soak it up and feel nourished by it—you will also be very sensitive to people *criticizing* you. As our earlier definition of narcissism suggested (and life experience confirms), the more you need people's approval, the more you will feel hurt by criticism—and to the same degree. You can't have one without the other. So, if you're going to allow yourself to feel buoyed up by the applause of others, understand that you will also feel wounded by the unkind comments and put-downs that others make.

I think it's pretty clear that allowing our pride to get bloated by approval is very problematic. But how could it lead celebrities, or us, to the kind of conflict, dysfunction, anger, rage, and depression that might lead to drug addiction or even suicide?

Question: How do you think Elvis Presley really felt toward all his hysterical, adoring, worshipful fans?

On the surface, of course, he seemed to love them (*"Thank yewww, thank y'all vera much! You're a fantastic audience, thank yew, y'all are fantastic!"*). But just think back to a moment in your life when someone *way* overdid it when praising how beautiful, smart, talented, or generous you were, and recall the feelings of awkwardness and confusion you felt—and then multiply that by, oh, about 10 million and lay it on poor Elvis. If we get addicted to the drug of worship, it destroys us.

Remember, what keeps us sane, happy, and moving in the right direction in this life is living in the light of constant, good-natured self-awareness. It is that self-awareness, with our conscience brightly shining through it, that becomes the regulator of our life and makes our perceptions and decisions right and wholesome. It's like God's manna from the invisible realm, which appears in our lives to nourish us just when we need it, as long as we are transparent and honest.

When we worship someone, whether it's a movie star or our spouse, we are, in effect, robbing them of this precious relationship with the real God. Although a part of them loves (is addicted to) the drug of praise, another deeper and more innocent part of them longs to be treated normally, honestly, soberly.

Truth be told, a great deal of what passes as "love," especially between couples, is not really love at all—not in the highest sense, at least—but rather amounts to ego stroking, which usually involves lying. But we get used to this, because after all, it feels good to both the giver and recipient of the "love," making the recipient feel great, and making the giver feel secure because the recipient needs him/her.

The same process goes on between us and our celebrities, although it's much easier to recognize the syndrome with them because the results are so extreme and obviously negative. Think about this: We have these people in society who sing songs, or tell jokes, or who make their living by wearing other people's clothes and acting like heroes or villains, pretending to be something they're not, repeating lines others have written for them—and we worship them. We call them "stars." We pump their pride up to the point of madness, and then we judge them when they fall.

Haven't you ever wondered why so many of the royal families of Britain and Europe throughout the centuries were full of intrigue and murder? Royal brothers and sisters always seemed to be plotting or poisoning or stabbing or betraying each other. But they had wealth beyond imagining, power, prestige—they had everything, so why weren't they happy? As I said, humans don't make very good gods. Worship destroys us, and drives us mad.

As with most problems, there is always a way out. Celebrities don't all become basket cases as a result of fame, fortune, and the adoration of the masses. In fact, there are many famous political leaders, actors, sports heroes, and music superstars who have stayed perfectly sane, among them Charlton Heston, who died in 2008. Although their fans may have inadvertently served up the drug, these "stars" accepted it gracefully, but apparently didn't swallow it.

A while back, I had a casual conversation with my friend Sean Hannity, certainly a media "superstar," outside the Fox News building in Manhattan after I had been a guest on his TV show. When I mentioned his phenomenal success, Sean had this to say: "God has blessed me. It's been great, and I appreciate the position He's put me in. But I don't take credit for it, and I know it could come to an end at any time."

Sean had the right attitude. Grateful, unassuming, both feet firmly on the ground, and recognizing that "Triumph" and "Disaster" are both equally impostors.

When we develop real character, rooted in ever-growing loyalty to the kingdom of heaven within, we find that "neither foes nor loving friends"—that is, neither condemnation nor praise—have much effect on our happiness. This is the simple truth Kipling was portraying with such warmth and grace:

> *If you can talk with crowds and keep your virtue,*
> *Or walk with kings—nor lose the common touch,*
> *If neither foes nor loving friends can hurt you;*
> *If all men count with you, but none too much,*
> *If you can fill the unforgiving minute*
> *With sixty seconds' worth of distance run,*
> *Yours is the Earth and everything that's in it,*
> *And—which is more—you'll be a Man, my son!*[23]

CHAPTER 5

✦

DOCTORS, DRUGS, AND DEMONS

Why So Many Americans
Are Labeled "Mentally Ill"

*Severe, Chronic, Disabling Mental Illnesses . . . Collectively Affect
Estimated 40 Million Americans*
  —*Hospital Business Week*, JUNE 15, 2008

Suicides Rising Among Those 10 to 19
  —*Pittsburgh Post-Gazette*, SEPTEMBER 3, 2008

Homicidal Thoughts Tied to Drug Yates Took Before Deaths
  —*Chicago Tribune*, JULY 10, 2006

"When I was lying in my bed that night, I couldn't sleep because my voice in my head kept echoing through my mind telling me to kill them."[1]

The words are those of twelve-year-old Christopher Pittman, struggling to explain why he murdered his grandparents, who had provided the only love and stability he'd ever known in his turbulent life. He was angry with his grandfather, who had disciplined him earlier that day for hurting another student during a fight on the school bus. So later that night, he shot both of his grandparents in the head with a .410 shotgun as they slept, then burned down their South Carolina home, where he had lived with them.

"I got up, got the gun, and I went upstairs and I pulled the trigger," he recalled. "Through the whole thing, it was like watching your favorite TV show. You know what is going to happen, but *you can't do anything to stop it.*"[2]

His lawyers would later argue that the boy had been a victim of "involuntary intoxication," since Pittman's doctors had him taking the antidepressants Paxil and Zoloft just prior to the murders.

Paxil's known "adverse drug reactions"—according to the drug's FDA-approved label—include "mania," "insomnia," "anxiety," "agitation," "confusion," "amnesia," "depression," "paranoid reaction," "psychosis," "hostility," "delirium," "hallucinations," "abnormal thinking," "depersonalization," and "lack of emotion," among others.[3]

Andrea Yates, in one of the most horrifying and heartbreaking crimes in modern history, drowned all five of her children—ages seven years down to six months—in a bathtub. Insisting inner voices commanded her to kill her children, she had become increasingly psychotic over the course of several years. At her 2006 murder retrial (after a 2002 guilty verdict was overturned on appeal), Yates's longtime friend Debbie Holmes testified: "She asked me if I thought Satan could read her mind and if I believed in demon possesion." And Dr. George Ringholz, after evaluating Yates for two days, recounted an experience she had after the birth of her first child:

"What she described was feeling a presence . . . Satan . . . telling her to take a knife and stab her son Noah," Ringholz said, adding that Yates's delusion at the time of the bathtub murders was not only that she had to kill her children to save them, but that Satan had entered her and that *she* had to be executed in order to kill Satan.[4]

Yates had been taking the antidepressant Effexor. In November 2005, more than four years after Yates drowned her children, Effexor manufacturer Wyeth Pharmaceuticals quietly added "homicidal ideation" to the drug's list of "rare adverse events." The Medical Accountability Network, a private nonprofit focused on medical ethics issues, publicly criticized Wyeth, saying Effexor's "homicidal ideation" risk wasn't well publicized and that Wyeth failed to send letters to doctors or issue warning labels announcing the change.

And what exactly does *rare* mean in the phrase "rare adverse events"? The FDA defines it as occurring in less than one in one thousand people. But since that same year 19.2 million prescriptions for Effexor were filled in the United States, statistically that means thousands of Americans might experience "homicidal ideation"—murderous thoughts—as a result of taking just this one brand of antidepressant drug.[5]

Effexor is Wyeth's bestselling drug, by the way, bringing in over $3 billion in sales in 2008, accounting for almost a fifth of the company's annual revenues.[6]

Columbine mass killer Eric Harris was taking Luvox, which like Paxil and Zoloft (and trendsetter Prozac) is a modern and widely prescribed type of antidepressant called selective serotonin reuptake inhibitors, or SSRIs. Harris and fellow student Dylan Klebold went on a hellish school shooting rampage in 1999 during which they killed twelve students and a teacher and wounded twenty-four others before turning their guns on themselves.

Luvox manufacturer Solvay Pharmaceuticals concedes that during short-term controlled clinical trials 4 percent of children and youth taking Luvox—that's 1 in 25—developed mania, a dangerous and violence-prone mental derangement characterized by extreme excitement and delusion.[7]

The inescapable truth is that perpetrators of many of the most horrendous murder rampages in recent years were taking, or just coming off of, prescribed psychiatric drugs.

Most recently, authorities investigating Seung-Hui Cho, who murdered thirty-two at Virginia Tech in April 2007, disclosed that "prescription medications related to the treatment of psychological problems had been found among Mr. Cho's effects," according to the *New York Times*.[8] The state's toxicology report released two months later said "no prescription drugs or toxic substances were found in

Cho Seung-Hui," according to the *Collegiate Times*. However, the killer's roommate Joseph Aust told the *Richmond Times-Dispatch* that Cho's routine each morning had included taking prescription drugs.[9]

What kind of meds might Cho have been taking—or recently have stopped taking (a notoriously unstable, unpredictable time period)? Curiously, despite an exhaustive review by the commonwealth of Virginia, which disclosed that Cho had taken Paxil for a year in 1999,[10] specifics on what meds he was taking prior to the Virginia Tech massacre have remained elusive, prompting critics to suggest the omission may be to protect the drug companies from liability claims.

Indeed, pharmaceutical manufacturers are nervous about lawsuits over the "rare adverse effects" of their mood-altering medications. To avoid costly settlements and public relations catastrophes—such as when GlaxoSmithKline was ordered to pay $6.4 million to the family of sixty-year-old Donald Schell, who murdered his wife, daughter, and granddaughter in a fit of rage shortly after starting on Paxil—drug companies' legal teams have quietly and skillfully settled hundreds of cases out of court, shelling out hundreds of millions of dollars to plaintiffs.[11] Pharmaceutical giant Eli Lilly fought scores of legal claims against Prozac in this way, settling for cash before the complaint could go to court while stipulating that the settlement remain secret—and then claiming it had never lost a Prozac lawsuit.

Meanwhile, the list of killers who happened to be taking psychiatric medications is long and chilling. Remember these headline names?

- Patrick Purdy went on a schoolyard shooting rampage in Stockton, California, in 1989, which became the catalyst for the legislative frenzy to ban "semiautomatic assault weapons" in California and the nation. The twenty-five-year-old Purdy, who murdered five children and wounded thirty, had been on amitriptyline, an antidepressant, as well as the antipsychotic drug Thorazine.[12]

- Kip Kinkel, fifteen, murdered his parents in 1998 and the next day went to his school, Thurston High in Springfield, Oregon, and opened fire on his classmates, killing two and wounding twenty-two others. He had been prescribed both Prozac and Ritalin.[13]

- In 1988, thirty-one-year-old Laurie Dann went on a shooting rampage in a second-grade classroom in Winnetka, Illinois, killing one child and wounding six. She had been taking the antidepressant Anafranil as well as lithium, long used to treat mania.[14]

- In Paducah, Kentucky, in late 1997, fourteen-year-old Michael Carneal, son of a prominent attorney, traveled to Heath High School and started shooting students in a prayer meeting taking place in the school's lobby, killing three and leaving another paralyzed. Carneal reportedly was on Ritalin.[15]

- In 2005, sixteen-year-old Native American Jeff Weise, living on Minnesota's Red Lake Indian Reservation, shot and killed nine people and wounded five others before killing himself. Weise had been taking Prozac.[16]

- In another famous case, in 1989, forty-seven-year-old Joseph T. Wesbecker, just a month after he began taking Prozac, shot twenty workers at Standard Gravure Corporation in Louisville, Kentucky, killing eight and then himself. Prozac maker Eli Lilly later settled a lawsuit brought by survivors.[17]

- Kurt Danysh, eighteen, shot his own father to death in 1996, a little more than two weeks after starting on Prozac.[18] Danysh's description of his own mental-emotional state at the time of the murder sounded strikingly similar to that of twelve-year-old Christopher Pittman, who had shot his grandparents while on psychiatric meds. "I didn't realize I did it until after it was done," Danysh said. "This might sound weird, but it felt like I had no control of what I was doing, like I was left there just holding a gun."[19]

- John Hinckley, age twenty-five, took four Valium two hours before shooting and almost killing President Ronald Reagan in 1981.[20] In the assassination attempt, Hinckley also wounded press secretary James Brady, Secret Service agent Timothy McCarthy, and policeman Thomas Delahanty.

These are only a few of the best-known offenders who had been taking prescribed psychiatric drugs before committing their violent crimes. There are many others.

SUBSTITUTING PILLS FOR COUCHES

When the subject of violent crimes and linkage to psychiatric drugs comes up, two distinct views emerge almost reflexively.

The mental health establishment's standard response is that these drugs have no "proven" role in enabling such horrific deeds, or at least that their benefits far outweigh whatever negative reactions may rarely occur. According to this view, of the millions of people taking these medications the vast majority are helped and the few who end up committing violent acts probably would have snapped anyway—with or without the drugs.

At the opposite extreme is the view that taking these medications is always harmful, turning previously nonviolent people into homicidal maniacs.

The truth, which is becoming increasingly hard to deny, is that these substances do indeed push some individuals, already living on the border of sanity, over the edge into violence. In addition to a growing corps of health professionals and a sizable pile of peer-reviewed studies corroborating this view, the drug companies themselves, compelled by FDA labeling requirements, bolster it with their "black box" label warnings of increased "risk of suicidal thinking and behavior" and other negative effects.[21]

But putting aside, for the moment, both the claims of the mental health establishment and the broad condemnations of antidrug activists, let us consider afresh what exactly we're dealing with here.

We are talking about human beings who have somehow developed a secret inner life dominated by exceedingly dark thoughts and compulsions. Wild mood swings. Horrible, consuming resentment teetering on the edge of violent frenzy. Paranoid delusions fueled by intense emotion. "Satanic visitations" and inner voices that torment them mercilessly, sometimes for years, commanding them to commit murder or suicide—or both.

Does this *really* sound to you like a person in need of drugs? Does it sound like a disease? A biochemical imbalance in the brain? Neurotransmitter activity that's too sluggish?

Or does it sound like something much more mental-emotional and even spiritual in origin?

The truth is that if we think we can solve problems like these with pills, we might be just as delusional as the people we're trying to help.

Before going further, let's state the obvious: sometimes psychiatric drugs, including antidepressants, are helpful—even necessary. But in the overwhelming majority of cases, of which there are *tens of millions* in the United States alone, these dangerous substances are recklessly being relied upon to solve Americans' mental-emotional-spiritual problems.

In search of a quick, painless fix for the problems we develop when we fail to deal well with the stresses of life, we've become a nation of drug takers. Millions of us "medicate" the pain of life away by taking illegal drugs, and millions more take prescription drugs to accomplish much the same thing. *Scientific American*'s February 2008 issue featured a shocking report under this headline: "Close to 10 percent of men and women in America are now taking drugs to combat depression. How did a once rare condition become so common?"[22]

And *Fortune* magazine notes that SSRI antidepressant brands such as Zoloft, Paxil, Celexa, and Luvox, which have become "household names," have "done more than any other class of drugs to spur psychiatry's substitution of pills for couches." In fact, reports *Fortune,* "we're popping so many SSRIs that their breakdown products in urine, gushing into waterways, have accumulated in fish tissues, raising concerns that aquatic animals may be getting toxic doses, according to recent research at Baylor University."[23]

When we've gotten to the point of poisoning fish, you know we're talking about a *lot* of drugs.

Even our soldiers, deployed in war zones around the world, are now being pumped up with psychiatric drugs as never before. According to a 2008 *Time* magazine cover story, "America's Medicated Army":

> For the first time in history, a sizable and growing number of U.S. combat troops are taking daily doses of antidepressants to calm nerves strained by repeated and lengthy tours in Iraq and Afghanistan. . . . [A]ccording to an anonymous survey of U.S. troops taken last fall, about 12 percent of combat troops in Iraq and 17 percent of those in Afghanistan are taking prescription antidepressants or sleeping pills to help them cope.

Reporting that "about 20,000 troops in Afghanistan and Iraq were on such medications"—roughly half on antidepressants and the other half on sleeping pills like Ambien—the *Time* article noted ominously:

> Last year the U.S. Food and Drug Administration (FDA) urged the makers of antidepressants to expand a 2004 "black box" warning that the drugs may increase the risk of suicide

in children and adolescents. The agency asked for—and got—an expanded warning that included young adults ages 18 to 24, the age group at the heart of the Army. The question now is whether there is a link between the increased use of the drugs in the Iraqi and Afghan theaters and the rising suicide rate in those places. There have been 164 Army suicides in Afghanistan and Iraq from the wars' start through 2007, and the annual rate there is now double the service's 2001 rate.

At least 115 soldiers killed themselves in 2007, the Army reports, including thirty-six in Iraq and Afghanistan—the highest toll since such record keeping started in 1980. And almost 40 percent of the Army's suicide victims in recent years had been on psychiatric drugs, especially SSRI antidepressants such as Paxil, Zoloft, and Prozac. "The high percentage of U.S. soldiers attempting suicide after taking SSRIs should raise serious concerns," Harvard Medical School's Dr. Joseph Glenmullen told *Time*.[24]

And remember, antidepressants are only one type of drug. What about all the other types of psychiatric meds we consume, including the tens of millions of prescriptions for Ritalin and other controversial stimulants taken by children and adults diagnosed with attention deficit disorder (ADD) or attention deficit hyperactivity disorder (ADHD), a condition that didn't even exist until the 1980s?

It wasn't too long ago when the counseling arts recognized that people suffering from mental-emotional and developmental problems needed self-understanding first and foremost. This was a noble and vital goal. But today, as *Fortune* points out, psychiatry has substituted "pills for couches." Like mad scientists, our "experts" fool around with the intricacies of people's brains, tinkering with the levels of neurotransmitters such as serotonin and norepinephrine to artificially "elevate mood."

Thus we have the spectacle of troubled people coming to mental health experts with serious personal problems: addictions, debilitating emotional conflicts, depression and anger problems rooted in early trauma, or in seriously flawed family relationships, or in buried resentments toward cruelty that were never resolved but just festered and grew. Yet instead of being helped to understand where their negative programming came from or how their unhealthy relationships and destructive attitudes developed, so they can correct them and find genuine healing, they're given drugs designed to chemically trick the body and mind into "feeling better." And worse, according to the Food and Drug Administration itself, people taking these drugs "may be more likely to think about killing themselves or actually try to do so."[25]

Then later, when they eventually stop taking the drugs, they risk serious deterioration of their condition. But what else should we expect when we just mask symptoms and ignore root causes?

And that begs the next big question: Why do so many mental health experts today seem to ignore root causes? Why do they prefer pills to couches?

DON'T WORRY, IT'S NOT YOUR FAULT

Until the last fifty years or so, Western culture strongly reflected the core Judeo-Christian conviction that God created the human race and put us all here on this beautiful globe we call Earth, and that we, alone among all creatures, were given the ability—and destiny—to choose between good and evil.

That was then. Today's cultural elite, including those in the healing arts, basically no longer think of man in spiritual terms, of morality, character, self-understanding, repentance, and forgiveness. Rather, most of today's experts look at man and see a soulless animal whose behavior problems are mostly genetic or organic in origin and, in any event, usually manageable with drugs.

The truth is, most pill-dispensing mental health practitioners don't really understand why people experience clinical depression or other "mental illnesses." Go search WebMD and five or ten other websites on, let's say, postpartum depression (or any other syndrome). You'll be stunned at the lack of real substance with regard to *what causes it*. Instead, you'll see statements like "The causes haven't been pinpointed yet," along with reams of authoritative-sounding data on symptoms and predisposing factors and what drugs to take and how valuable it is to have a support group and what vitamins help in recovery and so on. But no one will tell you what on earth would make a mother want to kill herself after she gives birth to her child. They don't know.

Yet can there be any doubt that *somewhere* there are real, understandable reasons for this and other syndromes—reasons a normal person with common sense could comprehend and act upon, and which might even lead to genuine healing, if only the "experts" counseling them knew what they were talking about?

While understanding is in short supply today, the mental health establishment is great at naming syndromes and conditions—maybe to give the rest of us the impression they know more than they really do.

Are you an angry volcano inside? You may have "intermittent explosive disorder."

Hostile toward authority? You could be suffering from "oppositional defiant disorder."

Worry too much? Probably a case of "generalized anxiety disorder."

Do you suffer from "road rage"? It's now a mental illness, according to some psychologists, called "aggressive driving spectrum disorder."

Are you a normal boy who fidgets because you don't like shutting up and sitting still at a desk for six hours a day listening to a teacher? You may be diagnosed, as millions of American children already have been, with "attention deficit hyperactivity disorder." After it became widely known that public school administrators and other nonmedical personnel were coercing multitudes of American children—between 4 and 9 million, by most estimates—into taking

Ritalin and similar psychostimulant drugs, experts finally got concerned and put the brakes on the rampant overdiagnosis of ADHD.[26] The U.S. Congress as well as many individual states passed legislation to halt what can fairly be described as an orgy of overprescription of Ritalin and similar meds for the nation's children. Though the legislation wrested power away from school personnel and returned it to parents, every year still sees millions of new "cases" diagnosed.

What about addiction? Do you compulsively get drunk when the stress seems too great? While such was once considered a moral flaw or a character weakness, it is now widely categorized as a disease—which logically would make addiction to all other drugs, legal or illegal, a "disease" as well.

Are you a lying, cheating jerk? Then you have a disease—especially if you have tattoos. I'm not kidding. Research conducted at Michigan's Center for Forensic Psychiatry has determined that "certain criminals with tattoos are more likely to suffer from anti-social personality disorder," or ASPD:

> A study of forensic psychiatric patients in Michigan—half of whom were deemed unfit to stand trial and half of whom were found not guilty through insanity—revealed that 73 percent of the survey group that were tattooed also exhibited strong signs of ASPD. Sufferers of the disorder are characterized by a lack of empathy and shallowness and are prone to pathological lying, cheating, stealing, physical aggression and drug abuse.[27]

Do you get it? Everything bad, from temper tantrums, drunkenness, and road rage to "pathological lying, cheating, stealing, physical aggression and drug abuse," is now a disease. *Everything* is physiological or genetic and treated with drugs. *Nothing* is your fault. You're an innocent victim.

Furthermore, many of us like it that way. We like the idea that whatever is wrong with us amounts to an organic disorder, that there's no sin, no weakness, no deficit of character on our part. Our egos love that; it comforts us.

In July 2005, actress Brooke Shields wrote a piece for the *New York Times* about her postpartum depression: "In a strange way, it was comforting to me when my obstetrician told me that my feelings of extreme despair and my suicidal thoughts were directly tied to a biochemical shift in my body. Once we admit that postpartum is a serious medical condition, then the treatment becomes more available and socially acceptable. With a doctor's care, I have since tapered off the medication, but without it, I wouldn't have become the loving parent I am today."[28]

Brooke Shields is a lovely and principled lady, but I assure you that God did not design us to be depressed and suicidal after childbirth. Wouldn't it really be better if we stopped blaming all our psychological-spiritual problems on chemical imbalances, hormones, genes, and newly minted "mental illnesses," and instead looked more deeply for real causes—and real cures?

DRUGGING OUR CONSCIENCE

I began to suspect psychiatric meds were problematic three decades ago after a conversation with a friend who, to relieve her anxiety, had been taking the sedative Valium, then the nation's top-selling pharmaceutical. A very perceptive woman, she summarized her experience this way: "Do you know what the Valium did for me? It deactivated my conscience."

And just recently, another Christian lady anonymously wrote a highly thought-provoking essay, primarily for the benefit of other female members in her church, on the effect antidepressants had on her.

Stressed-out and depressed, she had sought her pastor's spiritual counsel—but he responded by advising her, just as he had done with other members of the congregation, to go on antidepressants.

"Not a word was said about my sinful attitudes regarding my responsibilities, and there were no offers of practical help," she wrote. "Just go to the doctor. He proceeded to tell me about many other women in our church who had taken his advice and were doing great. In retrospect, this makes sense—ours was a 'happy church.' No one seemed to struggle with any serious life issues. Only smiling, happy greetings and small talk. Imagine the 'Stepford Wives' at church and you'll get the picture." [29]

Within weeks, she wrote, she was feeling better. "By two months into treatment I was doing swimmingly, smiling and small-talking with the best of them. . . . I was handling the stress better and sleeping well. Most of my physical complaints were gone, and I felt very capable. Life went on."

Five years later, unhappy with their "happy" church, she and her husband sought out and joined a more traditional and biblical church "where sin is called sin, and people are held accountable."

At the new church, she said, "I met people who grieve over their sin. . . . This was foreign to me. I have never cried over my sin. I have felt bad for my sin, but I have never truly grieved over it. . . . I began to think that perhaps that little pill that was meant to 'take the edge off' was preventing me from grieving over sin. One thing I had noticed since being on it was that I could not cry. Nothing could bring me to tears, and I mean *nothing*. I didn't even cry when my dad died, not even as I watched him take his last breath, uncertain where he would spend eternity. No tears."

After much thought and prayer, she finally decided to get off her medication. As a result, she wrote:

> Last week, after I sinned in anger at my son, I was grieved! I had asked for forgiveness from him and from the Lord, but I could not deny a deep sense of grief in my soul as I real-

ized this had been a pattern of sinful anger for years. I had committed this same sin many times before, but felt justified, either by stressful circumstances in my life or by my son's bad behavior. I had never before felt such grief over my own sin, and I knew I could not indulge one more outburst like this.[30]

The antidepressants, she concluded, had "blurred the ends of the emotional spectrum, so that I experienced neither deep sadness nor great joy. I have now come to appreciate that both are vital to the Christian life. Oh, I was somewhat happy, and able to cope with life quite well, but the edge was off, not only from my sadness, but from my joy as well."

She added:

In the beginning, the drug was good, because it enabled me to think rationally and come out of my basement. If I had used that rational thinking to get a grip on the sin that was pulling me down into depression, I could have dealt with it biblically, and been off the drug in short order. But I did not. I became dependent on those pills and was gradually numbed to the seriousness of my sin. By God's grace, I came to the recognition that this drug could be stunting my spiritual growth, and that turned out to be exactly the case.[31]

The notion that psychiatric drugs might impair our conscience should not come as a shock. We're all too aware that people do bad things under the influence of alcohol, crack cocaine, and methamphetamine that they wouldn't do otherwise. Is it so hard, then, to comprehend that some *legal* drugs can also obscure or eliminate our awareness of conscience? After all, what does "feeling better" often involve but the elimination of conflict? And what is conflict but the evidence inside us that we've done something wrong—something contrary to our conscience? Getting rid of conflict, then, often involves blotting out our conscience!

The problem with that, of course, is that conscience is literally the presence of God in us, the friction between the way we are and the way we could be. We experience this correcting and illuminating presence—which is actually our greatest friend (like Jiminy Cricket in Disney's *Pinocchio*)—as a psychic pain when we deviate from its urgings. Thus, many of us ignorantly come to regard conscience as a problem, even an enemy, and strive to eliminate it any way we can.

HEALING THROUGH FORGIVENESS

Let's switch gears, set aside all our pill-prescribing psychiatrists, and for just a moment focus on another healer. Yes, Him. I wonder if it's just possible that the Lord's Prayer, the blueprint Jesus Christ gave the human race for how to approach God, could provide insight about how to heal what we call "mental illness." Does that sound crazy? Let's find out:

> *After this manner therefore pray ye: Our Father which art in heaven, Hallowed be thy name.*
> *Thy kingdom come. Thy will be done in earth, as it is in heaven.*
> *Give us this day our daily bread.*
> *And forgive us our debts, as we forgive our debtors.*
> *And lead us not into temptation, but deliver us from evil:*
> *For thine is the kingdom, and the power, and the glory, for ever.*
> *Amen. (Matthew 6:9–13)*

Reflect on this for a minute, please. Jesus starts out by telling us to honor God and humble our will before His and seek His continued sustenance. (*No problem,* we think.)

Later we're advised to ask God's protection as we acknowledge His supremacy in all things. (*Great, makes perfect sense,* we think.)

But in between comes one line that delivers the essential, life-changing commandment, the nuclear core of the Lord's Prayer, the fulcrum of change in our lives, the place where miraculous things happen to us—or don't, if we don't heed it:

And forgive us our debts, as we forgive our debtors.

This is where we live or die spiritually; it's where we find true happiness and innocence, or conflict and separation from God.

In fact, immediately following the Lord's Prayer, Jesus reemphasizes the forgiveness requirement in the starkest terms imaginable, to make sure nobody misses the most crucial point:

For if ye forgive men their trespasses, your heavenly Father will also forgive you; But if ye forgive not men their trespasses, neither will your Father forgive your trespasses. (Matthew 6:14–15)

Well, *that* gets my attention.

Forgiveness, that is, finding the grace to give up anger and resentment at injustice, is healing. The problem is that hostility and rage (unforgiveness) feed our pride, a part of our makeup that cannot live without constant meals of impatience, resentment, and emotional upset. So until we're ready to let the life of pride and sin inside us wither and die, we find it pretty much impossible to "listen to the right side" and truly forgive. Anger is like a drug—even worse, like a nutrient for our "wrong side."

ADVICE FROM AN ANGEL

A remarkably insightful description of the classic "tug of war" between the higher and lower nature in each of us is found in the second-century Christian book *The Shepherd of Hermas.* Though not part of the canon of the Holy Bible, *Hermas* was widely revered by the early Christians, praised by church leaders like St. Irenaeus, Clement of Alexandria, and Origen, and was frequently read publicly in early churches to edify the faithful.

A passage describing a conversation between a shepherd named Hermas and an angel who has been instructing him on how to live a life pleasing to God is titled "That every man has two angels and of the suggestions of both." The angel says to Hermas:

There are two angels with man; one of righteousness, the other of iniquity.

And I said unto him, Sir, how shall I know that there are two such angels with man? Hear, says he, and understand.

The angel of righteousness, is mild and modest, and gentle, and quiet. When, therefore, he gets into thy heart, immediately he talks with thee of righteousness, of modesty, of chastity, of bountifulness, of forgiveness, of charity, and piety.

When all these things come into thy heart, know then that the angel of righteousness is with thee. Wherefore hearken to this angel and to his works.

Learn also the works of the angel of iniquity. He is first of all bitter, and angry, and foolish; and his works are pernicious, and overthrow the servants of God. When therefore these things come into thine heart; thou shalt know by his works, that this is the angel of iniquity.

And I said unto him, Sir, how shall I understand these things? Hear, says he, and understand; When anger overtakes thee, or bitterness, know that he is in thee:

As also, when the desire of many things, and of the best meats, and of drunkenness; when the love of what belongs to others, pride, and much speaking, and ambition; and the like things, come upon thee.

When therefore these things arise in thine heart, know that the angel of iniquity is with thee. Seeing therefore thou knowest his works, depart from them all, and give no credit to him: because his works are evil, and become not the servants of God.

Here therefore thou hast the works of both these angels. Understand now and believe the angel of righteousness, because his instruction is good.[32]

Reading insight like this makes one wonder how many people who have suffered from what we today call "bipolar disorder," "depression," "anxiety disorders," "schizophrenia," and other serious conditions have mysteriously gotten better. Oh, we don't hear about such things in the news—but it happens. Somehow, privately, they discover how to listen to the right side, and to shrink from the wrong side. And they allow the light of God to come into them and shine on their conflicts and untangle their mess—mostly by discovering forgiveness. Having truly given up their resentments and rage, no longer getting upset all the time, they simply get better.

We need to revisit the practice of drugging troubled souls. Psychiatry has largely bought into the drugs-instead-of-understanding paradigm and may not take kindly to my questioning the mad-scientist approach to dealing with emotional problems. But the sad truth is, they're taking the crown of God's creation, the human mind, and acting like Dr. Frankenstein engaged in some grandiose but profoundly ill-conceived experiment, playing God, pulling people's mood strings chemically. There's another way.

No doubt there are appropriate times and places to use these medications—but not the hundreds of millions of annual prescriptions we're seeing today. Indeed, our ever-increasing reliance on them is creating untold suffering of a kind and magnitude we can barely imagine. All because of a blindness that dominates our age—a blindness that obscures that which every child knows naturally: we all have a "good side" (conscience) as well as a "bad side" (sin nature). And we need to be careful which side we heed. If we listen to the wrong side, terrible consequences follow.

ADVICE FROM AN INDIAN

Toward the end of one of my son's Boy Scout troop meetings, the scoutmaster stood up and used his customary "Scoutmaster Minute" to retell the famous story of an old Cherokee chief talking to his grandson. The chief said:

"A fight is going on inside me. It is a terrible battle—between two wolves. One wolf represents fear, anger, pride, envy, lust, greed, arrogance, self-pity, resentment, lies, and cruelty.

"The other wolf stands for honesty, kindness, hope, sharing, serenity, humility, friendship, generosity, truth, compassion, and faith.

"This same fight is going on inside you, and inside every other person, too," he added.

The grandson reflected on these words for a minute and then asked his grandfather, "Which wolf will win?"

The old chief simply replied, "The one you feed."

CHAPTER 6

✦

FALSE GODS

What's Behind the Popularity of Paganism, Witchcraft, and New Age Religions

Neopaganism Growing Quickly: Numbers Roughly Double Every
18 Months in United States, Canada and Europe
 —*Denver Post*, JUNE 26, 2008

Sorcery Sells, and the Young Are Buying
 —*Atlanta Journal-Constitution*, JUNE 10, 2007

Wicca is believed to be one of the fastest-growing religions among high
school and college students
 —NATIONAL PUBLIC RADIO, MAY 13, 2004

So there I was, listening intently to local radio talker Bob White interviewing a witch.

Yes, a real witch—and a male one at that. The guest sounded New Agey and effeminate, but harmless enough, and painted a colorful picture of what modern-day witches, or Wiccans, believe and do. You know, god and goddess worship, preparing herbal remedies, casting spells, caring for the earth, and so on—all couched in terms that sounded almost reasonable, or at least tolerable in a diverse society like ours.

But then he got to the part about their nighttime ceremonies, during which participants, both men and women, would get stark raving naked, dance and chant in the moonlight, worship Gaia, cast spells, invoke the blessing of various spirits, and sometimes engage in sex!

When he finished describing this bizarre scene, there followed a long, pregnant pause before Bob White responded. Assuming the host to be as taken aback as I was, for a moment I savored the prospect of his imminent rebuke—or at least some sort of expression of surprise.

But when White finally responded, he exclaimed approvingly: "I can't *imagine* anyone having a problem with that!"

Wow. Here I was, living in "conservative" rural Oregon, and a local talk show host expresses dismay that anybody could be bothered by naked witches sexing each other in the moonlight while summoning spirits and casting spells.

Now, the really interesting part of this story is that "Bob White" was actually the on-air radio name for none other than Neale Donald Walsch, who shortly thereafter became the mega-bestselling author of *Conversations with God* and several sequels. With two and a half years on the *New York Times* bestseller list and book sales of over 7 million copies in thirty-four languages, the author became a full-fledged, world-renowned, millionaire New Age guru speaking to enthralled audiences everywhere. Obviously, a whole bunch of people are in love with whatever Neale Donald Walsch—I mean, "God"—is telling them. Here's a sampling:

> There is no judgment in what you call the afterlife . . . there is no accounting, no one giving "thumbs up" or "thumbs down." Only humans are judgmental, and because you are, you assume I am. I cannot tell you my truth until you stop telling me yours.[1]

Remember, this is supposed to be God talking. When Walsch asks about sin, here's the response from "on high":

This alleged state of imperfection in which you are said to come into this world is what your religionists have the gall to call original sin. . . . Some of your religions have built up whole theologies around this misconception. . . . For anything I conceive—all that to which I give life—is perfect; a perfect reflection of perfection itself, made in the image and likeness of Me.[2]

So far, it sounds like everyone on Earth can pretty well do whatever they want—there's no divine judgment because there's no sin, so party on!

When Walsch asks about reincarnation, "God" tells him: "You have had 647 past lives, since you insist on being exact. This is your 648th. You were everything in them. A king, a queen, a serf . . ."[3]

Wait a minute, you might be wondering about now. *How exactly did Walsch receive all this very specific info directly from God?* "On a blank sheet of paper," the author reveals, "I would merely write a question . . . and no sooner was the question written than the answer would form in my head, as if Someone were whispering in my ear. I was taking dictation!"[4] Although "channeling" and "automatic writing," such as Walsch employed to produce his "with God" books, are considered by many to be dangerous occult practices, when Walsch asks "God" whether it's okay to develop and exercise such "powers," of course he's told it's fine: "Using psychic ability is nothing more than using your sixth sense. Obviously, this is not 'trafficking with the devil,' or I would not have given this sense to you. And, of course, there is no devil with whom to traffic."[5]

Okay. There's no devil, no hell, no sin, and no judgment. So, let's see, what does "God" say about sex, always a hot-button issue with the human race? Judaism and Christianity have strict moral codes when it comes to sex, but when Walsch asks, "Is sex okay?" his "God" sounds a lot more like Alfred Kinsey:

Of course sex is "okay." . . . Play with sex. Play with it! It's wonderful fun. . . . Sex is sacred, too. . . . But joy and sacredness do mix (they are in fact the same thing). . . . You have repressed sex, even as you have repressed life, rather than fully Self expressing with abandon and joy. You have shamed sex, even as you have shamed life, calling it evil and wicked, rather than the highest gift and the greatest pleasure.[6]

By golly, I think I'm beginning to understand why millions of people love Neale Donald Walsch and his "God." There's no sexual immorality, no sin to run afoul of, no devil, no judgment, no hell. Everyone goes to heaven.

But wait, what about people like Hitler? Surely *he* didn't go to Heaven? Surprise, according to the "God" of Neale Walsch: "I do not love 'good' more than I love 'bad.' Hitler went to heaven. When you understand this, you will understand God."[7]

What?! Can it really be true that everything turns out swell in the next life no matter how evil you've been in this one, that even Hitler went to heaven? It kind of makes you wonder if it's *really* God talking to Walsch. After all, it would just ruin everything if it turned out it was only Neale's subconscious mind talking to him—or whatever malevolent, deceitful spirit might be lurking down there just beyond his subconscious mind. Remember, channeling spiritual entities, which pretty much *always* claim to be good, is very common in the New Age world.

Interestingly, during an interview on CNN's *Larry King Live*, Walsch admitted that maybe it's *not* God after all that he's been channeling these many years:

KING: How do you know you weren't, one, hallucinating? People do that.
WALSCH: Yes.
KING: Imagining this voice?
WALSCH: Yes.

KING: Two, your own subconscious, in a sense, talking to you, you have put it into words.

WALSCH: I don't know, Larry.

KING: You don't know that.

WALSCH: I don't know.

KING: So maybe it wasn't God.

WALSCH: Maybe it wasn't. And the day . . .

KING: But you wrote a book called *Conversations with God*.

WALSCH: Because I think that it was. I sincerely think that I was inspired by the divine.[8]

So, let's sum up: millions of people are being sold an amoral, illogical, unbiblical, and manifestly preposterous view of God and life, which will possibly—if they don't wake up—determine their very destiny for eternity, all based on the murky spirit channeling of a former local talk show host who admits, "Maybe it wasn't [God]."

Amazing.

In any event, it's now clear why Walsch, in his former persona as radio talker Bob White, had no problem with the naked-witches-sexing-in-the-moonlight thing. After all, if *Hitler* is beamed up to heaven after his hellish romp through life on Earth, why not a peaceful, nature-worshipping witch who might occasionally engage in bizarre and immoral behaviors, but hey, never murdered millions of people?

To find out why New Age beliefs and practices are exerting such a powerful hold on so many people today, let's focus our microscope on witchcraft, a particularly popular and growing segment of the neopagan world.

GOOD WITCH, BAD WITCH

Actually, my first experience with witchcraft was as a young child. The witch was frightfully ugly, wore a black robe and hood, had a hook nose with a big wart on it, and was obsessed with killing Snow White. There was also the witch who morphed into a dragon in *Sleeping Beauty,* as well as all the pointy-black-hatted hags who were out and about every Halloween. It was pretty clear to *this* little boy that all witches are "wicked."

But then I saw *The Wizard of Oz,* which challenged my previous belief about total witch wickedness, since it featured equal numbers of wicked witches (East and West) and good ones (North and South).

Today's young people, of course, have been immersed for years in Harry Potter books and movies, featuring beautiful, heroic young wizards and witches zooming about on broomsticks and waving their magic wands while barking ancient-Latin-sounding spells like "Wingardium Leviosa!" (to make things levitate) or "Expelliarmus!" (to disarm an opponent) or—my favorite—"Stupefy!" (to render one's adversary unconscious).

All this is very entertaining, but alas, has nothing to do with real witchcraft.

So, what *is* witchcraft? Is it the same as Wicca? Is it, as critics allege, a form of Satan worship? Or can witches be good? The ones I've seen and heard certainly seem nice and well-intentioned enough, a far cry from the malevolence of the Satanist. Can witches really cast spells that somehow call forth hidden forces beyond the world of nature to help them accomplish their will—whether good or evil? And what's the deal with going naked? Most of all, what's the powerful appeal—why do so many people today aspire to be witches?

As a working journalist, I see many stories on witches, but they don't have hook noses or poisoned apples. Rather, reports abound that increasing numbers of modern-day Americans—housewives, students, professors, even soldiers, believe it or not—self-identify as witches or Wiccans. There are many news reports of Wicca being an official, legal religion and a fast-growing one at that, about judges ruling that witches must be allowed to lead prayers at official government meetings, and that Wiccan convicts must be provided with requested "sacred objects" so they can perform spells in their cells.

Here's a quick course, Witchcraft 101: Wicca and witchcraft are often used interchangeably, but they aren't exactly the same. While witchcraft goes back into ancient times, with many varieties springing from diverse cultures and worldviews, Wicca is a relatively modern nature-based religion first popularized in the 1950s by an Englishman named Gerald Gardner. Most "witches" today, at least in the Western world, are followers of the Wiccan religion.

Here's how the U.S. Army's chaplain's manual, *Religious Requirements and Practices of Certain Selected Groups: A Handbook for Chaplains,* describes Wicca. (Be aware that, as with all religious groups described in this Army reference book, the description of Wicca was written by Wiccans themselves.)

Wiccans worship the sacred as immanent in Nature, often personified as Mother Earth and Father Sky. As polytheists, they may use many other names for Deity. Individuals will often choose Goddesses or Gods from any of the world's pantheons whose stories are particularly inspiring and use those Deities as a focus for personal devotions. Similarly, covens will use particular Deity names as a group focus, and these are often held secret by the groups.

It is very important to be aware that Wiccans do not in any way worship or believe in "Satan," "the Devil," or any similar entities. They point out that "Satan" is a symbol of rebellion against and inversion of the Christian and Jewish traditions. Wiccans do not revile the Bible. They simply regard it as one among many of the world's mythic systems, less applicable than some to their core values, but still deserving just as much respect as any of the others.

Most Wiccan groups also practice magic, by which they mean the direction and use of "psychic energy," those natural but invisible forces which surround all living things. Some members spell the word "magick," to distinguish it from sleight of hand entertainments. Wiccans employ such means as dance, chant, creative visualization and hypnosis to focus and direct psychic energy for the purpose of healing, protecting and aiding members in various endeavors. Such assistance is also extended to non-members upon request.

What about Wiccan morality and behavioral standards? Says the Army handbook:

> The core ethical statement of Wicca, called the "Wiccan Rede," states *"An it harm none, do what you will."* The Rede fulfills the same function as does the "Golden Rule" for Jews and Christians; all other ethical teachings are considered to be elaborations and applications of the Rede. It is a statement of situational ethics, emphasizing at once the individual's responsibility to avoid harm to others and the widest range of personal autonomy in "victimless" activities.

How do Wiccans worship, and why the nudity?

> Wiccans usually worship in groups. Individuals who are currently not affiliated with a coven, or are away from their home coven, may choose to worship privately or may form ad-hoc groups to mark religious occasions. Non-participating observers are not generally welcome at Wiccan rituals. Some, but not all, Wiccan covens worship in the nude ("skyclad") as a sign of attunement with Nature.[9]

Readers who grew up exposed to the wicked, wart-nosed witches of the *Snow White* variety may be relieved to hear that the "Wiccan Rede" prohibits witches from harming others—although the "Rede" (or rule) is more akin to the 1960s hippie counterculture ethic ("Dude, I can do whatever I want as long as it doesn't hurt anyone else") than the much nobler Golden Rule.

Fine, you might be thinking. *But where do the moonlit sex orgies fit in?*

Exhibit A: "The Ritual of the Great Rite." In keeping with Wiccan cosmology, this is a ceremonial enactment of the creation of the universe in the union of the god and goddess. As explained by Vivianne Crowley, a prominent Wiccan high priestess, author, university lecturer, and psychologist, "The outer rite involves a linking of the male and the female, the God and Goddess. The inner symbolism is a uniting of the initiate with the animus or anima. The sacred marriage is outwardly a marriage of two people, but inwardly it is a marriage of the two within one person."[10]

So, what seems to a mere *muggle* (that's Harry Potter lingo for a nonmagical person) as just a chance to have sex in the woods, to a Wiccan has a much more sacred purpose—that of unifying and integrating the practitioners' inner selves through the union of opposite polar energies. And if that isn't esoteric enough for you, one Wiccan website explains the Great Rite as "the opening of the gateway to the womb of the Goddess that the Self may be reborn."

In any event, this could be one more reason men are increasingly joining this woman-dominated religion.

CASTING SPELLS

What about spells, rituals, and magic? Where does the notion come from that we can make our desires come true by the conscious direction of psychic energy—helped along by the beneficent influence of the Wiccan goddess and god? Imagine for a moment that you're a witch, intent on channeling the powers within nature and beyond nature for the purpose of solving your own problems, getting your boyfriend back, becoming rich—or, more altruistically, to bring peace and harmony to your family or the world.

You would begin by establishing a "purified magic circle," during which you'd invoke spirits or "guardians" of the north, east, south, and west, representing earth, air, fire, and water, respectively. You'd also use special "tools," including candles and incense, a broom, cauldron, chalice, wand, altar cloth, pentacle, and other items to help focus the energy. After placing the ritual tools on an altar in the circle, you'd perform the ritual. Here's a "typical invocation of the elements":

> *Air, Fire, Water, Earth,*
> *Elements of astral birth,*
> *I call you now, attend to me!*
> *In the Circle, rightly cast,*
> *Safe from curse or blast,*
> *I call you now, attend to me!*
>
> *From cave and desert, sea and hill,*
> *By wand, blade, and pentacle,*
> *I call you now, attend to me!*
> *This is my will, so mote it be!*

Then you'd thank the goddess, god, and guardians and close the circle.

Now, why in the world should the forces of nature—"Air, Fire, Water, Earth"—"attend" to you? This is a vital question, which, if we can answer it, will lead us to a profound understanding of occultism, including Wicca.

By the way, neophytes can dispense with the "tools" and other rigmarole and just follow the simple directions like a recipe while casting the spell of their choosing. Here, for instance, is a typical "love spell," one of thousands from the multitude of websites offering free spells for an ever-growing cadre of witches and wannabes:

DESIRE ME SPELL

A simple candle spell to bring desire to the eye of your beholder

First you need to scoop some soil.

Sprinkle this around the base of a red candle anointed with your
spit and some patchouli oil.

Light the candle and focus on you being desired. See you in
another's arms and bed.

When the vision is strong, intone as many times as you like:

Come to me
My will is great
Your new fate
You can't escape.

Do this every night until the next full moon.

Here's another spell, this one designed to bring good fortune:

GOOD LUCK SPELL

Make a fire outside and throw on seven big handfuls of leaves and
seven big handfuls of dried chamomile. Do not light the fire yet.

Now have a cold shower and go outside. Light the fire and leap
through the smoke seven times as you say:

Away Away
Bad luck and woe
The tide is turned
My fortune grows.

When the fire dies down, turn the ashes into the soil to bury your
old bad luck.

You may well be wondering what is accomplished by jumping through a fire while chanting, "Away away, Bad luck and woe." How can anyone really believe this stuff works?

Wicca is intentionally shrouded in mystery. In fact, many initiates maintain a hallowed, hand-copied book of spells, rituals, and magical information called, mysteriously, the *Book of Shadows.* Yet in the news business we prefer sunshine to moonlight, because it reveals the truth plainly—plus it makes a much better disinfectant. So, why don't we now pull the veil of mystery off Wicca? Let's let the sun shine. Let's set aside all the esoteric, intoxicating words that beguile our minds and seduce our senses, take off the amethyst-colored glasses, extinguish the incense, and honestly, soberly look at our growing obsession with pagan spirituality.

Rewind to the "Good Luck Spell" we just discussed. It's actually not hard to understand why people might think an invisible spirit can somehow help them banish their "bad luck" and bless their lives with health, prosperity, and happiness—because that's the truth. There *is* such a God. But He's not the pagan god or goddess of Wicca, nor the bizarre, all-excusing, "Hitler-went-to-heaven" deity channeled by Neale Donald Walsch or any other New Age guru. He is Almighty God—the real one—the all-powerful and all-knowing Creator and sustainer of the universe and everything in it, including us.

Moreover, each of us, created "in His image" and for His purpose, has an inner programming, put there by God, to seek His influence in our lives. This programming, as deeply engrained in us as though it were embedded in our DNA, impels us to discover and submit to His inner leading in all things, or else live meaningless, deluded, and ultimately wasted lives.

Here's the problem. If for any reason we're not ready or willing to submit to God—a state of honest transparency that tends to annihilate our selfish pride and bring us the blessings of genuine happiness, contentment, and understanding—then by default we find ourselves attracted to false gods. That is, to worldviews and weird religions that fill our spiritual void while also sustaining our secret rebellion against our Heavenly Father. And for many Americans today, that means New Age or pagan religion.

But why would anyone rebel against God?

PREFERRING MOTHER EARTH
TO FATHER GOD

In dysfunctional families, if you have a problem with your father, it's very easy to bond extremely closely—sometimes too closely—with your mother.

Goddess worshippers worship *creation*—"Mother Earth," with her flowers, trees, mountains, clouds, rocks, and rivers—because they're in rebellion against the *Creator* Father. They're totally identified with Mom because they have a problem with Heavenly Dad, the biblical, Judeo-Christian God who perhaps seems too "judgmental"—too stern and mean and out of touch with them.

And why would this be? To be painfully blunt, two of the biggest reasons for rampant rebellion against God the Father are the failure of many earthly fathers to be truly noble (which causes resentment and thus rebellion in children and wives) and the failure of many of today's Christian churches to be truly noble (which causes people to seek spiritual fulfillment elsewhere). Indeed, though America's news and entertainment media gave the New Age movement a huge boost during the 1960s and '70s with their enthusiastic and uncritical coverage, today's upsurge in neopagan religion has been fueled by the plasticness and shallowness of so much of the modern, institutional church.

Although some nevertheless discover genuine faith either inside or outside the church, others fall into agnosticism or atheism, while a great many more find themselves powerfully attracted to exotic religions that appear to be deeper and more personally spiritual—especially New Age religions such as Wicca. The Pew Forum on

Religion & Public Life's 2007 survey found that the percentage of practicing pagans in the United States is rapidly approaching those of U.S. Muslims, at 0.6 percent, and Buddhists, 0.7 percent.[11]

In many ways, the interest in Wicca among women (at least two-thirds of Wiccans are female) parallels the growth in feminism and lesbianism—all fueled by disillusionment with, and alienation from, men. Indeed, sociologist Helen Berger, who spent ten years researching and writing a definitive book, *A Community of Witches: Contemporary Neo-Paganism and Witchcraft in the United States,* reports that an astounding 32 percent of Wiccans and neopagans are homosexual, bisexual, or "other non-heterosexual."[12] Clearly, Wicca has become the spiritual home for many feminists, including lesbians.

There's a poignant irony here. While many hard-core feminist women resent men and reject what they see as the "repressive patriarchy" of Christianity, in reality the true Father in heaven is not only strong and just, but also kind, loving, and extremely patient. In other words, He's the dad they never had—the perfect Father every child wants and needs.

But why, then, does He condemn witchcraft? After all, the Old Testament says:

> There shall not be found among you any one that maketh his son or his daughter to pass through the fire, or that useth divination, or an observer of times, or an enchanter, or a witch, or a charmer, or a consulter with familiar spirits, or a wizard, or a necromancer. For all that do these things are an abomination unto the LORD: and because of these abominations the LORD thy God doth drive them out from before thee. (Deuteronomy 18:10–12)

Although scripture condemns witchcraft and sorcery in the strongest possible terms, miracles are evident in both the Old and New Testaments of the Bible—the same book that condemns magic. Did you ever wonder what the difference is? Though we use the word *miracles,* would it be correct to say Jesus performed "magic" when He turned water into wine, multiplied scant supplies of fish and bread to feed thousands of people, calmed storms, walked on water, and so on?

Biblical miracles didn't involve magic, witchcraft, or sorcery, and Jesus pinpointed the difference when He said: "I can of mine own self do nothing: as I hear, I judge: and my judgment is just; because I seek not mine own will, but the will of the Father which hath sent me" (John 5:30).

Therein lies the fatal flaw in witchcraft, magic, and occultism of every variety, and the very reason the Bible condemns them all: in the eyes of God, it's an abomination for human beings to attempt to harness and direct the hidden powers of creation to accomplish *their will*. Why? Because this whole notion of "your will" and "my will" is just an illusion. In reality, it is our core nature to serve another, higher (or lower) unseen will. We either serve God's will, or we are slaves of the unseen dark forces that helped us run away from Him—forces that pull on the strings of our mind and body (but which we think of as our own will) when we lack a deep commitment to what is right.

When Jesus performed miracles, it wasn't His will. When Moses parted the Red Sea, it wasn't Moses doing it. Standing there with his outstretched arms and staff, he was just the instrument. The true miracle worker experiences no personal sense of power; he knows it's not him. It's a paradox—like many other biblical paradoxes (for example, "The last shall be first" and "The greatest of you shall be the servant of all").

Magic spells are affirmations, ceremonial expressions of the Wiccan's will, of what she or he wants, typically sprinkled with the elements—earth, fire, and so forth—in hopes of subtly harnessing those powers by the force of their will. That is the aim of occult practices in the real world: to manifest our selfish will.

In *Magick in Theory and Practice, Book 3,* notorious British occultist Aleister Crowley, an important mentor to Wicca founder

Gerald Gardner, defined *magick* (he always spelled it with a *k*) as "the Science and Art of causing Change to occur in conformity with Will." [13]

"Will" was a big deal to Crowley, whose central credo took the issue to an absurd extreme: "Do what thou wilt shall be the whole of the Law." (Now, *that* is crazy.)

Thus Wiccans claim that magic spells, ceremonies, and rituals focus the practitioners' hidden reservoir of psychic energy, along with the aid of benevolent spirits, in the service of the witches' will.

Even though much of what passes as magic can be chalked up to hypnotic suggestion, affirmation, and outright delusion, we need also to realize that each of us is a spiritual being inside a physical body. So, much of what the occult world alludes to—the astral plane, spiritual entities, and the like—is quite real. And for the prideful, insincere "truth seeker," it's a realm offering a dazzling array of spiritual deceptions.

If you're enamored of such "signs and wonders" as channeling, astral traveling, clairvoyance, remote viewing, communicating with disincarnated spirits, near-death experiences, and other psychic phenomena, just remember that God is not the only one who can confer "gifts." So be careful about "looking up" to purveyors and recipients of such occult abilities, since they may well be much closer to hell than you are. After all, don't you think Satan knows many things? And if so, is it inconceivable that he could impart such knowledge to a gullible human helper, for the purpose of deceiving many others?

To bring forth an obvious example, let's consider one of the major New Age–inspired deceptions of our age, which has seeped big-time into mainstream culture, even impacting law and medicine.

ANGELS OF LIGHT

Come back in time with me to 1975, and picture this scene: South Carolina resident Dannion Brinkley, a former Marine and Vietnam vet, is talking to a friend on the phone when a bolt of lightning runs down the phone wire and strikes him in the neck, sending thousands of volts of electricity down his spine, through the bottoms of his feet into the nails in his shoes, which weld themselves to the nails of the floor.

For the next twenty-eight minutes, Brinkley has what is known as an NDE—"near-death experience"—which includes, he later says, a review of his entire life, a meeting with a celestial being, and 117 visions of events that would supposedly happen before 2004.

Moreover, Brinkley says, he has been "sent back" with a specific mission—to help other people facing death.

Incredibly, fourteen years later, during open-heart surgery, Brinkley "dies" *again* and once more experiences the same NDE. The "man who died twice" and lived to tell about it subsequently writes two books: *Saved by the Light* and *At Peace in the Light*.

In 1992, another near-death celebrity, Betty Eadie, writes *Embraced by the Light,* which becomes a national bestseller.

And Dr. Raymond Moody writes the all-time most influential book on the subject, *Life After Life,* in which he synthesizes the near-death experiences of many people into this summary:

A man is dying and, as he reaches the point of greatest physical distress, he hears himself pronounced dead by his doctor. He begins to hear an uncomfortable noise, a loud ringing or buzzing, and at the same time feels himself moving very rapidly through a long dark tunnel. After this, he suddenly finds himself outside his own physical body, but still in the immediate physical environment, and sees his own body from a distance, as though he is a spectator. He watches the resuscitation attempt from this unusual vantage point and is in a state of emotional upheaval.

After a while, he collects himself and becomes more accustomed to his odd condition. He notices that he still has a body, but one of a very different nature and different powers from the physical body he has left behind. Soon other things begin to happen. Others come to meet and help him. He glimpses the spirits of relatives and friends who have already died, and a loving, warm spirit of a kind he has never encountered before—a being of light—appears before him. This being asks him a question, nonverbally, to make him evaluate his life and helps him along by showing him a panoramic, instantaneous playback of the major events of his life. At some point he finds himself approaching some sort of barrier or border, apparently the limit between earthly life and the next life. Yet, he finds that he must go back to the earth, that the time for his death has not yet come. At this point he resists, for by now he is taken up with his experiences in the afterlife and does not want to return. He is overwhelmed by intense feelings of joy, love and peace. Despite his attitude, though, he somehow reunites with his physical body and lives.[14]

When we consider the incredible stories of people claiming to have "died"—that is, who had an NDE and came back to tell the world how the afterlife is so fantastic they really didn't want to come back—a couple of questions loom large:

1. Did they actually die?
2. If they didn't actually die, and therefore didn't experience the true afterlife, what then did they experience? A hallucination or delusion born out of the distress of life-threatening trauma and its accompanying mental, emotional, and physiological turmoil? The result of chemical shock, the effects of anesthesia, seizure, brain-oxygen deprivation, or neurological shutdown? Or could it be something else, perhaps even some sort of spiritual deception or demonic visitation?

In the news business, we constantly report cases of people pronounced dead who "wake up" a day later—in the morgue, in their casket at the funeral, sometimes even as they're being buried! It happens all the time. And as Tal Brooke, president of the Berkeley, California–based Spiritual Counterfeits Project, explains, "death" isn't quite as cut-and-dried as we might think:

> It appears from examining the results of our machine-diagnosed clinical death that we really do have a hit-or-miss situation. A subject is declared clinically dead before he has been found to be alive again after all. Did he die? . . . The most acceptable criterion for genuine and complete death occurs when the categories of "cardiac arrest," "respiratory cessation," "flat EEG," and "complete loss of vital signs" are satisfied and this condition remains permanent through rigor mortis and physical decay. When the body begins to smell from decay, one can be assured that it is dead, especially if it has been ice-cold for days and has gone through rigor mortis.[15]

However, adds Brooke, the only historical records of people recovering from this form of death are in the Bible: "Lazarus was stone cold and decaying for four days before he was brought back to live out the appointed remainder of his life. Death, apart from some really astounding miracle such as the case of Lazarus, is irreversible; that has to be the definition."[16]

If "near-death experiences" are only that—*near* death, but not the real thing—what, then, is actually going on during an NDE?

For a potent clue, consider this interview Brinkley did with nighttime radio talk host Art Bell, during which he told millions of listeners there is no hell. "If anybody was going to hell, I would have been going," he said. "I can promise you that, pal. And if I didn't go, the odds [that many others will] are slim to none."

What happened to him, Brinkley added, "is gonna happen to you too":

> Everybody that's listening. This is not just one guy from South Carolina. . . . This is how you leave this world, too. Not only

did I see and feel everything I went through; I literally *be-came* every person that I had ever encountered in my life, and I got to feel the direct result of my interaction between me and those people. I not only got to feel the anger, frustration, humiliation, pain—literally horror—that I had inflicted on thousands of people, you know, in lots of different countries. . . . That tells me there's justice, and there's fairness, and there's righteousness and there is a day of judgment. But guess who judges you. *You* judge you! It's you who looks at you. . . . People think that there's a God, or a devil, or they're gonna be judged by a force outside of themselves. They're makin' a mistake.[17]

EVERYBODY GOES TO HEAVEN?

And no marvel; for Satan himself is transformed into an angel of light.
—2 Corinthians 11:14

Okay, time for a little reality. Sorry to burst the velvety New Age bubble. First of all, these NDE folks have *not* died. Forget about "clinically dead," "legally dead," and other meaningless distinctions—*really* dead means you stay dead, unless a supernatural miracle occurs. So, if you flatlined on the operating table but were successfully resuscitated, you were not "dead"—period. As Miracle Max said famously in *The Princess Bride* (and you'll have to imagine Billy Crystal's voice here), "There's a big difference between *mostly dead* and *all dead*. Mostly dead is slightly *alive!*"

Since none of these people who "died and went to the other side and came back to tell us all about it" were ever really "all dead," what, then, did they experience?

In a world full to overflowing with illusions, deceptions, and counterfeits—counterfeit love, counterfeit sincerity, counterfeit religious experiences—is it unreasonable to consider that maybe these people are being treated to nothing more than a very elaborate sales pitch for death, presented by the great salesman for death himself?

After all, as scripture affirms, even "Satan himself" sometimes appears as an "angel of light."

How many people do you suppose have committed suicide after reading such books as those referenced here or listening to the wondrous testimony of those singing the praises of death? How many people, unhappy with their lives, have taken the easy way out, crossing irrevocably the line between this life and whatever lies beyond it, in the belief they will find inexpressible joy and relief—all based on delicious NDE tales of those who have returned?

Returned, yes—but from where?

We've all seen, especially since 9/11, how a powerful delusion of a glorious afterlife can entice some people to give up their lives. How many radical Muslims have committed mass murder in the vain belief it would purchase them a one-way ticket to a sensual paradise filled with earthly delights?

Is it any wonder, then, that primed with stories of universal peace and light awaiting us whenever we check out of this life—no matter what sort of life we have lived—death has become strangely attractive for many people, including many in the right-to-die and euthanasia crowd, which is powerfully influenced in turn by New Age spirituality and sensational tales of people returning from the land of the dead?

So attractive, says Brooke, that this view of the afterlife is the crowning glory of a new religion on its way. "In the 'scientific supernatural' near-death experience," he says, "we also see the makings of a spiritual module waiting to be plugged into any world religion. It seems to span world religions by using the afterlife as its bridge. Thus it is the new inclusive faith that judges no one and admits all universalism. It is the sort of great deception that the pages of the Bible have warned about for 2,000 years. It looks good, but it is lethal." [18]

So, please, let's not give too much credence to wild tales of a universal New Age afterlife that seductively make death sound so attractive that we almost can't wait to send the old and infirm there before their time—or to leap there ourselves in hopes of shedding the difficulties of this life for something better. We might just find we've jumped foolishly from the frying pan into the fire.

"YE SHALL BE AS GODS"

For false Christs and false prophets shall rise, and shall shew signs and wonders, to seduce, if it were possible, even the elect.
—Mark 13:22

Hopefully it's becoming more clear why the Bible prohibits sorcery, witchcraft, and talking to dead people, and why even so-called white magic is not blessed by God: not only because it doesn't serve His will, but also because it invites evil and deception to invade our world. There's a fantastic complexity to the "spiritual mechanism" of the human being. But just like a sophisticated new piece of electronics, it's not supposed to be user-serviceable or modifiable. That's the realm of the Manufacturer alone. Instead of meddling with the Maker's sacred matrix of Life, we're meant to share in an entirely different kind of "magic."

For this magic to bless our lives—the seemingly effortless walk through difficult circumstances, with the aid of a hidden hand we call grace—we need to abandon pride and "wait" patiently on God in each moment of our life. In this state of grace, we are in effortless alignment with His will and thus the creative powers of the universe, and not the other way around. We have a sense of well-being, a lack of time pressure, a knowing that the future is being rolled out before us by God, and that we just need to be there to discover it in each moment, in endless inner obedience.

It's a sort of "magic," yes, but we're not the magician making it happen. We're just the grateful receiver, full of wonder as our life unfolds, because to ourselves we don't seem very worthy, and we're not—another divine paradox. Much of what we see from moment to moment, in fact, is our very real faults and weaknesses. But then, that's the very humility that connects us up with the real-life "force" of God.

However, sorcery, witchcraft, occultism—where we're literally trying to play god, harnessing the hidden forces of creation to accomplish *our* will—is indeed an abomination, and a doorway through which hell readily enters this earthly realm. We're playing with a level of trickery and seduction way beyond our ability to comprehend.

Ask yourself: How is it that millions of people can basically worship Neale Donald Walsch, who seems to have channeled an ungodly spirit entity claiming to be God? How can they follow such a profoundly counterintuitive and deluded path to "enlightenment"?

It's because most of us are unconsciously addicted to the power of lies that keeps our pride alive—our love of the great illusion of life that says we ourselves can be our own gods.

This, of course, was the original lie in the biblical account of Adam and Eve. Remember the story? God gave the first two people a test in obedience: "Of every tree of the garden thou mayest freely eat: But of the tree of the knowledge of good and evil, thou shalt not eat of it: for in the day that thou eatest thereof thou shalt surely die" (Genesis 2:16–17). Shortly thereafter, the story goes, Satan in the form of a serpent approached Eve and said, "Ye shall not surely die: For God doth know that in the day ye eat thereof, then your eyes shall be opened, and ye shall be as gods, knowing good and evil" (Genesis 3:4–5).

Adam and Eve couldn't resist the promise that they would be "as gods," and we've been falling for the same lie ever since. This is the flaw in Eastern and New Age religions that claim we are all gods, and that, just as Neale Donald Walsch and other gurus teach, our only problem is that we haven't yet realized our own greatness and divinity.

So, the Wiccans are right when they say Satanism and witch-craft are different. I agree: Wiccans are *much* nicer. But the truth is, Satanism and Wicca are just different forms of rebellion against God. One is male in nature—overtly angry, arrogant, selfish, cruel, and rebellious. The other is female, a seductive version of the same rebellion—smiling, passive, and powerfully alluring. But both are separated from the love of God, obsessed with magic (playing god), and clothed in the beguiling philosophies of the serpent. Yet what a sad, pathetic, shadowy reflection of the real power we're supposed to freely enjoy in our lives, when we truly live in the sunlight of the One True God.

CHAPTER 7

REJECTING GOD

Why Militant Atheism
Is Becoming a Badge of Honor

Are Atheists Becoming the Hot New Political Force?
    —*Los Angeles Times*, APRIL 27, 2009

In God They Don't Trust: Nonbelievers Spreading a Different Faith
    —*New Haven Register*, FEBRUARY 11, 2007

Following Atheist Trend, Britons Seek "De-baptism"
    —AGENCE FRANCE-PRESSE, MARCH 29, 2008

A while back, while looking out over the vast Pacific Ocean from a cliff top on the Oregon coast, I conducted a little thought experiment. Taking it all in—the endless expanse of water as far as my eyes could see, the seagulls, the salt air, the hypnotic sound of the waves and the pounding surf, ultimate power and ultimate serenity all in one timeless moment—I asked myself, *How can one possibly experience all this without believing in a Creator?*

So I tried, really tried—just as an experiment, mind you—to conceptualize the existence of the magnificent creation I was beholding, yet without a Creator. I attempted to adopt an atheistic worldview, even for just a minute or two, to see what it was like.

The result of my brief mental exploration shocked and amazed me, and opened my mind to something I had never before understood.

Before I share the outcome with you, however, let's take a fresh look at this whole atheism issue, because it's rapidly undergoing a remarkable transformation right before our eyes.

Somehow, in recent years, atheists have gone from being a near-invisible pariah class on the fringe of civilized society to a confident, unapologetic, and increasingly vocal minority, publishing bestseller after bestseller condemning and mocking religion, coalescing into a genuine political force and comparing their "plight" to that of gays combating "discrimination." The evidence is hard to miss:

- Newspaper headlines trumpet atheists' new confidence and activism, as in the *New York Times*'s front-page story "More Atheists Shout It from the Rooftops." [1]
- The American Religious Identification Survey, released in early 2009, shows that atheists are increasing in number, with those claiming "no religion" being the only demographic group to expand in all fifty states over the last two decades. [2]
- Almost half of Americans—45 percent, according to one Gallup poll—say they'd be willing to vote for an atheist for president of the United States. [3]
- President Barack Obama "regularly puts nonbelievers on the same footing as religious Americans," notes the *Wall Street Journal*. [4] Even in his inaugural address, Obama declared: "For we know that our patchwork heritage is a strength, not a weakness. We are a nation of Christians and Muslims, Jews and Hindus, and nonbelievers." [5]
- Atheism is so big in the United Kingdom that more than one hundred thousand Britons downloaded "certificates of de-baptism" off the Internet to make official the renunciation of their Christian faith. [6]

- Illustrating atheists' increasingly public "liberation" from religion, Richard Dawkins, the charismatic evolutionist-author, is selling a whole line of "Scarlet Letter" T-shirts with a giant red A—for *Atheist*—on his website (and bumper stickers, too).[7]

Atheism, just like homosexuality—once considered shameful by the larger culture—is now becoming hip, sophisticated, even a badge of honor.

While it's difficult to gauge exactly how many atheists there are in America, exit-polling data clearly indicate their numbers are growing dramatically. "The bloc of voters identifying themselves as religiously unaffiliated—which does not directly translate into nonbelievers but includes their ranks—has risen in every presidential election since 1988: from 5.3 percent that year to 12 percent in 2008," writes Paul Starobin in the nonpartisan *National Journal*. "That 12 percent share amounts to 15 million voters—a bigger bloc than the Hispanic vote (9 percent), the gay vote (4 percent), and the Jewish vote (2 percent), and just a notch smaller than the African-American vote (13 percent)."[8]

Even more impressive are the data compiled by Roger Finke, a Pennsylvania State University professor who directs the Association of Religion Data Archives:

> The share of Americans who report no religious preference hovered around the 5-to-6 percent level from the early 1970s through the 1980s, jumped to 9 percent in 1993, rose to 14 percent in 1998, and is now about 16 percent. . . . By that count, the no-preference bloc is nearly equal to the share of mainline Protestant churches, from which it is probably poaching members.[9]

Until recently, atheists had zero political clout, having to content themselves with being more of an "intellectual club," the *Journal* report says, "reflecting on the meaning of a life without God (and the patent absurdity, as many of these folks think, of a life with God). But those days are over."

Now the Godless are making a crucial transformation toward the status of a my-time-has-come movement with a political and legislative agenda to enact—and with this shift, a host of contentious national issues is being engaged, with the potential to ignite a new round of culture wars in American society.[10]

Today's atheist activists "liken their strategy to that of the gay-rights movement," adds the *New York Times,* "which lifted off when closeted members of a scorned minority decided to go public."

"It's not about carrying banners or protesting," said Herb Silverman, a math professor at the College of Charleston who founded the Secular Humanists of the Lowcountry, which has about 150 members on the coast of the Carolinas. "The most important thing is coming out of the closet."[11]

In fact, just as homosexuals co-opted the word *gay* to facilitate their cultural and political mainstreaming, atheists have adopted their own euphemistic label, many now calling themselves "brights."

And how, exactly, do atheists want to change American society and government?

"The end result," atheists claim, would be "a more peaceful and modern society," reports the *National Journal,* since presumably our nation would be "less willing to embark on violent conflicts of a religious character" such as those in Iraq and Afghanistan. Euthanasia would be widely permitted—no ethical problems there. Pharmacists couldn't legally refuse to fulfill birth control prescriptions (or, presumably, chemical abortion prescriptions, either) as a matter of conscience or religious faith. School science classes would be prohibited from teaching anything about the origins of life except evolution—no mention of "intelligent design" allowed. And "the Boy Scouts would lose all forms of federal support for teaching that a good Scout has a 'duty to God.'" [12]

It gets even more controversial. At least some influential atheists reportedly want to clone humans. "In a sign of the culture warfare to come," reports Starobin, atheists are "emerging as an enthusiastic voice on behalf of scientific efforts to clone human beings, a technology with the potential to 'conquer mortality.'" Seeing themselves as very pro-science, atheists "tend to think that mindless religious scruples prevent the development of such techniques as cloning that could extend the boundaries of human life." [13]

RELIGIOUS EVIL

So, how has our once Judeo-Christian culture birthed and nurtured a growing movement intent on eliminating God from our lives and instead pursuing immortality through mad-scientist research? What is responsible for this new wave of atheism sweeping the Western world?

Dennis Prager, the brilliant radio talker and writer, ferrets out some key reasons for the major backlash against religion.

"First and most significant," he points out, "is the amount of evil coming from within Islam." Even if jihadists "who slaughter innocents in the name of Islam" represent only a small percentage of Muslims worldwide, "they have brought religious faith into terrible disrepute."

> How could they not? The one recognized genocide in the world today is being carried out by religious Muslims in Sudan; liberty is exceedingly rare in any of the dozens of nations with Muslim majorities; treatment of women is

frequently awful; and tolerance of people with different religious beliefs is largely nonexistent when Muslims dominate a society.

If the same were true of vegetarians—if mass murder and violent intolerance were carried out by vegetarians—there would be a backlash against vegetarianism even among people who previously had no strong feelings about the doctrine.[14]

Understand that to atheists, the "big three" religions of Christianity, Judaism, and Islam are all pretty much the same—dangerous monotheistic fairy tales that induce people to kill and oppress each other, the only difference being the particular myths, superstitions, and rules they impose on followers based on each religion's traditions and supposed "holy books."

Thus the fanaticism and extreme violence exhibited by jihadists around the world today are readily associated by atheists with all religions.

Another major, if more long-term, factor contributing to the popularity of atheism, notes Prager, is the "secular indoctrination of a generation," thanks to a de facto atheistic public school system:

Unless one receives a strong religious grounding in a religious school and/or religious home, the average young person in the Western World is immersed in a secular cocoon. From elementary school through graduate school, only one way of looking at the world—the secular—is presented. The typical individual in the Western World receives as secular an indoctrination as the typical European received a religious one in the Middle Ages. I have taught college students and have found that their ignorance not only of the Bible but of the most elementary religious arguments and concepts—such as the truism that if there is no God, morality is subjective—is total.[15]

Finally, Christianity and Judaism have, with some notable exceptions, failed to provide any effective contrast to the ever-growing atheistic secularism of the Western world. "It is virtually impossible to distinguish between a liberal Christian or Jew and a liberal secularist," says Prager, who notes that all three "regard the human fetus as morally worthless; regard the man-woman definition of marriage as a form of bigotry; and come close to holding pacifist beliefs, to cite but a few examples."

Thus, with religious evil increasing in the world—thanks to Islamic radicalism—and fewer and fewer people willing and able to confront it, Prager concludes that "the case for atheism will seem even more compelling."[16]

"THIS IS ATHEISM'S MOMENT"

Clearly, the most public manifestation of atheism's current explosion, as well as the intellectual wellspring nourishing many of today's unbelievers, is the spate of bestselling books taking turns pummeling religion.

In the news business, we often cite a nation's current top-selling books—for example, the popularity of anti-Semitic titles in Arab countries—as evidence of the present mind-set of the people. And in the United States of America these days, some of the most bought, most read, and most discussed books are angry, in-your-face atheist manifestos.

Journalist Christopher Hitchens sets the tone in his number-one *New York Times* bestseller, *God Is Not Great,* when he calls organized religion "violent, irrational, intolerant, allied to racism, tribalism, and bigotry, invested in ignorance and hostile to free inquiry, contemptuous of women and coercive toward children."[17]

Beyond Hitchens's book, which dominated nonfiction bestseller charts for months, there's the popular *Letter to a Christian Nation* by atheist author Sam Harris, sequel to his earlier tome *The End of Faith.* And then there's *God: The Failed Hypothesis: How Science Shows That God Does Not Exist,* by Victor J. Stenger; *Breaking the Spell: Religion as a Natural Phenomenon,* by Daniel C. Dennett; and *Atheist Universe: The Thinking Person's Answer to Christian Fundamentalism,* by David Mills.

Then of course there's Oxford biologist Richard Dawkins's mega-seller *The God Delusion.* Dawkins, the scientist and evolutionist who likes to call religion a "virus" and faith-based education "child abuse," almost makes the pugnacious Hitchens sound tame. Here's the opening sentence of chapter 2 of *The God Delusion:* "The God of the Old Testament is arguably the most unpleasant character in all fiction: jealous and proud of it; a petty, unjust, unforgiving control-freak; a vindictive, bloodthirsty ethnic cleanser; a misogynistic, homophobic, racist, infanticidal, genocidal, filicidal, pestilential, megalomaniacal, sadomasochistic, capriciously malevolent bully." [18]

Remember, millions of people are reading these books.

"This is atheism's moment," crows David Steinberger, CEO of Perseus Books, in a *Wall Street Journal* interview. "Mr. Hitchens has written the category killer, and we're excited about having the next book." He was referring to *The Portable Atheist: Essential Readings for the Nonbeliever,* edited by Hitchens, giving the publishing world yet another opportunity to cash in on the anti-God juggernaut.[19]

Since today's growing repudiation of God is being turbocharged by this steady stream of bestsellers, let's take a quick jaunt through the world of atheist manifestos. For a crowd priding itself on purely rational thinking, some of their arguments are surprisingly nonsensical.

For instance, if atheism is inherently so progressive and tolerant, and religion so ignorant and violent as the current crop of atheist Pied Pipers tells us, how do they explain the 100 million–plus innocent men, women, and children slaughtered by their own atheist governments during communism's twentieth-century reign of terror?

Simple. Hitchens simply declares atheistic communist dictatorships to be "religious." Quoting his hero George Orwell, Hitchens says "a totalitarian state is in effect a theocracy," thus making Stalin's mass murders of tens of millions of his countrymen not the work of an atheist, but of religion![20] And what about Reverend Martin Luther King, Jr., whom Hitchens admires? How does he square the effectiveness of the 1960s civil rights movement's leader with his having been a Christian minister? Well, you see, explains Hitchens, whatever good works King accomplished were due to his humanism, not Christianity. "In fact," notes the *Washington Post* in its review of Hitchens's book, "King was not actually a Christian at all, argues Hitchens, since he rejected the sadism that characterizes the teachings of Jesus."[21]

So—just in case you missed that—the millions of innocents murdered by atheistic communists during the last century don't count against atheism in Hitchens's book, since communism isn't really atheistic—its atheist leaders being so delusional that they're sort of, you know, *religious*. But Reverend King, whom Hitchens likes, wasn't really a Christian at all, since he didn't embrace the "sadism" of the most compassionate, virtuous, and self-sacrificial being ever to walk the earth.

Another major talking point of the atheist authors is that God isn't needed to make man moral, since even unbelievers often have a strong innate moral sense. In fact, during his nationwide book tour, Hitchens made a practice of confronting every audience with the same question. "My challenge: Name an ethical statement or action, made or performed by a person of faith, that could not have been made or performed by a nonbeliever," he wrote in *Vanity Fair*. "I have since asked this question at every stop and haven't had a reply yet."[22] Author Sam Harris makes the same argument, forcefully stating the obvious point that human beings are born with an ethical sense of right and wrong—even if they *don't* believe in God.

I wonder, do our atheist standard-bearers ever pause to consider that, if perchance there actually were a God, logically He would put this moral sense, or conscience, into each person whether or not that person was aware of his Creator? After all, a little child innately knows it's wrong to kill a playmate even though he or she is too young to have any knowledge or belief about God. Moreover, most people's inborn sense of right and wrong operates as intended—just as their arms, legs, heart, lungs, liver, and pancreas do—even if they're not mindful of their Creator's existence. Thus, when atheists see an old woman fall down in the middle of a street, they of course stop to help her as readily as anyone else. It's called common decency.

So the very evidence of God—in the form of a mysterious moral sense within us of right and wrong that transcends time, place, culture, education, and conditioning, a trait shared by no other animal—becomes for the atheist proof of just the opposite, that there is no God.

MOCKING "UNINTELLIGENT DESIGN"

A key battleground for all of atheism's champions, of course, is evolution. Dawkins, nicknamed "Darwin's Rottweiler," strongly condemns belief in creationism as "evil." Hitchens mockingly catalogs various parts of the human body, taking witty pot shots at their "poor design." And Harris, with stunning chutzpah, writes in *Letter to a Christian Nation* that "nature offers no compelling evidence for an intelligent designer and countless examples of *un*intelligent design."[23]

Sam, what are you thinking?

A single dandelion, considered from a strictly clinical, scientific perspective, displays more unimaginable complexity and spellbinding design brilliance—from its atomic and molecular design to its cellular and plant structure—than all the man-made supercomputers in the entire world combined.

"No compelling evidence for an intelligent designer"? Since that conclusion is embarrassingly nonsensical, perhaps we may speculate that Harris has uncritically imbibed a "religious" doctrine that doesn't square with reality. That's right, evolution is extraordinarily like a religion, full of incredible and unproven beliefs about man's origin, and by logical extension his destiny, and even his very nature.

Reality check: any theory or philosophy—especially an unprovable one—that purports to explain the origin, destiny, and nature of man is, by *definition*, religious. If you don't get that, you're not thinking.

Ironically, many of the same human weaknesses and societal pressures that induce some people to accept their religion unthinkingly—a criticism atheists rightly level at organized religion—also cause many atheists to embrace evolution's belief system every bit as unthinkingly. For within the current science establishment there are overwhelming academic and professional pressures to embrace evolution, and outright persecution for not doing so. No room for honest inquiry or a good-faith challenge to today's rigid orthodoxy. Dare to criticize or question the utterly unproven theory of macroevolution (one species, like dinosaurs, morphing into an entirely new species, like birds) and you're belittled and ridiculed. And if you're employed as a scientist, you may well be fired.

Yet history's greatest scientists, from Galileo to Newton, would laugh incredulously at today's supposedly "scientific" notion that nature displays no evidence of an intelligent designer. In *The Marketing of Evil* I briefly explore this point:

> From the beginning of human life until Darwin came along in the mid-19th century, human beings would step outside their homes and survey with their eyes and minds the wonders of nature. . . . Looking in every direction, we humans beheld not only fantastic complexity, diversity and order, but also the supreme intelligence behind creation, as brashly evident as the noonday sun.
>
> This ubiquitous natural wonderland caused man to

acknowledge and honor the Creator of creation, as Coperni-
cus did when he wrote, "[The world] has been built for us
by the Best and Most Orderly Workman of all." Or as Galileo wrote, "God is known . . . by Nature in His works and
by doctrine in His revealed word." Or as Pasteur confessed,
"The more I study nature, the more I stand amazed at the
work of the Creator." Or Isaac Newton: "When I look at the
solar system, I see the earth at the right distance from the sun
to receive the proper amounts of heat and light. This did not
happen by chance." [24]

Since surveying the created universe makes the Creator's existence so extraordinarily obvious, I often wonder whether atheists are
really rebelling against God—or against religion. There's a big difference.

HYPOCRITES

Although God and religion are two fantastically different things,
they're inextricably entwined in the atheist's mind. Hitchens's book
is titled "God Is Not Great" and subtitled "How Religion Poisons
Everything," showing he equates "God" with "religion" from the
get-go. Yet this is absurd. God is God, but even the most noble religion is populated by imperfect people—often confused, and sometimes corrupt or even crazy.

If atheists are genuinely against God, they have an unsolvable
problem—unless they come to realize their error, as many do at
some point in their lives. But if they're rebelling against religion,
then clearly they deserve a little slack.

After all, religion in the modern world is little short of a disaster. And I'm not talking just about the cancerous jihad movement
spreading within Islam, or about evil committed around the world by
all sorts of exotic religious movements, sects, and cults. Even within

Christianity you have major scandals such as the Roman Catholic Church's epidemic of child sexual abuse by predatory priests,[25] as well as the Protestant world's abundance of high-profile scandals, sexual and otherwise. Then you have the absurdly unbiblical, leftist agenda of many so-called mainline Protestant denominations, including their outrageous attacks on Israel, the ordination of open homosexuals and lesbians as church leaders, and so on.

But even more troubling than these dramatic, headline-grabbing church scandals is the anesthetizing shallowness and superficiality of far too much of the modern Christian church.

One Saturday afternoon I was channel-surfing and ended up watching the notorious 2004 film *Saved*, a satire that mercilessly skewers evangelical Christianity and features in the lead role a vain, duplicitous, and downright mean teenage Christian girl. The movie has been understandably condemned by many believers.

Just for a lark, during commercials I flipped over to some of the religious television networks to catch a little "real" Christian programming. It was eerie, almost surreal, how similar the "real" preachers, fund-raisers, and sidekicks were to the "caricatures" of the same types portrayed mockingly in the film.

Nothing in this world will more readily turn even decent people away from God (at least for a time) than religious leaders who are phonies. Unfortunately, it's easy for guilty, denial-steeped people, those who aren't yet ready to genuinely face themselves, to clothe themselves with the appearance of religiosity while secretly preserving their selfish, sinful nature. This hypocrisy is profoundly confusing to people who are looking up to such "leaders" for guidance and example.

Let me put it even more bluntly, since it's at the root of a great deal of disillusionment with religion in the modern world: a smug, self-righteous, phony, Bible-thumping hypocrite is enough to tempt all but the most mature to run as far away as possible from religion— as well as from the great Being religion endeavors to represent.

In the same way, when parents are religious hypocrites, or emotionally "high" on their religion, or pretentious, or impatient and willful, or just confidently parroting "truth" they've heard but don't really understand, their kids can sense something wrong. They really can. But because children are not yet mature and are easily influenced, they almost always end up either conforming (out of a need for approval) to their parents' mold and becoming just like them, or eventually rejecting religion altogether.

These may be tough words, but if we're ever going to understand why so many people are turning not only to atheism, but to pagan and New Age religions and myriad other strange spiritual philosophies and practices, then we need to face the sad state of the modern church.

YELLING AT GOD

The number-one argument, not only today but throughout history, against the existence of God is this: "If there's a loving and all-powerful God, how can He allow the human race—His children, made in His image—to suffer so terribly?" This question has often been called "the rock of atheism."

In *Letter to a Christian Nation,* atheist scientist Sam Harris hammers this point relentlessly. "At this very moment," he writes, "millions of sentient people are suffering unimaginable physical and mental afflictions, in circumstances where the compassion of God is nowhere to be seen, and the compassion of human beings is often hobbled by preposterous ideas about sin and salvation." Attempting to rub the reader's nose in the age-old mystery of suffering, Harris continues: "Somewhere in the world, a man has abducted a little girl. Soon he will rape, torture, and kill her. If an atrocity of this kind is not occurring at precisely this moment, it will happen in a few hours, or days at most. Such is the confidence we can draw from the statistical laws that govern the lives of six billion human beings. The same statistics also suggest that this girl's parents believe—as you believe—that an all-powerful and all-loving God is watching over them and their family. Are they right to believe this. Is it *good* that they believe this?"

"No," answers Harris, who adds cryptically: "The entirety of atheism is contained in this response."[26]

From the day's news, Harris calls forth still more examples of great suffering as proof God doesn't exist:

> The city of New Orleans, for instance, was recently destroyed by a hurricane. More than a thousand people died; tens of thousands lost all their earthly possessions; and nearly a million were displaced. It is safe to say that almost every person living in New Orleans at the moment Hurricane Katrina struck shared your belief in an omnipotent, omniscient, and compassionate God. But what was God doing while Katrina laid waste to their city? Surely He heard the prayers of those elderly men and women who fled the rising waters for the safety of their attics, only to be slowly drowned there. These were people of faith. These were good men and women who had prayed throughout their lives. Do you have the courage to admit the obvious? These poor people died talking to an imaginary friend.[27]

Mankind has grappled for millennia with the mystery of suffering, and how it can be compatible with an all-powerful and benevolent God. Let's take a fresh look at this question for a few minutes and see if perhaps we can catch a glimpse of an elusive but far greater reality.

To do this, I'd like to introduce one more famous voice angrily condemning God as cruel and sadistic. See if you can guess who the speaker is:

> What reason have we, except our own desperate wishes, to believe that God is, by any standard we can conceive, "good"?

Doesn't all the prima facie evidence suggest exactly the opposite? . . .

If God's goodness is inconsistent with hurting us, then either God is not good or there is no God: for in the only life
we know He hurts us beyond our worst fears and beyond all
we can imagine.[28]

So, who do you think this is, ranting and raving about God's cruelty? The ever-fuming journalist Christopher Hitchens? The haughty
Oxford professor Richard Dawkins?

No, actually it's another Oxford professor, far more famous than
Dawkins, and whose intellect and writings dwarf Hitchens's. It's
C. S. Lewis, one of the twentieth century's most influential authors
and defenders of the Christian faith.

As you may know, Lewis was an atheist for the first part of his
life. But through a gradual awakening during his early thirties, he
became convinced of the existence of God, and later—with the
help of *The Lord of the Rings* author J.R.R. Tolkien and another
colleague—embraced the Christian faith. Through his books, such
as *Mere Christianity* (voted the best Christian book of the twentieth century by *Christianity Today*), *The Screwtape Letters,* and many
others, including of course his beloved *Chronicles of Narnia* series—
he has helped countless people in their journey toward God.

So, you must be thinking, *these angry anti-God words from the
great C. S. Lewis must have come from his early, whacked-out atheist
years—right?*

Wrong.

They were written after *Narnia,* after *Mere Christianity,* after all
the acclaim of an appreciative Christian world. They were written,
to be precise, after the 1960 death of Lewis's wife, Joy.

For most of his life, well into his fifties, Lewis had been a bach-
elor. Then he met Helen Joy Davidman, a gifted American writer
and poet of Jewish background who had converted from atheistic
communism to Christianity, in part due to Lewis's writings. After

they corresponded for several years, she moved to England and they married in 1956, when Lewis was fifty-seven.

Both of them knew Joy had bone cancer—in fact, they were married at her hospital bedside.

Amazingly, Joy experienced a dramatic remission, during which time the couple lived together happily, and traveled and enjoyed each other to the fullest. But this blissful period was short-lived, and Joy died when her cancer returned with a vengeance in 1960.

In his 1961 book, *A Grief Observed,* Lewis records for posterity his intense bereavement, including his very real angers and doubts about everything he had written and taught about a "loving God" for decades, and does it in such a raw and uncensored manner that he originally released the book under the pseudonym of N. W. Clerk, so readers wouldn't associate it with him.

Let's see how Lewis responded to this severe personal suffering, and what conclusions they brought him to regarding God.

After first expressing his anguish over Joy's death, Lewis gets straightaway to the big question: Where is God when you need Him? When you're happy, the author muses, so happy that you don't even seem to need His help, God is there welcoming you "with open arms." But when you're desperate, when no one else can possibly help or console you and you turn to Him, what do you get? "A door slammed in your face"—and then, silence. Wait all you like, but all you get is more silence.

"Not that I am (I think) in much danger of ceasing to believe in God," Lewis writes. "The real danger is of coming to believe such dreadful things about Him."

Indeed, sounding like Sam Harris and other atheist authors, Lewis asks, Who or what can possibly make us conclude that God is actually good, when most everything that happens in this life seems to "suggest exactly the opposite"?

What about Christ? Doesn't his selfless life and sacrificial death demonstrate God's goodness, as all Christians affirm? Maybe so, says the tortured Lewis, but then, what if Jesus's words on the cross—

"My God, my God, why hast thou forsaken me?" (Mark 15:34)—
were actually the evidence of God's malevolence? What if the dying
Jesus had "found that the Being He called Father was horribly and
infinitely different from what He had supposed" and that the whole
savior-of-mankind thing was just a "trap," one "long and carefully
prepared" and "subtly baited" by God, who at the last minute, with
Jesus nailed to the cross, finally sprung it? "The vile practical joke,"
he speculates darkly, "had succeeded." [29]

Wow. What happened to the wise, deep, and enlightened
C. S. Lewis, the one who for a generation introduced millions to the
Christian faith?

In his literary fit of despair, Lewis goes on to ruminate about
another "vile practical joke" God appears to have played—this time
on him and his beloved. Every attempt he now makes at prayer, he
complains, is "choked" by memories of all the prayers he and Joy
had offered and all the false hopes they had clung to, encouraged
by "false diagnoses, by X-ray photographs, by strange remissions,"
including one "temporary recovery" that seemed almost miraculous. So, although he and Joy had once dared to believe that perhaps
God's grace was guiding her recovery, writes Lewis, it now seems
evident that while thus leading them on, God "was really preparing
the next torture." [30]

The next morning, Lewis thinks better of his agonized rant, asking if it is really rational to believe in a "bad God," or as he puts it
more pungently, "the Cosmic Sadist, the spiteful imbecile?" [31]

Starting now to come back to his senses, he asks, "Why do I
make room in my mind for such filth and nonsense?" Isn't all this
fuming just a miserable attempt to transform pain into something
more bearable, "the senseless writhings of a man who won't accept
the fact that there is nothing we can do with suffering except to suffer it?"

"KNOCKED SILLY"

Eventually, his grief and doubts about God fully vented, his rage spent, Lewis begins to reconnect with his natural understanding and reverence for his Creator. A few weeks have passed, he's recovered from his physical exhaustion, and he's more lighthearted. His inner relationship with God now restored, Lewis affirms the truism that "these things are sent to try us," quickly clarifying that he realizes God wasn't "trying an experiment on my faith or love in order to find out their quality. He knew it already. It was I who didn't." [32]

Finally, Lewis admits a shattering but liberating personal truth:

> He always knew that my temple was a house of cards. His only way of making me realize that fact was to knock it down. . . . [33]

And he offers a useful metaphor to explain the powerfully redemptive use God makes of human suffering: Bridge players, he says, insist there must be money on the game or else no one will take it seriously. Life is just like that, he explains. One's "bid" for good or evil, for eternal life or oblivion, won't be serious if there is nothing clearly at stake. It is only, he says, when we realize "the stakes are raised horribly high," when we see unmistakably that everything we have, everything we are or ever will be, is staked on the "game," that we'll take it seriously.

"Nothing less will shake a man—or at any rate a man like me—out of his merely verbal thinking and his merely notional beliefs," Lewis confesses. "He has to be knocked silly before he comes to his senses." [34]

Why do you suppose one person who suffers a tremendous personal loss also loses his belief in God, while another goes through the same experience and—despite all his transient doubts and angers—emerges with his faith intact and stronger than ever?

Why did some people survive the Nazi Holocaust only to conclude there is no God—or no God worth knowing if He would allow such suffering—while other Holocaust survivors emerged from that ordeal with a deeper faith in the Almighty?

What words can describe this mysterious quality? Humility, blessedness, grace? It's actually beyond words, perhaps some unexplainable connection between our soul and God, some back channel that enables us to keep attuned to a proper perspective regardless of difficult circumstances.

That special quality—C. S. Lewis had it—is the secret ingredient that makes the good things that happen to us truly good, and the bad things also "good" in the sense that they have a redemptive value, because God uses them to perfect us. In the same way, for people who live from the energy and motivation of pride, which in turn is connected to the invisible realm of evil, the bad things that happen remain bad (nonredemptive), but even the "good" things (success, wealth, fame) aren't ultimately good, either, because they just build pride, in ever-increasing conflict with God.

But if we find this special quality I'm talking about, our lives, including all the difficulties and suffering, can become part of what Lewis called God's "grand enterprise," full of adventure and discovery. I'm not talking necessarily about our outer journey of life, which may or may not be particularly exciting. I'm referring to the inner adventure we're meant to experience, whereby through progressive realization and repentance, we are inwardly transformed in our Creator's image, and for his purpose. The beauty of such a life is subtle and private—no one else will know about it—but it's surely more magical than anything in *The Chronicles of Narnia* or *The Lord of the Rings* or the Harry Potter books or any other fantasy from the mind of man. Because we are living characters, set in a story not from the mind of man, but from the mind of God. And that story is full of wonder.

After all, said Einstein, "There are only two ways to live your life. One is as though nothing is a miracle. The other is as though everything is a miracle."

We're surrounded by miracles of God. An acorn falls to the ground and effortlessly grows into a towering oak tree—a transformation that, if it occurred in a few seconds, we'd consider pure magic. The entire world would be transfixed by this dramatic, paranormal phenomenon, news organizations from all continents would converge on the locale of the "miracle tree," and all would be wonder and awe. But, since that exact same miracle unfolds in slow motion over the course of fifty years, we think nothing of it. We constantly walk past such marvels, oblivious.

In the same way, we also bypass the potential miracles of character growth within each of us because we don't understand God's methods. They can take years. And sometimes our miraculous transformation is brought about by adversity and loss—but only if we endure it with patience and dignity, and not with resentment.

To put it plainly, God works miracles through the things we suffer. Even Jesus Christ "learned obedience" that way, according to the Bible: "Though he were a Son, yet learned he obedience by the things which he suffered; And being made perfect, he became the author of eternal salvation unto all them that obey him" (Hebrews 5:8–9).

So, even if we are hurting, even if we are "knocked silly" like C. S. Lewis, all is not lost. Like the acorn that dies to itself but is transformed into a giant oak tree, when we die to pride and come alive as something better—a change often brought about by the things we endure patiently—there's magic in the air, the magic of a genuine walk with God.

And what of the atheist? He also breathes a kind of magic air, but from a very different realm. Freedom *from* God—or more accurately, the illusion of being free from accountability to a higher power—has a sort of sweet stench, a little like those green Christmas-tree-shaped air fresheners people hang from their car's rearview mirror, meant to improve the smell but actually emitting an offensive odor. Just so, the "sweetness" of pride, the delusion that you are your own god and ultimate master of your destiny, has a spiritual scent that is noxious to sincere seekers of truth.

THOUGHT EXPERIMENT

This brings me right back to my little thought experiment on the Oregon coast. You remember, I described how I tried my hardest to experience the exquisitely beautiful Pacific Ocean, with all its lovely sights, sounds, and smells, without God—to see creation without its Creator.

What happened then was something I hadn't anticipated. I experienced a psychic shock, along with a headache—you could almost say it was a momentary contact with another realm—an empty, prideful, appalling dimension of hell-on-earth, masquerading as enlightenment and freedom.

It was a profound experience, and one more personal confirmation for me of the reality of God. It also helped me to realize why the conflict between theism and atheism, and between intelligent design and evolution, is not just an academic, philosophical topic for polite debate over tea. It's a spiritual war of the worlds.

That high anxiety I felt momentarily, as I tasted the "other dimension" that animates those who reject the very idea of God, was minor and transient. But I'm quite sure hard-core, militant atheists feel *terror* when the opposite happens to them—that is, when they chance to experience a fleeting moment of realization that God does indeed exist, and that they are ultimately accountable to Him.

This would explain the volatile emotions that always surround this "objective, scientific" subject. Underneath all the academic pretension, something deep down inside the atheist scientist is troubled, threatened, nagged at, by the very notion of God, the Creator of all.

World-renowned astrophysicist Robert Jastrow explained this "fear of faith" brilliantly in his book *God and the Astronomers*. Describing modern science's quest to understand the origin of the universe, Jastrow, the founding director of NASA's Goddard Institute for Space Studies, was attempting to make sense of the extraordinarily emotional responses his colleagues had to the scientific consensus that the universe didn't somehow "evolve," but rather, burst into being ages ago in one cosmic event—kind of what you might expect a God to do.

"There is a strange ring of feeling and emotion in these reactions," he wrote. "They come from the heart whereas you would expect the judgments to come from the brain. Why?"

Jastrow answers his own question with remarkable insight and honesty:

> I think part of the answer is that scientists cannot bear the thought of a natural phenomenon which cannot be explained, even with unlimited time and money. There is a kind of religion in science, it is the religion of a person who believes there is order and harmony in the universe, and every effect must have its cause; there is no First Cause. . . .

"No First Cause," of course, translates into "No Creator, no God." Jastrow goes on to bare the soul of the secular scientist, including himself:

> This religious faith of the scientist is violated by the discovery that the world had a beginning under conditions in which the known laws of physics are not valid, and as a product of forces or circumstances we cannot discover. When that happens, the scientist has lost control. If he really examined the implications, he would be traumatized. As usual when faced with trauma, the mind reacts by ignoring the implications—in science this is known as "refusing to speculate"—or trivializing the origin of the world by calling it the Big Bang, as if the Universe were a firecracker.[35]

"Consider the enormity of the problem," says Jastrow, pursuing the question. "Science has proven that the universe exploded into being at a certain moment. It asks, What cause produced this effect? Who or what put the matter and energy into the Universe?

Was the Universe created out of nothing, or was it gathered together out of pre-existing materials? And science cannot answer these questions. . . ."[36]

"Now," he continues, "we would like to pursue that inquiry farther back in time, but the barrier to further progress seems insurmountable. It is not a matter of another year, another decade of work, another measurement, or another theory; at this moment it seems as though science will never be able to raise the curtain on the mystery of creation."

Jastrow's ultimate conclusion is astonishingly candid, particularly in light of his own professed agnosticism: "For the scientist who has lived by his faith in the power of reason, the story ends like a bad dream. He has scaled the mountain of ignorance; he is about to conquer the highest peak; as he pulls himself over the final rock, he is greeted by a band of theologians who have been sitting there for centuries."[37]

CHAPTER 8

THE WAR ON FATHERS

How the Feminization of America
Hurts Men and Boys

Why Boys Are Lagging Behind Girls
—*London Daily Telegraph*, January 23, 2008

Money and Power Shifting to Women
—*Birmingham (England) Post*, January 21, 2006

Women Initiate Divorce Proceedings Two-Thirds of the Time
—*Ottawa Citizen*, May 1, 2004

"Father knows best."

How do those three words make you feel? Turn them over in your mind a couple of times and be aware of the subtlest of feelings. Be honest.

Do they make you feel slightly squeamish? Produce a little discomfort in your solar plexus? Is something deep down inside you *repelled* by those words?

If so, you're not alone. Contempt for male authority—as if to say, "Give me a break, Father sure didn't know best in *my* life"—is everywhere around us. We're swimming in it. The fact is that men, boys, and masculinity itself have been under withering national assault, both cultural and legal, for decades.

Father Knows Best, of course, was a popular TV show during the 1950s. Set in the wholesome midwestern town of "Springfield," insurance agent Jim Anderson (played by Robert Young) would come home from work each evening, trade his sport jacket for a nice, comfortable sweater, and then deal with the everyday growing-up problems of his family. Both Jim and wife Margaret (played by Jane Wyatt) were cast as thoughtful and mature grown-ups. Jim could always be counted on to resolve that week's crisis with a combination of fatherly strength, lighthearted attitude, and good old common sense.

Today, more often than not, television portrays husbands as bumbling losers or contemptible, self-absorbed egomaniacs. Whether in dramas, comedies, or commercials, the patriarchy is dead, at least on TV, where men are fools—unless of course they're gay. For instance, on the hit show *Queer Eye,* now in syndication, the "fab five" are supremely knowledgeable on all things hip, their life's highest purpose being to help those less fortunate than themselves—that is, straight men—to become cool.

However, it's not only in Hollywood, but on Main Street, that men and boys are having a hard time of it. The evidence is everywhere.

To begin with, in public school classrooms across America, in every category and every demographic group, boys are falling behind:

- "For years, educators were concerned that girls were not keeping up in the classroom," reports CBS News. "Now the worry is that boys are falling behind in almost every academic category from standardized test scores to college enrollment rates." [1]
- "Boys in the U.S. bring home 70 percent of poor or failing grades and receive the bulk of school suspensions," adds Voice of America. [2]

- The problem is much the same in the United Kingdom, where London's *Daily Mail* reports what it calls "truly shocking" statistics: "White working-class boys are doing significantly worse at school than almost all other groups of pupils. A mere 15 per cent finish compulsory education having mastered the three Rs, official statistics show."[3]

Family therapist and author Michael Gurian provides some disturbing specifics in his bestselling book, *The Minds of Boys:*

- Boys make up 80 percent of our discipline problems.
- Of children diagnosed with learning disabilities, 70 percent are boys.
- Of children diagnosed with behavioral disorders, 80 percent are boys.
- Over 80 percent of schoolchildren on Ritalin or similar drugs are boys.
- Of high school dropouts, 80 percent are young males.[4]

"What we have done," says Thomas Mortenson, senior scholar at the Pell Institute for the Study of Opportunity in Higher Education, "is we have a K–12 school system that seems to work relatively well for girls and does not work for a very large share of boys."[5]

Echoes former U.S. assistant secretary of education Diane Ravitch, "In the view of elementary and high school students, the young people who sit in the classroom year after year and observe what is going on, both boys and girls agree: Schools favor girls."[6]

Taking it one step further, Alvaro de Vicente, headmaster of the Heights School, a Washington, D.C.–based private all-boys school, says: "I think that in many cases boys are falling behind because there has been a process over the last 20 years, a process of education becoming more feminine. And I mean that in sort of a realistic factual sense. Because if you look at the statistics there is a majority of women teachers and a majority of girls in the school that everything gets tailored to the girls and the young women."[7]

How does our society respond to such disconcerting data? Do we focus seriously on understanding boys' actual makeup and crafting an educational experience to better fit their needs? No.

Instead, when millions of boys, who perhaps don't thrive sitting practically motionless in a classroom all day, manifest symptoms of their distress—difficulty paying attention, being easily distracted, forgetting, fidgeting, getting up frequently to walk around, talking excessively, procrastinating, running or climbing excessively when inappropriate, having difficulty awaiting their turn, frequently interrupting others, blurting out answers (yes, these normal-sounding boy behaviors are all clinical symptoms of ADHD)[8]—we eagerly diagnose them as suffering from a mental illness and put them on drugs.

Between four and nine million American children diagnosed with attention deficit hyperactivity disorder—mostly boys—are taking Ritalin or similar dangerous psychostimulant drugs. Yes, dangerous. Here's what the Drug Enforcement Administration says about Ritalin, a trade name for methylphenidate: "Methylphenidate, a Schedule II substance, has a high potential for abuse and produces many of the same effects as cocaine or the amphetamines."[9] Indeed, other Schedule II substances include cocaine, amphetamines, opium, methadone, oxycodone (as in OxyContin), morphine, codeine, and barbiturates. "The controlled substances in this schedule," the DEA adds, "have a high abuse potential with severe psychological or physical dependence liability, but have accepted medical use in the U.S."[10]

Yet because of disturbing evidence, including dozens of suspicious deaths, that Ritalin and similar stimulants are harmful to the heart, members of a federal advisory panel announced in 2006 that they "wanted to slow the explosive growth in the drug's use."[11]

Alarmingly, Dr. Steven Nissen, a cardiologist at the Cleveland

Clinic and FDA panel member, said, "I must say that I have grave concerns about the use of these drugs and grave concerns about the harm they may cause."[12] Another panel member, Curt Furberg, a professor of public health at Wake Forest University, said, "Nowhere else in the world are 10 percent of 10-year-old boys diagnosed and treated for ADD."[13]

Let's back up for a moment. Is "attention deficit hyperactivity disorder" actually a mental illness? Almost everyone writing on the subject stakes out one of two positions: either it's a well-established psychiatric disorder whose validity is beyond question, or it's a myth, a panacea for clueless school administrators or a plot of greedy pharmaceutical companies. The truth is somewhere in between. Without question, people with serious cases of ADHD suffer from significant behavioral and cognitive problems that adversely impact their lives. But labeling millions of children with ADHD and drugging them to make their behavior more acceptable is nothing short of a national scandal.

Yet parents and educators somehow feel compelled to drug Johnny when they see him constantly fidgeting and squirming at his desk. Surprise—after years of medicating millions of kids for their restless behavior and seeming inability to focus, it turns out fidgeting is okay! Mark D. Rapport, a clinical psychologist, professor, and longtime ADHD researcher at the University of Central Florida, conducted a meticulous, four-year study demonstrating that boys learn *better* if they're simply allowed to fidget and move around all they want.[14] As *Time* reported:

[C]hildren with attention-deficit/hyperactivity disorder (ADHD) often squirm constantly, even when other kids can remain still. Many parents and teachers respond by trying to get ADHD kids, at any cost, to stop fidgeting. The assumption is that if they could just stop wriggling, they would be able to focus and learn. But a new study suggests that a better approach for ADHD kids (at least those who are not hyperactive to the point of breaking things) is to let them move all they want. That's because many kids use their movements—like swiveling in a chair or folding a leg underneath themselves and bouncing in a desk seat or repeatedly lolling and righting their head—the way many adults use caffeine: to stay focused. In other words, it may be that excessive movement doesn't prevent learning but actually facilitates it.[15]

So extreme is this reflexive intolerance for boys' natural behavior that a top British mental health expert insists "Winston Churchill would be put on Ritalin if he was a schoolboy today." Dr. Tim Kendall, joint director of the National Collaborating Centre for Mental Health, notes the famous British wartime leader was inattentive and disorganized as a schoolboy—a perfect candidate for Ritalin. As Kendall quipped on the BBC radio show *The Medicalization of Normality*, "Almost every possible human behavior can be classified as being in some way aberrant."[16]

As a result of these factors and many others, boys have fallen so far behind girls in American society that many colleges are concerned about maintaining a normal ratio between young men and women. Currently, about 3 out of 5 college students are girls.

"It's led to what some college counselors call education's dirty little secret," reports the *Denver Post:* "affirmative action programs for men, no matter their color. Admissions directors at many schools are bypassing girls with better grades and more extracurricular activities in favor of boys who don't have similar credentials, just to keep male numbers up."[17] Actually, it's no longer a secret: affirmative action admissions of "lesser qualified" males into the nation's institutions of higher learning are being widely reported in the press.[18]

LOSING THEIR CHILDREN

After boys have made it through school, sooner or later they usually get married and start a family. So how does "equality of the sexes" work out at this stage?

We've all heard that close to half of America's marriages are ending in divorce, but did you know that most of those divorces—2 out of 3—are initiated by the wives?[19]

Typically, divorce means one thing to fathers: they lose their children. It's widely acknowledged that the American judicial system is blatantly biased in favor of the mother in child custody disputes. This reality was confirmed in a report by the New Hampshire Commission on the Status of Men. Nowhere, according to the state government panel, is society's bias against men so obvious as in matters of child custody and support. Fathers get custody of children in uncontested cases only 10 percent of the time and 15 percent of the time in contested cases. Women get sole custody 66 percent of the time in uncontested cases and 75 percent of the time in contested cases.[20]

How does this make sense? "Given the plethora of evidence documenting the benefits of involved fathers with their children, and the present rate of female participation in the workforce, the custody imbalance between fathers and mothers seems difficult to justify," concluded the state panel.

What about the reported national epidemic of "deadbeat dads" we're always hearing about from the government and news media? After all, the Clinton administration gave us the Deadbeat Parents Punishment Act[21] and President George W. Bush requested tens of millions of dollars annually for programs to "promote responsible fatherhood"—while also promising to aggressively increase collections from all those "deadbeat dads."

So great is the official obsession with irresponsible fathers that Fox developed its notorious *Bad Dads* reality TV show (later rechristened *Deadbeat Dads* and taken over by Lifetime), designed to humiliate on national television fathers whom the show's producers deemed "deadbeats."

As the *Hollywood Reporter* describes the show, "Jim Durham, director of the National Child Support Center, functions as a sort of 'Dog the Bounty Hunter' for tracking deadbeats. . . . [H]e goes into their life, finds out what kind of assets they have and makes their lives miserable—foreclose on their house, repossess their car. He will squeeze them until the women get paid." [22]

Hold on, says syndicated columnist Kathleen Parker of the *Washington Post* Writers Group, who calls the show "neither accurate nor fair." Insisting the program's stereotype of "the rich pig who leaves his wife and kids for a pole-dancing aerobics instructor—or who enjoys extended martini lunches with his golf pals—is far from the norm," Parker provides a much more realistic and poignant slice of reality:

> The more accurate picture of a deadbeat dad is an unemployed or underemployed bloke who sees more jail cells than golf courses. A common sequence of events for the poorest deadbeat dads goes something like this: Fall behind in child support, get arrested and put in jail, lose your job, fall further behind in child support . . .
>
> Clearly, some men are sinners and some women are saints. But sometimes the reverse is true. In fact, noncustodial mothers are 20 percent more likely to default on child support than noncustodial fathers, according to U.S. Census data. But we don't see a reality show aimed at humiliating moms. [23]

Why? As Parker observes, "civilized people would strenuously object to the public ridicule of moms whose children may be watching. . . . The question is why we feel no such decency toward men and the children who love them."

In the end, comments Parker:

Bad Dads is just the latest insult to men and especially fathers who feel, appropriately, that they've been maligned and minimized through television programming and advertising. In sitcoms, men are typically buffoons. And fathers, if they exist, are inept and unreliable, while Mom is a paragon of virtue and competence. Television executives and advertisers may profit from such "entertainment," but who's having fun? Apparently, women are. Four out of five network sitcom viewers are female.[24]

Not only is the "deadbeat dad" theme being exploited for entertainment. "In fact," writes Stephen Baskerville, Ph.D., "no evidence exists that large numbers of fathers voluntarily abandon their children." A Howard University political science professor and board member of the American Coalition for Fathers and Children, Baskerville says categorically: "No government or academic study has ever demonstrated such an epidemic, and those studies that have addressed the question directly have concluded otherwise. In the largest federally funded study ever conducted on the subject, psychologist Sanford Braver demonstrated that very few married fathers abandon their children."

Baskerville adds that, overwhelmingly, "it is mothers, not fathers, who are walking away from marriages and thus separating children from their fathers."[25]

How on earth did we get here? What happened to the great feminist revolution that was supposed to make ours a better, more equal society? Women were being "liberated"—or so we were assured—from "bondage" to their traditional roles, and thereby enabled to develop themselves personally, professionally, and spiritually as never before. Men were also supposedly "freed" to express their more sensitive, nurturing, and feminine side. In this fuzzy utopian fantasy, society was supposed to evolve into a great big happy androgynous paradise where everyone is equal to everyone else in every way.

Even if such radical "equality" were possible and desirable—and it is neither—why do we now find men being demeaned as never before? Why are boys falling behind girls in school? Why are family courts so scandalously biased against fathers? Why, in short, if this is all about equality, is there such an unrelenting war against boys and men?

"STRAITJACKET OF MASCULINITY"

"It's a bad time to be a boy in America," states Christina Hoff Sommers at the outset of her groundbreaking book, *The War Against Boys.*[26] The Ph.D. scholar cites example after example of how America's cultural, academic, and political elite have had an extended field day maligning and redefining masculinity, going back to their analysis of the 1999 student massacre at Columbine High School:

> "The carnage committed by two boys in Littleton, Colorado," declares the *Congressional Quarterly Researcher,* "has forced the nation to reexamine the nature of boyhood in America." William Pollack, director of the Center for Men at McLean Hospital and author of the best-selling *Real Boys: Rescuing Our Sons from the Myths of Boyhood,* tells audiences around the country, "The boys in Littleton are the tip of the iceberg. And the iceberg is *all* boys."[27]

Sommers shows how the chic, politically correct 1990s "discovery" that *girls* are being shortchanged by American society is largely unsupported by research or experience. Rather, she says, it is actually boys who not only are being shortchanged but also are being targeted for radical reprogramming by academics offended by masculinity itself.

The belief that boys are being wrongly "masculinized" is inspiring a movement to "construct boyhood" in ways

that will render boys less competitive, more emotionally ex-
pressive, more nurturing—more, in short, like girls. Gloria
Steinem summarizes the views of many in the boys-should-
be-changed camp when she says, "We need to raise boys like
we raise girls." [28]

Indeed, Sommers explains, an obsession with "how our culture
binds boys in a 'straitjacket of masculinity' has suddenly become a
fashionable topic":

> There are now conferences, workshops, and institutes ded-
> icated to transforming boys. Carol Gilligan, professor of gen-
> der studies at Harvard Graduate School of Education, writes
> of the problem of "boys' masculinity . . . in a patriarchal so-
> cial order." Barney Brawer, director of the Boys' Project at
> Tufts University, told *Education Week:* "We've deconstructed
> the old version of manhood, but we've not [yet] constructed a
> new version." In the spring of 2000, the Boys' Project at Tufts
> offered five workshops on "reinventing Boyhood." The plan-
> ners promised emotionally exciting sessions: "We'll laugh and
> cry, argue and agree, reclaim and sustain the best parts of the
> culture of boys and men, while figuring out how to change
> the terrible parts." [29]

"Terrible"? Just what sort of qualifications do these "critics of
masculinity" bring to their project of "reconstructing the nation's
schoolboys," Sommers wonders aloud. "How well do they understand and *like* boys? Who has authorized their mission?"

Despite the deplorable attempts by social revolutionaries to feminize and reprogram boys to be more like girls, in reality, as Sommers affirms, there is nothing wrong and a very great deal right with
boys—testosterone, competitiveness, aggressiveness, fidgeting, and
all—just as there is a great deal right with girls. Even maverick feminist Camille Paglia courageously reminds her men-hating colleagues

that masculinity is "the most creative cultural force in history."[30] Think about that statement: this "force" we call masculinity—which for millennia has tamed the wilderness, constructed civilizations, revolutionized life through dazzling inventions, and sacrificed its own life to protect women and children—is what our feminist-inspired experts want to destroy, so they can "construct a new version." Yikes.

GENDER REVOLUTION

Why would our culture so denigrate masculinity? And why—this is the flip side of the same question—are we becoming so increasingly feminized as a society?

Today's high level of gender confusion and role reversal, manifested most obviously in the dramatic upswing—and near celebration—of homosexuality, is one of the great cultural mysteries of our time. The bending and sometimes breaking of traditional gender roles permeates our society in obvious and subtle ways.

Popular culture promotes sexual confusion at every turn. The fashion industry, for example, has long been steeped in androgyny, exploiting the shock value of clothing that creates sexual ambiguity. Likewise, gender confusion has been a central feature of rock music for decades. First, the "British invasion" featured the long-haired, "choir boy" Beatles, who "helped feminize the culture," writes author and 1960s culture analyst Steven D. Stark;[31] and the "bad boy" Rolling Stones, featuring the prancing, pouting Mick Jagger with his long hair, skin-tight jeans, eyeliner, and (after a while) dangling earrings.

Later this feminization of performers led to outright androgyny, with the likes of David Bowie, Boy George, and of course Michael Jackson, virtually worshipped by millions of fans, as well as heavy metal rock groups such as Mötley Crüe, Kiss, and Ozzy Osbourne who exploit sexual ambiguity for their shock and entertainment value.

Then there's the national fad of teen and college girls "trying out" lesbianism/bisexuality just because it's "chic," in response to the behaviors they see in their favorite entertainers. "Some see it as the latest cool trend among girls in America's high schools," reports London's *Guardian* newspaper. "Others claim it is just teenagers doing what they do best—being rebellious. Either way, a wave of 'bisexual chic' is sweeping the United States. Emboldened by such images as Madonna kissing Britney Spears and Christina Aguilera on a TV awards show, girls are proudly declaring their alternative sexualities at a younger age than ever before." [32]

At the far extreme of gender confusion is the mainstreaming of transgenderism, referring to people who literally want to become the opposite sex, and who often mutilate their bodies by cutting off breasts and other body parts in a sad and desperate effort to surgically accomplish that goal. These obviously troubled people, much more in need of enlightened counseling than body mutilation, were celebrated by President Barack Obama when he set aside an entire month to honor them, declaring: "I, Barack Obama, president of the United States of America, by virtue of the authority vested in me by the Constitution and laws of the United States, do hereby proclaim June 2009 as Lesbian, Gay, Bisexual, and Transgender Pride Month." [33]

"To the sexual liberal, gender is a cage," explained author George Gilder in his classic book *Men and Marriage*. "Behind cruel bars of custom and tradition, men and women for centuries have looked longingly across forbidden spaces at one another and yearned to be free of sexual roles." [34]

Those gender-role "prison bars" were broken during the 1960s "cultural revolution." "Sexual liberation" during the '60s and '70s, promoted by an army of supposed experts, encouraged women to adopt a more aggressive and promiscuous role "equal" to men's, one made possible by the birth control pill and legalized abortion, which freed women from the natural restraints that previously had bolstered traditional, Bible-based morality. Today, after decades of progressive destruction of traditional standards, the sexual mores that once formed the foundation of Western civilization have pretty much been reduced to rubble, on top of which has been erected a secular, sophisticated but extraordinarily sexualized culture. (As Thomas Paine observed, "The palaces of Kings are built upon the ruins . . . of Paradise.")

Without question, the crowning glory of America's gender revolution has been the virtual normalization of homosexuality—no small feat for a lifestyle once regarded morally as a sin, medically as a psychiatric disorder, and legally as a crime. "Gay rights" has come a long way since the Stonewall riots and nascent "gay liberation" movement of the 1960s. Same-sex marriage, literally unthinkable a generation ago, has evolved into a major "civil rights movement," buoyed by activist judicial opinion that it's constitutionally mandated.

No matter that the vast majority of Americans have strongly and repeatedly rejected same-sex marriage in state elections. No matter that a comprehensive review of nine different studies of same-sex couples shows that children raised by homosexuals are "seven times more likely to develop homosexual or bisexual preferences than children raised by heterosexuals."[35] The gay rights juggernaut, aided by a sympathetic government and compliant press, rolls on.

Most Americans do in fact support equal rights (though not special rights) for homosexuals. The problem is that the official "normalization" of homosexuality has progressed to such an intolerant extreme that just criticizing it on moral/religious grounds is increasingly portrayed as equivalent to racism or anti-Semitism. This is an ominous development, as it may well lead—and indeed already has in several other nations—to the de facto criminalization of traditional Christian expression, which holds that homosexual acts are sinful, just like adultery, fornication, and all other extramarital sex. Such beliefs, however sincerely held or compassionately shared, are increasingly being cast as "hate speech" by gay rights activists and their fellow travelers in the press and government. Surely America can discover an enlightened way to treat everyone justly, including homosexuals, without demonizing and criminalizing the religion on which the nation's laws, traditions, core institutions, and fundamental freedoms are based.

Perhaps the most obvious and direct root of the modern cultural antipathy toward men and boys is another 1960s revolutionary movement, running parallel to "gay liberation" and "sexual liberation"—namely, "women's liberation."

Although that movement's public face was a laudable quest for equal pay for equal work, equal opportunity, and so on, the movement's leaders were motivated by rebellion against traditional patriarchy and rejection of "stereotypic" gender roles—or, to put it more plainly, hatred of men—with frequent fiery condemnations of marriage as "slavery" and "legalized rape." (You don't suppose this hostility toward men could be animating the pious efforts of today's "critics of masculinity," whom Sommers describes—you remember, the ones who want to reprogram boys to be more like girls?)

To understand this bizarre mentality, let's look a bit more closely at one prominent feminist author and antipornography crusader, Andrea Dworkin, who died in 2005. "Like prostitution," she wrote, "marriage is an institution that is extremely oppressive and dangerous for women."[36] Such a radical view becomes immediately more understandable when we realize Dworkin had been severely abused by the men in her life. At nine, an unknown man reportedly molested her in a movie theater, and when she eventually married, her anarchist husband would frequently punch, kick, and burn her, sometimes beating her head against the floor until she was unconscious. No wonder she developed a hatred for men.

Andrea, if you could hear me, I would say to you: "I am truly sorry for the things you suffered at the hands of violent and abusive men in your life. But you erred greatly in concluding therefore that getting married and having a family is 'oppressive and dangerous for women.' That belief understandably emanated from your rage toward those who victimized you—yet in your anger you sadly extended that condemnation to apply to *all* men, and then spent years persuading other women to join you in shunning them."

When all is said and done, there is something about resenting, rejecting, and demeaning men that seems to accompany the overall growth of suffering and evil in society. Not only do fatherless families lead directly to more oppressive and intrusive government, as the welfare state "moves in" to become a surrogate husband/breadwinner and father, but myriad social plagues, from gang proliferation to violent crime, have their roots directly in homes without fathers.

Very simply, when the bond between fathers and their families is encouraged, society thrives. When fathers are separated from their families, due to destructive feminist philosophies, subversive no-fault divorce laws, and the like, society not only fragments, but loses its very identity and direction, which is exactly what we see happening today.

When we were little children, most of us intuitively understood that "Father"—if he's a decent, principled, conscience-driven human being—usually "knows best." I'm talking about an ordinary man living in the light of constant, honest self-examination, progressively giving up his own selfishness and impatience and accepting full responsibility for the lives of his family members. Such a man is worthy of being respected, followed, and loved. One indication of his worthiness for this role comes when he sees that his wife is right and he is willing to submit to her correct discernment. A good man, like a good woman, serves a Higher Right, so what's important to him is not *who* is right, but *what* is right. Therefore, sometimes "Mother knows best," but it is *Father* who decides the question. Otherwise no one is ultimately responsible.

"WHAT IF HE'S A JERK?"

But—some women readers may now be asking, or possibly screaming—what if he is not a good man? What if your man is unprincipled, hostile, selfish, and dense? How can you respect such a man, let alone follow him?

This is the same dilemma many people experience over the commandment "Honor thy father and thy mother: that thy days may be long upon the land which the Lord thy God giveth thee" (Exodus 20:12). It's easy enough to honor your parents if they are good people, but how do you honor someone who's just not honorable? This question begs for an answer, because there's something vital and actually life-giving ("that thy days may be long upon the land") about honoring your father and mother, but how do you do so if they're not good people?

Here's the secret: If you're fortunate enough to have a decent father (or husband, since the principle is the same), respect and appreciate him for the good you see in him. But if he is so deeply flawed that he has badly hurt you, then you can still "honor" him—and thus obey God's law—by giving up your resentment for him.

We're talking about forgiveness, of course. But forgiveness doesn't mean you conclude that his treatment of you was okay, because it may have been thoroughly rotten. Rather, to truly forgive means, as a Christian counselor I know once said memorably: "Feel the hurt—but not the hate."

Think about this. It could revolutionize your life.

When someone wrongs you, there's a critical difference between the "hurt" and the "hate" you feel, although the two always tend to be mixed together into one big pain. Yet a truly sincere person who desires to obey that commandment can rise above the hate component.

For a powerful object lesson in this principle, watch the movie *The Passion of the Christ*. Jesus was flogged, mocked, tortured—but while he certainly felt the *hurt* of that awful abuse, he didn't fall to experiencing *hate*. Rather, he prayed, "Father, forgive them; for they know not what they do" (Luke 23:34).

Perhaps your response is "Well, that was Jesus. He can forgive, but I can't." Wrong. We *all* can forgive, completely and totally—in fact, are commanded to do so: "For if ye forgive men their trespasses, your heavenly Father will also forgive you: But if ye forgive not men their trespasses, neither will your Father forgive your trespasses" (Matthew 6:14–15).

Let's bring this down to earth with a simple, uncomplicated example. Suppose I thoughtlessly, or even maliciously, trip you and cause you to sprain your ankle. You will, of course, feel pain in your ankle, but you'll also very likely resent me for causing the injury. That hostility toward me is a separate pain, distinct from the physical pain in your ankle. And of course, your anger toward me just increases your overall discomfort level.

Forgiveness means you give up the anger toward the person who caused the injury. Although part of you really wants to hold on to the anger, just let it go—and you'll be left with a much more tolerable pain in your ankle. Who knows, you may even recover faster; forgiveness has a way of bringing God and healing into the picture.

Thus, ladies, if you have been hurt by your husband (or father), just realize that, if you are willing, you really can give up the resentment that always seems to accompany violation, cruelty, or betrayal, and which clings to us even years afterward like some sort of parasite on our soul. This resentment slowly destroys our spirit while secretly feeding our pride.

Mercifully, the opposite of this syndrome is also true: if you can just discover how to genuinely forgive, the "dark side" of you will die a little bit and the bright side will grow stronger. Just "feel the hurt" while you quietly "let go of the hate." Have a little compassion; it will make it easier to truly forgive. Realize that the man who hurt you was a victim himself—traumatized and confused and shaped by forces he couldn't overcome or even understand during his own flawed upbringing.

This genuine forgiveness toward your father or husband actually exerts a powerful, unseen force on him, mysteriously helping him (if he's willing) to recognize his own long-invisible faults and to grow beyond them.

Gentlemen, don't blame women for giving up on you and divorcing you. A lot of the blame rightfully belongs to you. Your intense need for their emotional and sexual support, your selfishness and impatience, your immaturity—all this and much more literally creates and feeds the resentment within your beloved. Remember, women are much more vulnerable than men. You must be strong for your wife, which will eventually inspire her to be strong for you. So give up your own "hurt feelings"—really anger—toward her for being so emotional and perhaps unreasonable; it's the result of a frustration you've had a large part in creating.

America needs to get a handle on its divorce epidemic. We're committing national suicide, one family at a time. Often, both spouses are decent people, yet they develop such conflict and pain between them that they just can't bear to live together anymore.

But how many marriages could be saved if the spouse intent on divorce were just to learn to give up all that anger toward the other?

This brings us back full circle to our question of what's behind the war on men.

The angry spirit of the radical feminist basically says: "Men are selfish dogs who use women for their own gratification. Christianity is a man's religion, used for centuries to oppress women. Women are better off without these selfish men, and without the god of selfish men." Although few people reading this would identify consciously with such radical views, in reality millions of us have embraced the secret rebellion against God and patriarchy represented in those sentiments.

The solution to all this is disarmingly simple. Men, stop looking at women as though they were created to serve your ego. They weren't—they really weren't. Care about them for themselves, and not for what you're getting from the relationship.

And women, give up the anger against your men. Their failure to find real, selfless love for you is their serious flaw. But your resentment toward them for that failure is your serious flaw. Give each other a break. Bring the best out of your spouse—and your kids and everyone else for that matter—by discovering how to be both patient and strong at the same time. There's magic there.

Most urgently of all, reject divorce as an option. Statistics prove second marriages are even more likely to fail, and you will lose forever the youth you shared and the life you lived—and your children will suffer most of all.

When we break the bond between fathers and their children, we're breaking the bond between God the Father and our nation. When we restore that connection, our society will be healed. It's as simple as that.

That's God's way. Listen to Him. He's your Father, and believe me, He knows best.

CHAPTER 9

✦

THE MYSTERIOUS POWER OF HATE

How Innocent Children
Become Murderers and Rapists

Children Trained as Suicide Bombers in Iraq
    —*Australian*, APRIL 22, 2009

5,750 People Killed in Gang Violence in Last 10 Years
    —*LAist*, APRIL 17, 2009

Neo-Nazis Screaming "Heil Hitler" Attack Concentration Camp
Survivors
    —*Daily Mail* (LONDON), MAY 12, 2009

Growing up in a family of genocide survivors as I did, I got to hear stories—lots of stories—about just how depraved human beings can get.

Although my father and grandmother passed down these often-vivid recollections to us in the comfort of a warm suburban family room, worlds apart from the nightmares of their youth, their painful psychological scars remained ever fresh. And to a young boy like me, those stories—of cruel soldiers and bandits hell-bent on mayhem, as well as their intended victims' resourcefulness and sometimes even heroism—provided a glimpse into a scary, alien dimension of evil.

But rather than tell any more family stories here—and most

Armenian families have them, just as Jewish Holocaust survivors and their kin have their stories—I'll quote the U.S. ambassador to Turkey at the time, Henry Morgenthau, whose published memoirs exposed the horrors he witnessed firsthand during the twentieth century's first genocide. Incredibly, he described how Turkish officials bragged to him about their nightly meetings where they would enthusiastically share the latest torture techniques to use on the Armenians:

> Each new method of inflicting pain was hailed as a splendid discovery, and the regular attendants were constantly ransacking their brains in the effort to devise some new torment. He told me that they even delved into the records of the Spanish Inquisition and other historic institutions of torture and adopted all the suggestions found there. . . . [1]

I'll spare you the details, except to say that Morgenthau, father of FDR's treasury secretary of the same name, summed up the "sadistic orgies" of the Armenian genocide by declaring: "Whatever crimes the most perverted instincts of the human mind can devise, and whatever refinements of persecution and injustice the most debased imagination can conceive, became the daily misfortunes of this devoted people. I am confident that the whole history of the human race contains no such horrible episode as this." [2]

Unfortunately, more such "horrible episodes" followed apace throughout the twentieth century. In the 1930s, Stalin ordered his military to confiscate all of Ukraine's food and then sealed her borders to prevent any outside sustenance from getting in, thereby intentionally starving 7 million men, women, and children to death. This was followed soon by Japan's demonic "rape of Nanking," during which 300,000 Chinese were butchered in their nation's capital, including up to 80,000 women and little girls gang-raped by Japanese soldiers and then stabbed to death with bayonets. The Nazi Holocaust in the 1930s and '40s, of course, tops most people's list of genocidal horrors, with its death-camp crematoria, extermination of

6 million Jews, and unspeakable "medical experiments." For sheer numbers of dead—tens of millions during the 1960s and '70s—China's Mao Zedong has been called history's worst mass murderer. Pol Pot's maniacal communist purge of Cambodia in the late 1970s led to the deaths of 2 million of his own people, while Rwanda's tribal genocide in the 1990s resulted in the club-and-machete massacring of 800,000. Today's ongoing Sudanese genocide, backed by the Islamist government in Khartoum, has resulted in at least 400,000 dead.

We frequently ask ourselves how human beings can sink to this level of cruelty. There's no precedent for it among even the most fearsome predators in the animal kingdom. What, then, makes us capable of such extreme evil?

Genocidal madness can't be blamed on a particular philosophy or religion. Stalin, Mao, and Pol Pot were atheistic communists. Imperial Japan and Nazi Germany were in the grip of quasi-religious personality cults that deified their leaders. And today's genocide in Sudan, like the Turkish military that tortured Armenians for sport a century earlier, is heavily motivated by Islamic jihadist fervor.

So what turns people into monsters? Since they obviously didn't start out that way, let's rewind back to the beginning of the story and see what causes an innocent child to morph into an instrument of great evil.

CHILDREN'S SONGS
THAT CELEBRATE MURDER

There's nothing more beautiful than a young child. Nothing. The brightness of spirit, the spontaneity, the natural intelligence—which Einstein called "the holy curiosity of inquiry"[3]—are breathtaking.

What, then, possesses a smart, handsome young five- or six-year-old boy to go on Palestinian television and sing, "When I wander into Jerusalem, I will become a suicide bomber"? Or a group of children, both boys and girls, to sing together, "How pleasant is the smell of martyrs, how pleasant the smell of land, the land enriched by the blood, the blood pouring out of a fresh body"?[4]

What? How does the horror and stench of death magically transform into the "pleasant smell" of life and glory for these kids? What happens to them in their earliest, most vulnerable years to induce some to later strap on explosive belts and vaporize themselves while murdering dozens of unsuspecting innocents?

Why, growing up in a "normal home" with a mom, dad, siblings, school, and friends, does a young man suddenly feel compelled to stab his own sister to death—knifing her not just once or twice, but over and over again in a murderous frenzy—just because somebody said she was walking down the street with a male who wasn't a relative?

Clearly, as these young people's indoctrination progresses from singing songs about atrocities to actually committing them, we're witnessing not only a toxic philosophy at work, but also the magic ingredient that makes that philosophy come to life—namely, *hatred.* Underneath all the smiles, underneath the "devout" faith, underneath whatever persona is masking the overwhelming fear, confusion, and jihadist programming that have been cultivated in them since birth, lies the core of their being—a smoldering fireball of suppressed rage.

Intense hatred has a way of morphing inexorably into full-blown, epic madness. Indeed, hate is like spiritual plutonium, possessing bizarre, explosive, and transformative qualities of which we are largely unaware. It is the means by which evil itself blooms on this earth, especially when rage is focused and magnified by a malignant worldview. If you think this is overstated, just contemplate with me the following news items:

- Popular Middle East television programming for children that features jihadist clones of Mickey Mouse, *Sesame Street* characters, and other kids' favorites, in which the lovable, cuddly stars teach children vicious lies and the virtues of mass murder.[5]

- Rape *victims* being flogged and imprisoned, as when a Saudi court in early 2009 sentenced a twenty-three-year-old female who had been gang-raped by five men to one hundred lashes and a year in jail. Her crime? Accepting a lift from a man who drove her against her will to his house and took turns, with four of his friends, raping her.[6]

- An epidemic of "honor killings"—at least five thousand per year according to the United Nations, but many more that go unreported—in which fathers, brothers, or mothers brutally murder their own daughter or sister merely for being seen in public with a male or similar "offense." For example, two Jordanian brothers used axes to murder their two sisters, ages twenty and twenty-seven, after the older sister left home to marry a man without her family's permission and the younger one ran away to join her. After someone tipped off the brothers as to their sisters' whereabouts, the men went into their home with axes and hacked them to death. "It was a brutal scene," one government official told the *Jordan Times*. "One victim's head was nearly cut clean off."[7]

- Maniacal, zombielike "religious police," such as those in Saudi Arabia who on March 11, 2002, allowed fifteen young girls to die horrible deaths when a fire broke out in their school in Mecca. The religious police, or Mutaween, literally blocked firefighters from saving the girls because they weren't dressed in the proper Islamic way for girls and women to be seen outdoors. With helpless firemen watching, the religious police literally beat the girls—those who were not wearing their headscarves or abayas—back into the inferno.[8]

What we're looking at here is criminally insane behavior—no less insane or criminal than that exhibited by severely deranged people we routinely lock up in maximum-security psychiatric hospitals or prisons in the United States.

Of course, by now we've all heard more than we care to know about radical jihad culture, with its pathological blame of Jews for everything, its condemnation of Western civilization, and its "die-while-killing-infidels-and-Allah-will-give-you-virgins" recruitment pitch. But distilling this "martyrdom" obsession down to its essence, common sense tells us no one murders innocent people or forces schoolgirls back into a burning building unless they're insanely angry. So, where exactly does this hate come from?

Let's understand that even a violent philosophy like that of radical Islam isn't necessarily sufficient, by itself, to create a rage-fueled jihadist. No, you become full of hate and driven to violate others only when someone else first *violates you*—when a parent, older sibling, teacher, cleric, or other authority figure intimidates, frightens, degrades, bullies, humiliates, or perhaps sexually abuses you. And such cruelty and degradation are, unfortunately, endemic in much of the Islamic world. Its rigid, authoritarian religious system, the near-slave status and abuse of women, the suffocating sexual repression, the widespread incidence of what can only be called the world's most flagrant child abuse (where even toddlers are groomed for future "martyrdom operations"), and the pervasive fear of flogging, amputation, or stoning if one runs afoul of the ultrastrict sharia legal code—all this creates an environment reeking of quiet terror. No wonder its victims take to terrorism so readily.

So, once these parents and other authorities, full of the madness and confusion injected into them during their own youth, succeed in passing it on to the next generation of youngsters by intimidating and indoctrinating them, it's child's play to focus the newly created jihadists' zeal onto the appropriate "hate object"—Jews, Americans, "infidels," etc.

This dynamic is not unique to radical Islam. In fact, believe it or not, it's the hidden fabric of all too much of our own lives—albeit usually in a far less extreme form. In a perverse mirror reflection of the Golden Rule, we all tend compulsively to do unto others what was done unto us. We effortlessly internalize the cruelty of others.

This is because, aside from the obvious effects being angry and upset have on us—making us emotional, clouding our judgment, and so on—it also throws us into "program mode." That's right: when we get upset at the intimidating words or actions of other people, their cruelty "infects" us in a very real way. So, for instance, if our parents angrily yelled at us all the time when we were children, we would tend to angrily yell at those smaller and weaker than us. A little bit of the bully gets inside of us, and we then bully others, in one form or another. We've all seen this, and we know that our prisons are full of molesters and abusers who were molested and abused as children.

Thus maniacal imams and jihadist teachers find it relatively easy to convert innocent children into suicide bombers. The first step is to indoctrinate them from birth with a poisonous belief system demonizing "infidels," a process explained by Israeli counterterrorism expert Itamar Marcus in an op-ed, "The Genocide Mechanism":

> Common to the framing of all genocide is a very specific kind of demonization. In Rwanda, the Hutus taught that the Tutsis were cockroaches and snakes. Tutsi women were portrayed as cunning seductresses who used beauty and sexual power to conquer the Hutus. . . . Radio Rwanda repeatedly broadcast a warning that Hutus were about to be attacked by Tutsis, to convince the Hutus that they needed to attack first to protect themselves.
>
> This demonization included two specific components. First, the victims had to be perceived as a clear and present threat, so that the killers were convinced they were acting in

self-defense. Second, the victims were dehumanized, so that the killers convinced themselves that they were not destroying real human beings.[9]

Teaching children virtually from birth that Jews are subhuman, evil oppressors of Muslims—fiends who grind up Arab youngsters to use as ingredients in their Passover matzoh—is epidemic in the Islamic world. A typical example: The Saudi satellite television station Iqraa broadcast an interview with a three-year-old Egyptian girl named Basmallah, who answered a question about Jews by declaring: "They are apes and pigs."[10]

But this little girl is not about to murder anyone. She's just repeating statements fed to her by adults for the sake of winning their love and approval. Dehumanizing indoctrination isn't quite enough to launch a genocide. There must also be hate, and lots of it—not merely to fuel the atrocity machine, but to allow the indoctrination to fully take root.

In other words, whatever the toxic programming may be—Hutus demonizing Tutsis as "cockroaches and snakes," Turks accusing Armenians of being "enemy collaborators," Nazis likening Jews to "vermin"—for such outrageous and counterintuitive falsehoods to be both believed and acted upon, those being indoctrinated must be kept in a very emotional state.

Recall that Hitler *always* kept his audiences superemotional; that's how he programmed them and guarded against their naturally coming back to their senses. He was always stirring up their emotions, and by so doing, his thoughts became their thoughts, his feelings became their feelings. It's Brainwashing 101: cause your intended victims to become upset, angry, emotionally riled up, and you have your hands on the control levers of their mind.

Children are so vulnerable, like spiritual sponges, that if they're treated with cruelty, if they're degraded sexually, if they're constantly confused and intimidated—and at the same time are indoctrinated with lies denying their neighbors' humanity, and also showered with promises of glory, reward, and brotherhood for believing and acting a certain way—well, it's not long before you've got yourself a newly minted jihadist, communist, or Nazi.

To understand why it's so easy for us to be programmed this way, let's briefly focus on a hate-based culture much closer to home.

COLOR WARS

As a journalist, I remember when I first reported on Southern California's gang epidemic back in the late 1980s. Fueled by rampant family breakdown in the black community—meaning no dad in the home (if there was a home at all)—Los Angeles County alone had upward of one hundred thousand gang members. The two biggest black groups, the Bloods (who wore red) and the Crips (who wore blue), were locked in a perpetual cycle of outright war. Crips would shoot or stab a member of the Bloods, followed by the predictable retaliatory strike and so on, each attack ratcheting the hate level upward. Entire communities came to resemble war zones where mayhem, murder, and drive-by shootings were a daily occurrence—with innocent bystanders frequently cut down by the cross fire. Sometimes, residents who just happened to be wearing red or blue were mistaken for members of the enemy gang and executed.

Today, decades later, the same war rages on. In south-central Los Angeles, ground zero for the Crips and the Bloods, "guns and color wars have killed more than 15,000 people over the last 30 years," reports *Newsweek*—"more than have died in the sectarian conflict in Northern Ireland in the same time."[11]

So, what's all the fighting about? Why do they hate each other so much?

No good reason. In fact, no reason at all.

Members of both groups think, speak, act, feel, and look

exactly the same as each other, except for their "colors" (and hand gestures and graffiti). Yet, with the exception of the occasional much-publicized "truce," they remain mortal enemies. Why?

There's no dispute between two religious and political camps as in Northern Ireland, or between two ideologies like Marxism and capitalism, or between "haves" and "have-nots." Indeed, while analysts and gang members themselves advance various theories—including turf disputes, boredom and unemployment, the prevalence of crack cocaine, and the cultural requirement to appear tough and command "respect"—the underlying reason for this never-ending war is that the gangbangers are simply addicted to hating. Feeling and expressing that hatred and degrading others reinforce their sense of self-worth, of identity, of life itself—the only life many of them know.

This is not hard to grasp when you consider that the initiation ritual to join one of these gangs typically involves being severely beaten with fists or clubs by multiple members of the gang. You also will likely be required to commit a violent crime, such as assaulting or knife-slashing a rival gang member or even an innocent stranger in the face. Females, if they're not "beaten in" to the gang, are "sexed in," which means they have sex with multiple male gang members, or they may be raped. There are even reports of females being "sexed in" by being required to have sex with someone who is HIV-positive.[12]

Why all the degradation and humiliation? Because being required to cross serious moral and legal lines by committing crimes and performing degrading acts bonds the new "initiates" on many levels to their new "family." Indeed, while committing a criminal act makes leaving the gang difficult, it also promotes a bizarre sense of growth and family belongingness.

That's right: inculcating hatred into a youngster—whether it's a Palestinian youth in Gaza or a fatherless gang wannabe in Los Angeles—actually provides a perverse kind of nurturing warmth because it's nourishing to his ego, his need to feel superior to others, and to feel powerful and important. Hatred of an "enemy" has a perverse way of fulfilling a person emotionally and enhancing his or her self-image, and of course there's absolutely nothing more unifying to a group of dysfunctional, hostile people than sharing a common enemy.

To understand better how extreme anger can generate such a convincing illusion of enlightenment and self-worth, join me for a guided tour inside the hater's brain.

ANATOMY OF AN ANTI-SEMITE

Before the 9/11 era and the ubiquitous fear of large-scale terrorism by angry jihadists, if the subject of "hate groups" came up most people would think reflexively of domestic organizations like the Ku Klux Klan and Aryan Nations. Ironically, the number-one target of "right-wing" hate groups and anti-Western Islamists is the same—Jews.

So, let's briefly examine this strange hatred of Jews that has so long infected the human race.

Thousands of books and articles in many languages describe the supposed subhuman character and dark machinations of "the Jews." Anti-Semitic "think tanks" devote years to the painstaking revision of history to eliminate or downplay the Nazi Holocaust. Newspapers throughout the Middle East and elsewhere regularly publish diatribes condemning Jews as Satan's cannibalistic offspring. Leftists fulminate over the brutal "apartheid" regime in the "racist" state of Israel. And angry pseudo-Christians excoriate Jews as "Christ-killers" while proclaiming themselves to be "God's chosen":

• The Aryan Nations, a white supremacist organization, condemns Jews as "the natural enemy of our Aryan Race. This is attested by scripture and all secular history. The Jew is like a destroying virus that attacks our racial body to destroy our Aryan culture and the purity of our Race." [13]

• Then there's the American Nazi Party (which invites website visitors to "Download Adolf Hitler's masterpiece 'Mein Kampf' HERE!"), whose founder, George Lincoln Rockwell, said: "We must have an America without swarming black filth in our schools, on our buses and in our places of work; an America in which our cultural, social, business and political life is free of alien, Jewish influence; an America in which White people are the sole masters of our own destiny." [14]

• And of course we've got the Reverend Louis Farrakhan, leader of the U.S.-based Nation of Islam, who said during a Chicago speech on February 25, 1996: "You are wicked deceivers of the American people. You have sucked their blood. You are not real Jews, those of you that are not real Jews. You are the synagogue of Satan, and you have wrapped your tentacles around the U.S. government, and you are deceiving and sending this nation to hell. But I warn you in the name of Allah, you would be wise to leave me alone. But if you choose to crucify me, know that Allah will crucify you." [15]

• But the prize for anti-Semitic rants goes to *Al-Akhbar*, the semi-official Egyptian state-run daily newspaper. In a column titled "Accursed Forever and Ever," Fatma Abdallah Mahmoud writes:

They [Jewish people] are accursed in heaven and on earth. They are accursed from the day the human race was created and from the day their mothers bore them. They are accursed also because they murdered the Prophets. . . . These accursed ones are a catastrophe for the human race. They are the virus of the generation, doomed to a life of humiliation and wretchedness until Judgment Day. . . . Their history always was and always will be stained with treachery, falseness, and lying. . . . Thus, the Jews are accursed—the Jews of our time, those who preceded them and those who will come after them, if any Jews come after them. [16]

What is wrong with these people? What benefit can they possibly derive from basing their entire existence on hating others?

Let's try a quick thought experiment, sort of like Einstein and Galileo used to conduct, except instead of focusing on some perplexing scientific conundrum, we'll mentally explore the mystery of anti-Semitism.

Imagine for a moment that you really, *really hate* "the Jews." You blame them for corrupting your society's culture, subverting its government, degrading its children, strangling its commerce, and generally poisoning everything they touch. Moreover, you are convinced that somehow, from far-off and unseen places, Jews are literally running—and *ruining*—the world. You believe and *feel* all this very deeply and powerfully.

Take a minute to conjure this up the best you can. (Just fake it, please.)

Okay. Now it's time to examine this supremely judgmental mindset objectively, dispassionately, clinically—as a scientist would. Are you ready?

What is this feeling you experience when you first breathe in Jew hatred—when you quietly, knowingly condemn "the Jews" and blame them for everything wrong in your life? What exactly is it you are experiencing?

Let me help you put it into words.

It's like the rush of a drug, but much more smooth, subtle, and refined, yet at the same time more potent and mind-altering. Before, you may have been wallowing in the anxiety and confusion many people feel over their problem-ridden lives. But now, having partaken of the consciousness-expanding "drug" of anti-Semitism, your thinking has been totally reorganized, revolving around your newly illuminated understanding of life. Suddenly everything makes sense. You are part of the world's elite, with esoteric knowledge of where all this evil is coming from. You totally understand both past and present.

But this "high" provides much more than just total clarity about who's good and who's evil. There is also a sense of what can truly be described as euphoria, exaltation, ecstasy, power, identity, "belongingness," a feeling of righteousness, a restoration of lost innocence. Yes, hatred and blame can confer counterfeits of all these qualities and more.

Confusion and ambivalence are replaced by noonday clarity. Helplessness is replaced by a sense of power. You feel as though the wisdom of the ages (after all, the Jews were always bad, weren't they?) courses through your veins, as the inexorable power of historical truth imparts to your previously wobbly thinking the strength of steel.

In short, the anti-Semitism drug has the power to transform a loser into a winner (only in his mind, of course). The way this is accomplished is the essence of simplicity. Instead of taking responsibility for our own problems, we blame them on others! Psychologists call it projection, or scapegoating.

Although, as we'll see, Jews make the best scapegoats, any person or group can serve the same basic purpose—someone on whom we can project guilt, blame, and hate.

But first, who would engage in such an unfair practice?

There are, in a sense, two types of people in the world: There are those who, regardless of how flawed or out of control they are, deep down want to face reality, want to understand what's wrong with them, and are willing to apologize to God or man for their offenses. Then there's everybody else—those who, despite all appearances to the contrary, don't really want to face reality and aren't truly interested in admitting their own failings or changing in any meaningful way. For the latter group, there's a tempting smorgasbord of options available to facilitate their escape from basic truth: drugs, alcohol, sex, even music and entertainment. The choices are virtually endless. But perhaps the most dangerous, certainly as addicting as any drug, is scapegoating.

In her book *The New Anti-Semitism,* author, feminist, and psychoanalyst Phyllis Chesler explains scapegoating this way:

[W]hen a man is angry at his boss, or at authority in general, but can't afford to express this anger directly lest he lose his job or his life, he might redirect his rage and frustration at his child or wife, who cannot hurt him and, as a vulnerable dependent, is a safe and ever-dependable target. Verbally abusing or beating his wife will not change his work conditions or the humiliation he may feel at work, but it may make him feel powerful over someone. Perhaps he has also internalized his boss's withering ways and when he visits such abuse on a wife or child, he may feel that here at least he is the boss.[17]

But what, asks Chesler, "if the problem one faces goes far beyond one's own working conditions and includes collective disasters such as plagues, earthquakes, sterility, and famine? Whom can an afflicted society then blame?" She recalls the European Catholic Church's executions of women accused of witchcraft—"that is," she writes, "of causing male impotence, miscarriages, abortions, crop failures, plagues, and other deeds that cannot be attributed to a loving, Christian God but only to Satan—and to his most intimate mortal companion, Woman."[18]

However, noting that the women thus accused of witchcraft "belonged to the same ethnic and national groups that denounced them and that then laid claim to their land and possessions," Chesler says the art of scapegoating was refined still further when later, in Spain and Portugal, "the Inquisition was carried out not against women but against Jews."[19]

Analyzing the advantages of targeting a separate group, as opposed to one's own group, Chesler concludes:

From a psychological point of view, if a man or many men—if entire nations—are suffering from poverty, disease, violence, and other conditions over which most individuals are helpless, perhaps the intimate family scapegoats—women, children, servants, and slaves, who may also be suffering—

cannot be targeted. Perhaps the more reliable scapegoat is not part of oneself, but a stranger, an outsider, not one's own wife or child. Nothing unites people who are otherwise and at all times divided as well as having a common enemy to scape-goat. . . .

Perhaps someone of a different race or religion might better serve as a scapegoat, the one who must suffer and atone for the people's sins. Perhaps perpetual evil may be perpetually embodied by one group in particular, a group that seems to exist everywhere but does not really fit in or belong. A group that resists fitting in, rejects belonging, prefers its own ways, its own kind; an indigenous, nomadic group—secretive, strange, "different," but worldly wise and well-traveled. Smart. Monied. Filled with ideas. Who better than the Jews?[20]

As we can see, projecting blame and guilt onto other people is a core survival strategy for the dark side of human nature. If we want to avoid taking responsibility for our own sins, we find a scapegoat. On the world stage, the Nazis blamed the Jews, the Turks blamed the Armenians, and the Japanese blamed the Chinese. But in our own lives, with infinite variations, most of us tend to play the same game—blaming each other for our problems.

SHOOTING THE MESSENGER

In fact, projecting our own inner darkness onto others is such a successful technique to avoid facing ourselves, we've even figured out how to turn inanimate objects into scapegoats—for instance, by attaching the hatred and violence within us to a lifeless piece of metal. I'm talking here about the fact that large numbers of us "hate," "are afraid of," or "are uncomfortable around" firearms.

Doesn't that seem odd? Guns are, without question, indispensable for restraining the evil intentions of criminals and tyrants.

Indeed, exhaustive research proves *more* guns in the hands of law-abiding citizens results in *less* crime.[21] Yet millions of us nevertheless consider guns almost inherently evil, and well-funded organizations are dedicated to banning them.

But the evil is not in the gun—it's in us. Nevertheless, if they make us feel uncomfortable, we conveniently blame the guns.

Do we dare examine the disturbing truth behind this common phenomenon? Warning: this is scary.

Microscope, please. Let's focus on the strange thoughts and feelings—never spoken, never acknowledged to anyone else, not even to ourselves—that arise from the depths of many of us in the presence of a loaded firearm sitting there on the table:

"Why don't you pick up that gun and blow your brains out?"
"You could kill a whole lot of people with that gun."
"Why not shoot her right now? That would shut her up!"

That's right. Dark thoughts and impulses, too horrible to dwell upon or even acknowledge, occur to many of us at the mere sight of a firearm or a naked blade. When we see the weapon, we sense the presence of evil—so naturally we assume the gun is its source, when actually the gun's close proximity caused our own buried, angry, violent tendencies to surface for a moment.

Thus many people who "dislike" or "are uncomfortable around" guns are actually afraid of *what they might do* if they had a loaded firearm in their hand. And I'm not talking about criminal types here. I'm talking about "nice" people—nice on the outside, and lots of buried and perhaps unrecognized rage inside. Again, the presence of the gun simply causes his or her own dark, angry propensities to "stir a little" deep down.

But the reality of all this is too heavy and "negative" for many of us to face, so we instantly and unconsciously project our own buried violence onto the gun, as though an inanimate hunk of metal, a tool, could somehow be intrinsically evil.

Obviously, a loaded gun has great potential for destruction and havoc—for evil. At the mere squeeze of a trigger there can be murder, suicide, terrorism. Even without being fired, the gun becomes the magic ticket to armed robbery, forcible rape, and every other form of coercion. For a person with lots of anger, albeit buried, a gun represents the shortest distance between two points: between the suppressed violent nature within him or her and the maximum expression of that nature. Therefore, the mere sight of a gun excites that dark part of us, causing it to beckon wordlessly, "Use me!"

Let's examine this admittedly spooky phenomenon a little more closely.

Have you ever stood close to the edge of a cliff, or out on a balcony of a tall building? Did you notice that some "force" almost seemed to want to pull you over the edge? Most of us have experienced something like this—a momentary loss of balance, an unexplainable fear, some mysterious pull toward the edge. We have a moment of disorientation and fear, then we pull back to safety.

In this life, the malevolent intelligence we call "evil" is constantly scanning each of us for opportunities to tempt or even destroy us. The Bible has a famous verse: "Be sober, be vigilant; because your adversary the devil, as a roaring lion, walketh about, seeking whom he may devour" (1 Peter 5:8). In critical moments of the sort I'm describing, evil seizes the opportunity to give us a mental "shove." Unfortunately, for some people that shove is strong enough, especially after a lifetime of giving in to anger, doubt, and despair, to pull them over the edge.

We'll never know how many "suicides," in which people tumbled off a cliff or a balcony, occurred this way—not because of a premeditated suicide plan, but because they were vulnerable to the opportunistic impulse of evil.

Similarly, how many head-on auto accidents occur because someone inexplicably crosses the centerline to crash at high speed into an oncoming car, having succumbed to a wordless, instantaneous mental suggestion from hell? All in a timeless fraction of a second the message impresses itself on your mind: *Crash your car into that one coming your way. Life sucks. Go out with a major bang! Everyone will be shocked! You have the power! Just do it! Do it now!*

Does this scare you? If so—if this description resonates with you even a little bit—it's only because you have the same problem to some degree. Don't worry, we're all in the same boat, all subject in some measure to the "dark side of the force." It's called being "born in sin." But some of us honestly face what's wrong with us, and quietly call out to God for help, and His help comes. Others live in denial—until tragedy and death end it all. (This is the central theme of the blockbuster film *Spider-Man 3*, by the way.)

In any event, this same phenomenon is at work with firearms, because of the potential they provide for immediate and ultimate destruction. Guns literally bring to the surface of the mind the suppressed potential for violence that exists inside every angry person. For that reason, they make a perfect scapegoat for people not ready to face their own darkness.

ALTERNATE DIMENSION

And what exactly is this "darkness" that plagues the human race, this subterranean, selfish, animalistic part of us that we labor so hard to suppress, disguise, deny, blame on others—or, justify as great righteousness?

What we need to understand is that becoming angry and resentful is literally like stepping into an alternate dimension. You think differently, you feel differently. When you're mad, your mind doesn't work the same as it normally does. It's almost as though you're connected to a different hard drive and a different operating system with different logic.

Different because, in a very real sense, the angry, resentful *you* is cut off from God, meaning disconnected from your usual calm, sensible mind that is overshadowed by conscience and intuition.

Instead, you're a conduit for something else—something not of God—that doesn't have your best interest at heart. After all, how many people are locked up in prison because they acted under the spell of anger, did something terrible, and later came to regret it for the rest of their lives?

We started off this exploration by looking at genocidal madmen, suicide bombers, and drug-dealing gangbangers. But truth be told, normal folks like you and me all have an anger problem, too. It's just a question of degree.

At one end of the anger continuum, you have utterly depraved people, consumed with rage, who have given themselves over to the lowest impulses and committed the most heinous acts imaginable. I'm talking about people like the Japanese solders in Nanking, gang-raping thousands of women and girls before slaughtering them, using the men as targets in bayonet competitions or else burning or burying them alive, and who sadistically perpetrated all manner of sexual atrocities on their victims, both male and female.[22] The only time we see comparable barbarity in Western society today is the infrequent news report of a lone serial killer or sadistic sexual psychopath.

But, moving along on our continuum now, for every one of those rare and extreme cases, tens of thousands of people every year commit serious violent crimes such as rape, assault, arson, armed robbery, and murder, and they all obviously have major anger issues. And for every one of those people, many more commit cruel, predatory acts below the radar of the criminal justice system. Likewise, for every one of *those*, many more are emotionally abusive to their families and others. You get the idea. That's a lot of people with anger problems. Eventually, though, we get to all the "normal" people. Right?

But what's really going on inside all these "normal" people?

Many of them are also full of hostility, but put a good face on it for the world; only their long-suffering families know the truth. Such emotional turmoil often leads to family breakdown and di-vorce, with millions of husbands and wives blaming each other for the disintegration of their marriages. Many "normal" people also smoke, drink, or take legal or illegal drugs to "take the edge off" all the accumulated anger inside.

"Normal" people's anger frequently causes or exacerbates illness, as reaffirmed in a major study in the *Journal of the American College of Cardiology,* which "links changes brought on by anger or other strong emotions to future arrhythmias and sudden cardiac arrests, which are blamed for 400,000 deaths annually," according to Science*Daily*.[23]

Who's left? What about those who don't commit crimes, don't smoke, drink, or take drugs to anesthetize their anger, aren't openly belligerent, or divorcing, or having a heart attack due to excessive emotion? Are they free of this inner darkness that, in larger concentrations, fuels genocides and destroys civilizations?

Microscope, please, this time focused on you and me, the "normal" person. Let's pick a simple, mundane activity—say, we're driving our car through town. As we observe the other drivers and pedestrians, many of us are secretly reacting emotionally to almost everything we see. It may be too subtle for us to notice, or maybe the stereo drowns out our perception, or maybe we're just so accustomed to reacting emotionally to everything we believe it's "normal." But for many of us, here's the subaudible "buzz" of our inner lives:

We notice someone driving a nicer car than ours: *twinge of envy.* We see someone behind the wheel of an older, banged-up car: *slight whiff of superiority.* Someone is driving too fast, causing a traffic hazard: *flash of resentment.* Or someone's driving too slowly, causing us to have to slow down: *annoyance.* And so on. There aren't enough words to describe all the subtle flits of negative emotion we generate each day as we move through life, but a great deal of it amounts to—and forgive me for dispensing now with all the euphemisms— resentment or hate. Envy is a tiny bit of hate. Contempt is a tiny bit of hate. Anger at an unaware driver who almost caused an accident is a tiny bit of hate. Impatience at the driver in front of us going too slowly is a tiny bit of hate.

Why do we experience such "tiny bits of hate"? Why do we compulsively become impatient with the slowpoke in front of us?

Impatience is literally our making *what we want* (to go faster) more important than *what is right* (God's commandment that we be patient with our neighbor's shortcomings). It's making our will more important than His will—in other words, playing god. Despite all the excuses we make to justify it, impatience is just a selfish, immature, unloving reaction to life. Sorry—truth hurts.

What's more, anger generates an illusion that we're strong, simply because it *feels* like strength. It's not. It's actually a terrible weakness, one that wreaks havoc on everyone around us.

My friend Rabbi Daniel Lapin comes to much the same conclusion when he writes, "anger is one of the most self-destructive of all human behaviors. It shatters romantic, social, and business relationships—and rightly so. Why should anyone have to endure the abuse regularly dished out by someone who can't control his temper?"

Interestingly, adds Lapin, "almost every human characteristic, both positive and negative, has its place, with the exception of anger":

> There is never any circumstance that demands that you become angry. Please note that I do not say, "Never *display* anger." Instead, I say, "Never *be* angry." In other words, there may well be many management situations, both at home and at work, where radiating an impression of being really upset, even angry, might be called for. But that is entirely different from really being angry. Being angry means you are out of control.
>
> What causes anger? Arrogance. Show me someone who readily loses his temper and showers those around him with angry yells and insults, and I'll show you a very arrogant man. Anger is the emotion you feel when you are not being treated with what you consider to be appropriate respect. When I erupt in obscene fury at a traffic jam that threatens to make

me tardy for an appointment, what I am really saying is, "How dare they! How dare they make me late! Don't they know how important I am?" Were I to be as humble as I should be, almost nothing would make me feel anger.[24]

Unfortunately, it's "human nature" for us to justify our own anger, as though someone else's wrongdoing gives us the moral right to be upset and resentful in response. But how, then, do we explain the most famous case of forgiveness in history, when Jesus Christ demonstrated total forbearance toward his tormentors, even asking God to forgive them? Moreover, he had earlier commanded his followers to do likewise, to love one another "as I have loved you," that is, to love each other with the brand of love he had—unselfish, without anger and frustration, indeed without the slightest irritation or impatience. "A new commandment I give unto you, That ye love one another; as I have loved you, that ye also love one another" (John 13:34).

If such forbearance is desirable and even vital to our ultimate happiness, why then is it so hard to stop being angry and to exercise real patience, which is pretty much the same as real love? Because letting go of hostility feels as though we're giving up something very important, something we need and *deserve* to feel, something necessary and justified. In reality, the reason our resentments feel so justified, so righteous, is that they're feeding our pride, which feels like life itself to us. Yet, whether we recognize it or not, we're just nourishing everything that's wrong with us.

Oddly, our own anger virtually always *appears* (to our pride) to be righteous, offering us a strange and shadowy illusion of genuine nobility. Thus irritation and snapping at our children are a perversion of firm but patient correction. Resentment at injustice is a perversion of genuine righteous indignation.

Even being a suicide bomber is a perversion of true godly martyrdom. Remember our inquiry into why radical Islamist indoctrination so effectively induces many to forsake their natural love of life and embrace death? Jihadist wannabes can buy into such murderous insanity precisely because their insanity happens to closely parallel the truth! After all, self-sacrifice, martyrdom—giving up one's life for God—*is* great and noble and honorable. *Foxe's Book of Martyrs,* an encyclopedic compilation of true stories of Christian martyrdom, was one of the most popular books in the Protestant world from the sixteenth through the nineteenth centuries. Genuine martyrdom is an exceedingly high calling, as is standing up and courageously opposing evil oppressors—exactly what jihadists are told they are doing when they're slaughtering innocent men, women, and children. What they're being taught has the resonance of truth, although they end up embracing a hideous perversion of truth.

IS THERE A WAY OUT?

Most of us live in something of an emotional prison for much of our lives. Like the man I know who, as a child, was shoved into the water by another child as a prank, and from then on, for the rest of his life, remained afraid of the water and never learned to swim. Why did that one experience result in such a lasting negative impact, and why didn't he get over it? Or the woman I know who, as a teenager, was betrayed by her first boyfriend, who pretended he truly cared about her but just exploited her sexually and then dumped her. After that, she did something many women do: she became very overweight to "protect" herself from the unwanted lustful attentions of other men, and she remained obese, and single, for the rest of her life. Why didn't she get over it and go on to better things and better relationships?

Why do some people recover from such traumas and others don't?

There's one powerful factor that good psychology, good religion, common sense, and experience all converge upon, and that's forgiveness. True forgiveness is healing. The individual who forgives can move on, while the other remains burdened by the trauma until he or she learns to let it go. As adults, many of us still harbor resentments against injustices and insults meted out to us decades earlier, and somehow that resentment—evidence of our failure to truly forgive the offender—keeps the trauma alive in us.

The first step to forgiving, which means giving up our resentment, is surely to realize deeply that the hostility we feel—or anger, irritation, impatience, upset, envy, contempt, exasperation, annoyance, aggravation, bitterness, "hurt feelings," "hard feelings," and all the other euphemisms we employ to avoid calling it what it really is: hate—is a bad thing, period. When we justify it, we keep it alive. Yet despite all the rationalizations we come up with—political, practical, psychological, and even biblical—to justify hate as okay, it's not. In fact, the very reason we all have an "anger problem" is that anger is the necessary food for pride, and pride is at the very core of most of our problems in this life.

For us to truly overcome the compulsion to become upset, for us to resolve buried rage and resentments, in other words, to discover forgiveness toward all the flawed people who have wronged us, hurt us, shaped our very lives, we need God's help. To recognize our own flaws, to repent truly, to forgive deeply, to be "cleansed of sin," we need God.

Yet for all the talk about God, and for all the pulpit reminders that Jesus Christ died to cancel out our sins, the world today is filled largely with broken people. In the next chapter we'll explore the question of how to have "a closer walk" with the Living God.

CHAPTER 10

SO, WHERE ON EARTH IS GOD?

Rare Insights from Persecuted Saints of the Past

Nearly Half of Americans Uncertain God Exists: Poll
  —Agence France-Presse, October 31, 2006

Born-Again Christians Mirror Nation's Divorce Trend
  —*Chicago Sun-Times*, August 10, 2001

Survey Shows Only 9% of Christians Have Biblical Worldview
  —WorldNetDaily.com, December 3, 2003

If there's a cure for the evil in our lives, most people assume it has to come from God.

But doing an entire chapter about God is pretty challenging, since all we have is words—hieroglyphs on a page—with which to explore realities and realms far beyond words. For example, how can the words *heaven* and *hell* possibly convey anything like what heaven and hell are really like? Moreover, most of the religious or spiritual words available to us in the English language have been sullied by overuse and misuse; so if I use one of them, the meaning or association that word conjures up in your mind might be very different from what I intended.

Thus trying to discuss the Almighty in a fresh and meaningful way can be a little like walking through a minefield—the minefield of our own minds. But let's give it a try anyway. Nothing is more important in this life than walking with God. And, as we'll presently see, many good and courageous people have suffered tremendous persecution to pass on some simple, life-giving truths to the rest of us.

To begin with, let's ask the obvious question: If God is everywhere, why do so few people seem to be able to find Him? By "find Him," I don't mean just clinging to a vague notion that God exists, but rather, experiencing an intimate, moment-to-moment flow of understanding, guidance, and the special energy called "grace," coming directly from Him to us. After all, not only is God omnipresent, but we're told His desire is to have a personal relationship with each of us, whom He created in His image—to direct our paths and become our ultimate destiny. In other words, to be our God.

Why, then, are so many of us so lost?

Jesus Christ made this mysterious imbalance painfully clear when he stated, "Broad is the way that leadeth to destruction, and many there be which go in thereat: Because strait is the gate, and narrow is the way, which leadeth unto life, and few there be that find it" (Matthew 7:13–14).

That's pretty tough talk for a soft generation like ours, where comfort is king and instant gratification is expected in all areas of life, including the spiritual. It grates on our psyches to hear that only "few" find the genuine path "which leadeth unto life." Such words, even from Jesus, just don't seem to be in sync with our modern notions of "cheap grace" and stadiums full of people being instantly "saved" in great crusades and the like.

Let's take a little journey of discovery together, past the babble and bombast of the modern institutional church with all its high-profile problems—from lesbian ministers to subversive leftist political agendas to emotion-drenched, entertainment-oriented "worship services"—and venture out into the open fields and fresh air of honest, uncomplicated reflection on the actual message of Christ.

If we're blessed, maybe we'll glean a better understanding of how to stay on the "strait and narrow" path through this life—so full of wonder and adventure, yes, but also full of temptations and predators intent on pulling us into the side brush and devouring us.

WIDESPREAD DISILLUSIONMENT

First, let's acknowledge a painful truth: though 4 out of 5 Americans today call themselves Christians, most don't seem to have a clue about what it means to "follow Christ."

For example, only 9 percent of those self-identifying as "born-again Christians" even hold a biblical worldview, according to Christian pollster George Barna, whose organization has been tracking believers for more than two decades. Almost half of "born-agains"— 45 percent—teach their children there are no absolute values.

"You might expect that parents who are born-again Christians would take a different approach to raising their children than did parents who have not committed their life to Christ, but that was rarely the case," Barna said.[1] In fact, said the pollster, "For years we have reported research findings showing that born-again adults think and behave very much like everyone else. It often seems that their faith makes very little difference in their life."[2]

This brings us to painful truth number two: our churches, wracked by scandals and controversy, don't seem to be doing a great job of shepherding a righteous nation. In fact, according to Barna's 2005 book, *Revolution,* "Committed, born-again Christians are exiting the established church in massive numbers."[3]

Why are they leaving? In *Why Men Hate Going to Church,* author David Murrow documents the feminization of the modern church, which the author says caters to women, children, and the elderly by creating a safe, boring, predictable environment. Although many men, he insists, really do desire an authentic faith experience, they consider run-of-the-mill church services to be tedious and irrelevant. (Interestingly, this is much the same observation critics of public education have made about today's schools—that they're geared more toward holding girls' attention than boys'.)

One result of this crisis is the growth of the home-church movement, something basically unheard-of a generation ago, but experiencing rapid growth in recent years. As the *Washington Post* reported, "A growing number of Christians across Washington and around the country are moving to home churches, both as a way to create personal connections in the age of the megachurch and as a return to the blueprint of the Christian church spelled out in the New Testament, which describes Jesus and the apostles teaching small groups in people's homes."[4]

How widespread is dissatisfaction with traditional churches? Barna "estimates that since 2000, more than 20 million Americans have begun exploring alternative forms of worship, including home churches, workplace ministries and online faith communities," reported the *Post*. Startlingly, Barna predicts that "over the next two decades, traditional churches will lose half their 'market share' to these alternative start-ups."

As we've seen in these pages, widespread disillusionment with modern Christianity has contributed to many other things, including an upsurge in the popularity of pagan, New Age, Eastern, and other religions and philosophies, not to mention a major escalation, and even growing cultural cachet, in militant atheism.

What's going on? If 80-plus percent of Americans are Christians, attending tens of thousands of church services every week brimming with music, prayers, sermons, ceremonies, and missionary outreaches, why is America rapidly losing her very identity as a Christian nation? With the country dangerously polarized, and millions of families disintegrating, including many Christian families, where is God? How come He's not infusing each believer's life with meaning and direction and joy and power, as all the clergymen say He will? How come so many "born-again Christians" are getting divorced, taking antidepressants, hooked on online porn, or just plain confused, resentful, and dissatisfied with life?

Even among those churchgoers who believe they're "full of the spirit," truth be told, many are just emotionally high on religious excitement, ever needful of being pumped up again every week at church. Yet in their quiet, honest, reflective moments they have to admit—if they're sincere—that something about their Christian walk is just not quite real. Not yet.

Somehow, too many of our churches have lost the essence of what it means to walk with God and have filled the vacuum with either excitement and entertainment or dry theology and ceremony. Bottom line, writes Murrow about today's churches: "If we want to shed our reputation as a place for little old ladies of both sexes, we must recapture the challenge of following Jesus."[5]

"Following Jesus." That sounds awesome. But what do those words really mean? How do we actually "follow Jesus"? We all parrot the same phrases ("I've committed my life to Christ," "I do it all for God") we've heard from others, who in turn are repeating what they've heard from still others. But how many of us really understand deeply, firsthand, what the heaven we're talking about?

Christianity is a spiritual religion, not a legalistic one like Islam, where you can please Allah by diligently performing rituals such as praying a certain number of times a day while kneeling in a certain position on a certain type of rug facing in a certain direction. Anyone, including someone with an unspiritual or even violently deranged mind, is capable of fulfilling such requirements—just out of fear, or desire for reward.

But the Christian faith is very different. How do you mechanically, legalistically "follow Jesus"? Where is he? Obviously, you can't accomplish this without genuine understanding from God. When scripture says, "Let this mind be in you, which was also in Christ Jesus" (Philippians 2:5), what does that mean? How do you get his mind in you? Brain surgery? When Jesus said, "Ye must be born again" (John 3:7), Nicodemus asked, "How can a man be born when he is old? Can he enter the second time into his mother's womb, and be born?" (John 3:4). He was thinking mechanically, not spiritually. When we read, "Be not conformed to this world: but be ye transformed by the renewing of your mind" (Romans 12:2), what do these instructions really mean? How do you renew your mind?

These scriptures aren't just feel-good religious mantras for us to nod our heads to as the minister recites them. They mean something—something powerful, essential, and thoroughly *real,* just as real as the sun shining overhead.

PERSECUTED

To try to shed some light on this, let's start by going back a few hundred years. Back before the shallowness and soullessness of the modern secular era. Back when being a "good Christian" wasn't quite so easy. Back when such things as introspection and repentance, moral character and "dying to self" were considered essential to living a righteous life, acceptable and pleasing to God.

Consider the advice one of America's Founding Fathers, William Penn, founder of Pennsylvania, gave his own children on the subject of finding God:

> So soon as you wake, retire your mind into a pure silence from all thoughts and ideas of worldly things, and in that frame wait upon God, to feel His good presence, to lift up your hearts to Him, and commit your whole self into his blessed care and protection. Then rise, if well, immediately; being dressed, read a chapter or more in the Scriptures, and afterwards dispose yourselves for the business of the day, ever remembering that God is present the overseer of all your thoughts, words, and actions, and demean yourselves, my dear children, accordingly, and do not you dare to do that in his holy, all-seeing presence, which you would be ashamed a man, yea, a child, should see you do.

And as you have intervals from your lawful occasions, delight to step home (within yourselves, I mean), commune with your own hearts and be still; and, as Nebuchadnezzar said on another occasion, One like the Son of God you shall find and enjoy with you and in you: a treasure the world knows not of, but is the aim, end, and diadem of the children of God. This will bear you up against all temptations, and carry you sweetly and evenly—through your day's business, supporting you under disappointments, and moderating your satisfaction in success and prosperity.[6]

"One like the Son of God you shall find and enjoy with you and in you"—that's an extraordinary statement. Penn, a Quaker and close friend of the movement's founder, George Fox, is quite dramatically saying God can somehow be found in stillness, echoing David the psalmist, who wrote, "Be still, and know that I am God" (Psalm 46:10).

However, for his insights, Penn was arrested and imprisoned several times in England, before deciding to seek refuge from religious persecution in America.

Then there's the famous sixteenth-century Catholic priest St. John of the Cross, who authored the Christian classic *Dark Night of the Soul* and others. He said this: "Love consists not in feeling great things but in having great detachment and in suffering for the Beloved." Excuse me, but that sounds basically *opposite* to virtually everything else written and said about happiness in today's world. St. John also said this: "If you purify your soul of attachment to and desire for things, you will understand them spiritually. If you deny your appetite for them, you will enjoy their truth, understanding what is certain in them."

This is pretty mysterious talk: either poetic religious babble, or profound insight. Which is it? We spend our entire lives coveting and acquiring the possessions and relationships we figure will make us happy. And now, here we're being told by some supposedly spiritual person that, to actually find true and lasting happiness, we must somehow forsake these very desires. How? Why?

By the way, for his efforts at religious reform, John was imprisoned by religious authorities and flogged publicly every week, only to be returned to isolation in a tiny cell barely large enough for his body.

And then there was Jeanne Guyon, the seventeenth-century French author of many Christian books, including *Experiencing the Depths of Jesus Christ*. She gently nudges believers in the direction of "retreating inward, and seeking after tranquility of mind" in order to do all things "as in the Divine presence." In *A Guide to True Peace,* Guyon and her two co-authors wrote:

> "Every man is tempted, when he is drawn away of his own lust, and enticed." Therefore, know your own state, and the need you have to be purified by means of temptation, and keep always on the watch, lest the unwearied enemy gain access to your souls by his insinuations and pleasing allurements, which he will suit to your present situation and condition: for, in your passage through life, there are many things which he will offer you as temptations; endeavoring to produce in you an inordinate inclination and desire for them; which if you give way to while you are in this manner tempted, great will be the danger of your being wholly overcome.
>
> If the malignant enemy is not resisted in his first attack, he enters by gradual advances, and takes entire possession of the heart: and so long as opposition is deferred by habitual negligence, the power of opposing becomes every day less, and the strength of the adversary proportionally greater. Therefore, when you feel in yourselves a strong and eager desire after anything whatsoever, and find your inclinations carry you too precipitately to do it, strive to moderate yourselves by retreat-

ing inward, and seeking after tranquility of mind. To do all things well, we must do them as in the Divine presence, otherwise we shall soon get off our right center, and be in danger of being wholly overthrown.[7]

There's that "give-up-your-desires" theme again. One might understandably wonder what's going on with these people—are they all against enjoying life? Quite the contrary, as will soon become clear.

Oh yes, for Guyon's so-called Quietist teachings she was sternly condemned as a heretic by the Catholic Church, and the French government imprisoned her in the Bastille from 1698 to 1703. Her co-authors, Michael Molinos and François Fénelon, were also punished for heresy. However, many prominent clergymen revered Guyon and her teachings—from John Wesley, founder of the Methodist Church, to Charles Spurgeon, dubbed the "prince of preachers" during the nineteenth century. Whatever doctrinal reasons the Catholic Church might have had for rejecting Guyon, it's hard to dispute the classic wisdom espoused here of seeking God in stillness.

Now let's try to make sense of what these and other deep Christian thinkers who have advocated self-awareness and repentance—many of whom were persecuted, imprisoned, and sometimes tortured and executed by religious or secular authorities—have been saying through the centuries about truly finding God. And let's talk about it not in flowery medieval verse or elusive metaphors, but in plain, modern English.

TUG OF WAR

First, we need to realize that there's a tug of war going on inside each of us. On one side there's our conscience, which is primarily how God makes His presence within us known. But there's also a malevolent intelligence within each of us that exists to confuse us, to cause us to doubt truth, to tempt us to become angry and upset, with the aim that we ultimately will rebel against our God-given conscience.

This is the fundamental dynamic of our lives. How we address ourselves to it determines our values, decisions, relationships, our very destiny. That's why a Judeo-Christian understanding of life—that man is indeed a "fallen being" and saddled with a "sin nature" in competition with our more sincere, searching side, which is compatible with God's influence—is essential. It's not just a "religion" or "philosophy." It's *reality*, the way things actually are, and without recognition of this reality, life never makes sense, we can't deal with stresses gracefully, we can't understand how evil works, and we can't find the "strait and narrow" way to true life.

Stated simply, our core problem is that we're all born with a troublesome nature called "pride." This is the part of us that wants to be like God. It loves being praised, quickly puffs up with angry judgment over the real or perceived wrongs of others, and as a rule is oblivious to its own faults. Moreover, we can think of pride as a "life-form"—a living, breathing "something" that like any other life-form or "creature," can be fed or starved. When it's fed, it grows and enlarges; when it is starved, it diminishes and dies. This is what Paul the apostle was talking about when he wrote, "I die daily" (1 Corinthians 15:31).

As our pride (or "sin self") diminishes and dies through our obedience to God, the direct result is that our "good side," our true, God-centered character and identity, enlarges.

We're not talking about matters of religious dogma here, nor is this just a matter of outward behaviors and "good works." This is about real change, about transformation, the mysterious heart of the true Christian life, about "dying to the world." That's not an archaic, poetic, or hopelessly idealistic notion, but rather the very heartbeat of a mature person's everyday life, as we deal with stresses and problems ("trials and tribulations") in our lives.

Thus these persecuted Christian teachers whose words we've just shared are simply focused on drawing closer to God by starving their pride—their "dark side," the "born-in-sin" nature that most of us are unwittingly feeding all the time. The selfish pursuit of comfort, security, and pleasure, the constant quest for new "highs," the lust for power and prestige, as well as escape into entertainment, food, porn, drugs, whatever, all have a way of enlarging our pride, which causes ever-growing conflict with our conscience. It also "protects" us from clearly seeing our sins and rising above them. This is what Jesus was talking about when He said, "He that loveth his life shall lose it; and he that hateth his life in this world shall keep it unto life eternal" (John 12:25). The apostle John expressed the same idea in this well-known verse: "Love not the world, neither the things that are in the world. If any man love the world, the love of the Father is not in him. For all that is in the world, the lust of the flesh, and the lust of the eyes, and the pride of life, is not of the Father, but is of the world. And the world passeth away, and the lust thereof: but he that doeth the will of God abideth for ever" (1 John 2:15–17).

I realize this is worlds apart not only from all that today's pop psychology teaches, but also from much of what the modern church preaches. Be that as it may, it is the deep core of what the godly life once was understood to be in Christendom. Let us, then, explore it further.

Many believers throughout the centuries have struggled to extinguish their desires for "all that is in the world" by separating themselves physically from temptation, for example, by living in a monastery, or overcoming selfishness by giving away all their money, or keeping away from the opposite gender to quell the "desires of the flesh."

But truly, God does not require this of us. We don't need to live in a cave, nor necessarily to fast from food. We do need, however, to discover how to "fast" from hatred, resentment, and unforgiveness, the food of pride, which sustains everything that's gone awry in us.

To better understand what Christian leaders of the past have suffered and died to tell us about Christ's message, consider now the words of Jesus himself. In fact, let's focus on a one-word command the Messiah urged his followers to take to heart on many occasions: The word is . . . *Watch*.

"WATCH AND PRAY"

As he prepared to pray in the garden of Gethsemane, shortly before his mock trial and execution, Jesus told a few of his disciples who were with him to "watch and pray."

> And he cometh unto the disciples, and findeth them asleep, and saith unto Peter, What, could ye not watch with me one hour? Watch and pray, that ye enter not into temptation: the spirit indeed is willing, but the flesh is weak (Matthew 26:40–41).

> And saith unto them, My soul is exceeding sorrowful unto death: tarry ye here, and watch (Mark 14:34).

One might be tempted to think, *Well, I guess Jesus was just telling Peter and the other disciples to stay awake and "watch" him during his hour of need in Gethsemane.* Or, in the context of a verse like this one—"Watch ye therefore, and pray always, that ye may be accounted worthy to escape all these things that shall come to pass, and to stand before the Son of man" (Luke 21:36)—we might conclude, *He must want us to watch current events so we can predict the end of the world before it actually arrives.* But this would be widely missing the mark. The instruction to "watch" is found throughout the New Testament.

On many occasions, Jesus gives this mysterious command to "watch": "And what I say unto you I say unto all, Watch" (Mark 13:37). Likewise, Paul said to the people of Corinth: "Watch ye, stand fast in the faith, quit you like men, be strong" (1 Corinthians 16:13). To the church in Colossae, he exhorted: "Continue in prayer, and watch in the same with thanksgiving" (Colossians 4:2). To the Thessalonians, Paul said: "Therefore let us not sleep, as do others; but let us watch and be sober" (1 Thessalonians 5:6). In his letter to Timothy, Paul wrote: "But watch thou in all things, endure afflictions, do the work of an evangelist, make full proof of thy ministry" (2 Timothy 4:5). Peter said dramatically: "But the end of all things is at hand: be ye therefore sober, and watch unto prayer" (1 Peter 4:7). Most sobering, in the Book of Revelation, is Jesus's admonition to the human race: "Remember therefore how thou hast received and heard, and hold fast, and repent. If therefore thou shalt not watch, I will come on thee as a thief, and thou shalt not know what hour I will come upon thee" (Revelation 3:3).

What is this special "watching" that Jesus and his disciples are talking about? What exactly does Paul mean by "Watch thou in all things"? Or Jesus, when He says, "Watch and pray, that ye enter not into temptation"? Clearly, this is an admonition to be watchful of what's going on *within us,* because that's where temptation makes its approach and attempts to overtake us.

Watching is introspection—literally, "looking inward." Our conscious mind—that's the part of us that's aware right now of the ticking of the clock on the wall, or the refrigerator humming—can either be totally absorbed in our thoughts and feelings (as in a daydream) or it can watch those same thoughts and feelings objectively.

God gave us the capacity to dispassionately observe our own thoughts, our emotional reactions to stressful situations, our upsets, angers, and so on—all that transpires in these mortal bodies and minds. To be a watcher, then, is to understand ourselves, and others. However, objectively observing our own thoughts and feelings takes a genuine commitment to Truth. Why? Because when we are honestly introspective, we tend to see what's wrong with us, and really prideful people can't stand to do that.

Yet if we're willing to be truly aware of the sometimes strange thoughts and feelings within us, to watch the ongoing machinations of our own sin nature, in other words, something amazing may start to happen. Once we're a little separate from our constant rehashing of the past and worrying about the future, and instead remain focused on what we are observing inside us right now, we're actually closer to God. And in that stillness and poise we're able to see our own flaws with a new type of clarity, insight, and innocence that leads to real change.

It's as though we're allowing a light to shine on our failings merely by quietly, faithfully watching them. This is actually not a metaphor, but an expression of reality. When we stand back and "watch all things" honestly, as Paul prescribed, we're literally allowing God's light to shine in our souls and purge the "things of the darkness." In contrast, when we're thrashing around "down there" in our thoughts and emotions, trying desperately to solve our problems with worry and frustration, we're literally blocking His light.

Here's an extraordinary description of this situation from John the apostle: "Here is the message we heard from him [Jesus] and pass on to you: that God is light, and in him there is no darkness at all. If we claim to be sharing in his life while we walk in the dark, our words and our lives are a lie; but if we walk in the light as he himself is in the light, then we share together a common life, and we are being cleansed from every sin by the blood of Jesus his Son" (1 John 1:5–7, NET). Do you get what he's saying? He's saying if we allow the light of God to shine within us on our sins, simply by our willingness to face them honestly, then we are at that very moment being forgiven and cleansed by Christ's sacrifice. What a magnificent truth!

FLOATING DOWN THE RIVER

Okay, let's bring this "watching" thing down to earth.

Suppose, for example, you suffer from back pain. Almost always, physical pain also gives rise to emotions: maybe resentment toward the discomfort, still more anger over the accident that led to the injury, and perhaps intimidation and fear with regard to possible future pain and disability. And so we wallow in this debilitating jumble of physical and emotional pain. But what if you were to stand back, so to speak, and observe the back pain objectively, as well as the emotions that surface? You might find that although the physical pain remains, the emotions—if you watch them diligently without wallowing in them or feeding them—gradually dissipate. And pain without the attendant resentment is far easier to endure.

Truth be told, our normal waking mental state is a turbulent, ever-churning mixture of thoughts and feelings and unconscious mental riffraff. If we think of our thought stream as a flowing river full of driftwood and debris, then we're accustomed to floating down the river with it, swept along with the swirl of our own thoughts. Where we really need to be, however, is sitting on the bank of the river, watching the thoughts and feelings go by.

What do we do if we're watching ourselves and notice something really ignoble or rotten inside us? Say we detect a subtle feeling of satisfaction over somebody else's misfortune. Or we may notice irritation or resentment toward little children for their carefree innocence, because it reminds us of our lack of those qualities. This is somewhat painful to realize, but there's a bit of darkness that's made a home inside us during all the years when the light of God wasn't so welcome in us and we were emotionally reacting to the cruelties and confusion of everyone around us. But it's all right: we don't have to do anything to "fix" it. Just relax and suffer it graciously, which means don't deny it and don't hate it. Rather, watch—and pray.

Suppose we become aware of a big ball of rage deep down inside us. Almost everyone reading these words has an anger problem of one kind or another—it's epidemic in the human race. We bury the angers and resentments of our youth, and then unknowingly continue to feed "the beast" with daily doses of irritation and upset. Although this rage is suppressed and often out of view, it's perfectly positioned to spill out and spoil our life and marriage, and perhaps to cause some dreadful disease to boot. But rage too can be observed, and if we're not intimidated by the big anger bully inside us, but calmly and steadfastly watch it, it too will gradually yield to the light of observation and slowly lose its hold on us.

What about lust? When a man sees an attractive woman and experiences lustful thoughts toward her, part of him knows it's wrong. He has a conscience—plus, Jesus said that "whosoever looketh on a woman to lust after her hath committed adultery with her already in his heart" (Matthew 5:28). And of course the Ten Commandments affirm the same thing, that "thou shalt not covet thy neighbor's wife" (Exodus 20:17). So, how to deal with this? By watching that lustful impulse in an objective way. If we just watch it, but don't get carried downstream with it, we observe it out of existence, by God's grace. We're actually being separated from the sin by patiently watching it and 1) no longer agreeing with it and wallowing in it, nor 2) resentfully struggling with it. Both just enlarge the problem, but simple, faithful watching weakens the hold sin has on us.

Impatience with what we observe in ourselves masquerades as some sort of righteous attempt to fix ourselves. But in reality it's just more pride and faithlessness. If we really had faith in God, we wouldn't have the compulsion to try to fix ourselves (which never works anyway) through anger and frustration.

What about worry? When Jesus says, "Which of you by taking thought can add one cubit unto his stature?" (Matthew 6:27), we understand him to mean that we shouldn't fall to worrying. But how do we not worry? It's a compulsive mental activity that plagues all of us when we're lacking in real faith. In an effort to stop worrying, do we just manufacture some sort of emotionalized faith, quote some Bible verses, and turn up the "praise" music on the radio? No, because underneath it all, the worry is still there, and when we lie down in bed at night the worry thoughts flood back into our mind. Just watch it—and pray.

Watching objectively can be painful, because we're literally moving *toward* our conflict with God, rather than running away from it toward comfort and distraction—which is basically what most everything else in the world offers us. Think of it this way: It's as though we're walking down the street and we see, far off, someone coming toward us whom we have previously wronged. The closer we get to him, the more anxious and agitated we feel. We have an urge to cross the street, or turn around and walk the other way. Excuses rise up in our mind as to why we shouldn't face him—"Not now; it's not the right time; he probably hasn't forgiven me; I'll be late for my appointment," etc. But if we don't wimp out, once we come right up to him and apologize plainly and guilelessly for what we did, it's over—and we feel lighthearted for the rest of the day, free as a bird, as if we've won a great victory. Indeed we have.

When the one we reconcile with is our Creator, the result is peace with God. The other kind of "peace" we can choose is peace apart from God. The more we get lost in distraction, pleasure, food, drink, entertainment, vice, or any of a thousand other possible escapes, the further we get from conscience and the necessary conflict it causes us.

That pinpoints the difference between the kind of "stillness" experience that Christian saints espouse and the counterfeit variety Eastern and New Age gurus offer. The former brings peace *with* God, because we've literally gone in the direction of conscience and conflict, by facing our sins. The latter facilitates peace *without* God by taking us in the opposite direction—away from conscience. Remember this: with false spirituality, despite all the nice talk about God and being one with the cosmos and all that, there is no repentance. And how could there be, when its very purpose is to relieve our inner conflicts by taking us as far away from our conscience as possible, which is exactly what mantra meditations do?

Thus "being still" in the Judeo-Christian tradition doesn't mean blocking thoughts or imposing some Eastern-type empty-minded stillness (by suppressing thought) or muttering a mantra under our breath. Rather, it simply means observing ourselves with the utmost sincerity: "watching" our thoughts, feelings, problems, and upsets, in a way that effortlessly calls out to God for help.

So you see, when St. John of the Cross says, "If you purify your soul of attachment to and desire for things, you will understand them spiritually," he's not spouting mystical mumbo jumbo. He's saying: when you separate yourself from temptation—not physically, but just by observing the subtle strings of temptation pulling on your frail body of sin, and allow God to do the rest—you're "purify[ing] your soul of attachment to and desire for things."

When Jeanne Guyon warns us, "When you feel in yourselves a strong and eager desire after anything whatsoever, and find your inclinations carry you too precipitately to do it, strive to moderate yourselves by retreating inward, and seeking after tranquility of mind," the "tranquility of mind" and "moderation" of our urges she's talking about are the natural consequence of watching patiently and faithfully.

Therefore, to overcome selfishness, we don't need to give away all our money to the poor. We just need to watch—that is, observe honestly—our selfishness, and resist the temptation to fix it (as though God needs help in fixing us). Don't try to compensate by being "generous"—that's phony. Don't get mad at yourself for being selfish—that's more pride (the cause of selfishness). Simple, honest observation of our compulsively sinful tendencies is sufficient for God to transform us through genuine repentance.

WHERE IS FAITH?

Our mind has an incredible capacity for fooling us, for manufacturing fake righteousness, "right" thoughts, and "right" behaviors. But it's all an act. It is only through soberly seeing and comprehending our own sin thoughts and feelings, and allowing ourselves to experience the natural, gentle embarrassment and pain God graces us with, that we change, that we are "transformed by the renewing of our minds" (Romans 12:2).

What about faith? The first step to discovering real faith is admitting honestly that we don't have it yet. Emotional excitement isn't faith. Sorry—it's just not. Singing praise songs, memorizing Bible verses, or even being a Bible scholar—none of these require faith. Don't get me wrong: there's absolutely nothing wrong with memorizing Bible verses and singing hymns and learning Greek and Hebrew. They're just not faith and don't require faith.

So where is faith? Well, remember that always crouching at our mind's doorstep is faith's nemesis—doubt. And the way to deal with doubt and the malevolent spirit behind it is by watching it objectively. We can't wrestle doubt to the ground, outthink it, outsmart it, out-trick it, or overpower it. We can't overcome it by getting mad at it, dialoguing with it, or struggling with it in any way whatsoever. That just enlarges the doubt. But here's the wonderful truth hidden in all of this: simply and quietly recognizing doubt as doubt is evidence of a little bit of real faith. Think about it.

Many of us have been led to believe that holding on to certain correct beliefs and doctrines will save us. But it's possible to affirm all the right stuff yet still remain full of pride, hypocrisy, and worse.

The "strait and narrow" path is not ultimately paved with doctrine, vital as sound doctrine is, but rather with humility, repentance, forgiveness, and effortless transformation. The good thief on the cross—to whom Jesus promised, "Today shalt thou be with me in paradise" (Luke 23:43)—didn't know anything about the trinity or any other doctrinal points, and he probably hadn't been baptized. All he had was a humble spirit, a contrite heart, and a relationship with Christ. We need to be more like the good thief.

Watching the sin nature inside us and deeply realizing what a hold it has on us, we are moved not only to repentance, but to forgiveness toward those who have wronged us. After all, seeing our compulsiveness makes it much easier to have compassion on others similarly in the grip of their own sinful behavior. And in all of this, we experience genuine appreciation for God's mercy in caring about us and saving us.

It is then, in those private moments of awkwardness, embarrassment, emptiness, and need, to which He responds with His infilling grace—which is true life—that we are closer to Him than at any other time. Closer than when our spouse and children embrace us and warmly say they love us and God loves us. Closer than in Yosemite in the springtime, beholding waterfalls cascading into more waterfalls. Closer than in a mighty cathedral with soaring organ music and choirs singing glorious hymns.

Because the most splendid choir on Earth is just a pale imitation of the angels. And it is the heavenly host themselves, we're told, that celebrate the private redemption of the sincere watcher. As Jesus put it, "I say unto you, there is joy in the presence of the angels of God over one sinner that repenteth" (Luke 15:10).

This repentance and forgiveness in the light, and the effortless renewing of our minds that follows, is how we bond with God, and break the bonds of temptation and evil in the world. It is then, as Paul told the believers in Corinth, that "we have the mind of Christ."

CHAPTER 11

+

TURNING THE TABLES
ON EVIL IN AMERICA

How to Prevail Against a Government
and Culture Gone Mad

Gun-toting Woman, 85, Nabs Burglar
—UNITED PRESS INTERNATIONAL, AUGUST 19, 2008

Half-Dozen Abortion Clinics Shut Down
—WORLDNETDAILY.COM, AUGUST 18, 2006

Congress Finally Heard the People
—*Tulsa World*, JULY 29, 2007

After I wrote *The Marketing of Evil,* which documents how Americans were sold on sexual anarchy, abortion, easy divorce, multicultural madness, an atheistic school system, and much more—all by means of brilliant marketing—many people asked for a sequel. Only this time, they said, focus on the marketing of goodness, of truth, of freedom.

Their thinking was, If agendas hostile and destructive to our nation's well-being could be made attractive through ingenious marketing, why couldn't a culture more akin to the original America—rooted in Judeo-Christian values and promoting expansive liberty and limited government (rather than the reverse, as we have today)—also be "sold" to the current generation in the same way?

After all, tens of millions of Americans are horrified by what they see today in their beloved country. They're confronted with an increasingly toxic and hypersexualized culture, major institutions in decline, and a power-mad government oblivious to the Constitution and growing like a cancer. And they're desperately seeking a way to fight back.

So, in this final chapter, we'll explore how to overcome the lies and deceptions that permeate today's government and culture, and how to reboot the original vision of America bequeathed to us by our forefathers.

It won't be easy. Over the last couple of generations, a vast web of organizations and agendas profoundly destructive to American liberty, morality, and prosperity have grown up in our midst. Major institutions, from our schools and churches to our news media and government, have been subverted. Millions of our fellow Americans have become confused and demoralized, their loyalties captured. Prevailing in the face of all this will not be easy, but it can be done.

Make no mistake: we are in the midst of a monumental war for the "hearts and minds" of Americans, yet we don't know how fortunate we are! There are very few countries where debate and persuasion have any influence on whether the people live under freedom or tyranny. Often, dissent is illegal and elections shams if they exist at all, as the ruling elite simply rely on intimidation and brutality to impose their will. Any "transcendent" ideologies they may tout—Islam in Sudan, Confucianism in North Korea, communism in Cuba—are just camouflage for raw totalitarianism. It is only America's extraordinary political stability, the same enlightened Constitution for over 220 years and a powerful tradition of the rule of law, that allow free speech and free elections to determine our national destiny. But not forever. The ruthlessness inherent in Marxist-inspired radicalism is slowly eating away at the fabric of American civilization.

In the war I'm describing, we're unlikely to win over the hard-core radicals leading our country astray, but we *can* reach many of the decent but confused people they've seduced. That's the goal: to expose them so effectively that a majority of Americans eventually shun them and their destructive worldview.

Like all "hearts and minds" conflicts, our war is really just a huge confrontation between deception and truth. Right now, the deceivers have the upper hand, with hordes of people and institutions dedicated to projecting their lies into our minds, from politicians (Government cares about you and will solve your problems) to activist groups (Abortion is good, gay is good) to activist judges (Prayer and the Ten Commandments are bad) to the popular culture (Hooking up is cool) to public education (You evolved from an amoeba). And so on.

To understand how all these layers of deception are generated, let's briefly explore some of the incredible weapons being used to win Americans' hearts and minds. First we'll focus on those working to negatively transform our nation. Then, having identified the adversary and his methods, we'll see more readily how to fight back—and do so effectively.

"AN INVISIBLE GOVERNMENT"

See if you can recognize who said the following, or at least identify his profession:

> The conscious and intelligent manipulation of the organized habits and opinions of the masses is an important element in democratic society. Those who manipulate this unseen mechanism of society constitute an invisible government which is the true ruling power of our country.[1]

Sound like some psychopathic cult leader? Or a member of a secret society of globalist billionaires meeting clandestinely in a

Bavarian castle? Or maybe a Russian brainwashing expert preparing to unveil the latest refinements in mind control?

Nope. Those are the words of someone so mainstream and so famous that *Life* magazine designated him one of the twentieth century's one hundred most influential Americans. But hang on. What he says next is even more shocking:

> We are governed, our minds are molded, our tastes formed, our ideas suggested, largely by men we have never heard of. . . . In almost every act of our daily lives, whether in the sphere of politics or business, in our social conduct or our ethical thinking, we are dominated by the relatively small number of persons . . . who understand the mental processes and social patterns of the masses. It is they who pull the wires which control the public mind. . . . [2]

Meet Edward Bernays, the acknowledged "father of public relations." A nephew of Sigmund Freud, Bernays capitalized on his uncle's insights about people's unconscious motivations—not by helping people become conscious of them, as a psychiatrist would attempt to do, but instead by perfecting the art of exploiting those unconscious motivations to benefit his corporate and governmental clients.

Setting up shop in New York City in 1919, Bernays pioneered mass public manipulation over the next several decades. One of his many campaigns, for example, helped the American Tobacco Company end the taboo against women smoking. He paid young models to march in a high-profile suffragette parade and, on a given signal, take out their hidden cigarettes and light them up—he had already informed the press that women's rights marchers would be lighting "Torches of Freedom." Result: a whole new market for cigarettes.

Another big Bernays campaign, on behalf of the United Fruit Company in the 1950s, actually led to the CIA's overthrowing the democratically elected government of Guatemala, resulting in the death of many people—all to benefit his client's banana business.[3]

Bernays liked to describe his work as "propaganda" (the name of his 1928 book), a word that didn't yet harbor the negative connotations it does today. That changed when he found out his methods had been employed by the Nazis to shape the mind-set of the German people. "In his memoirs," write John Stauber and Sheldon Rampton, "Bernays wrote that he was 'shocked' to discover that [Nazi propaganda minister Joseph] Goebbels kept copies of Bernays' writings in his own personal library, and that his theories were therefore helping to 'engineer' the rise of the Third Reich."[4] Oops. After that, Bernays avoided the now-tainted word *propaganda* and used a much more neutral-sounding term: *public relations.*

With Bernays and others like him leading the way, America's burgeoning industrial and manufacturing empires of the early to mid-twentieth century positively reveled in the discovery that emotionally manipulating people sells far more products than appealing to their reason and logic. Vance Packard, in his 1957 bestseller, *The Hidden Persuaders,* documented how the new science of "motivational research," based on the latest insights from psychology and psychiatry, amounted to analyzing Americans like Pavlov's dogs to determine what would induce them to "salivate" over the marketer's products:

> Certain of the probers, for example, are systematically feeling out our hidden weaknesses and frailties in the hope that they can more efficiently influence our behavior. At one of the largest advertising agencies in America psychologists on the staff are probing sample humans in an attempt to find how to identify, and beam messages to, people of high anxiety, body consciousness, hostility, passiveness, and so on. A Chicago advertising agency has been studying the housewife's menstrual cycle and its psychological concomitants in order to find the

appeals that will be more effective in selling her certain food products.

Seemingly, in the probing and manipulating nothing is immune or sacred. The same Chicago ad agency has used psychiatric probing techniques on little girls. Public-relations experts are advising churchmen how they can become more effective manipulators of their congregations. . . . [5]

What *The Hidden Persuaders* exposed half a century ago remains true today: too many of us meander through life in a mental-emotional fog, our subconscious sensitivities to words and images causing us to feel, act, purchase, and vote in conformity with, as Bernays put it, "they who pull the wires which control the public mind."

None of this is meant to condemn public relations professionals, advertising agencies, political consultants, or other marketers. These professions, like most others—including my own, journalism— are precisely as honorable or dishonorable as their practitioners. All of the preceding, rather, is meant to demonstrate two points: one, human beings have proven they are extraordinarily easy to manipulate, and two, there are lots of people engaged full-time in doing the manipulating.

THE SELLING OF THE PRESIDENT

Today, the marketing of everything from cigarettes to bananas to presidential candidates is engineered by hugely talented professional strategists, based on in-depth market research. Let's talk about presidential campaigns.

When Bill Clinton's liberal agenda endangered his 1996 reelection, then–presidential adviser Dick Morris saved the day by shrewdly "re-creating" Clinton as a centrist, persuading him to co-opt and champion GOP policies such as welfare reform. Karl Rove, "the greatest political mind of his generation and probably of any generation," according to the *Weekly Standard*'s Fred Barnes, was "the architect" of both of George W. Bush's presidential campaigns and senior adviser throughout his presidency. Clearly, both strategists exerted a huge influence on the direction our nation took.

With the 2008 election, however, we entered a whole new level of "the selling of the president." With Bernays-inspired mass persuasion developed to such a high art, and an American populace increasingly conditioned to make emotion-based decisions, it was no wonder a majority of voters could be induced to elect Barack Obama as president.

Adviser David Axelrod, the Chicago-based political consultant who served as chief strategist for Obama's presidential campaign, managed to overcome a host of extraordinarily negative factors, any one of which would otherwise have nixed the candidate's prospects of being elected. After all, Obama had virtually *no* experience or qualifications for the presidency (three years as a state senator and three more as U.S. senator, most of it spent running for president). His chief mentors (Frank Marshall Davis, William Ayers, Reverend Jeremiah Wright et al.) were Marxists, criminals, and America-hating racists. The nonpartisan *National Journal* rated Obama as having the most liberal-left voting record in the entire U.S. Senate.[6]

Yet in the past, Americans had overwhelmingly rejected ultraliberal candidates such as George McGovern, Walter Mondale, and Michael Dukakis—all far less radicalized than Obama. Why, then, did they elect the most left-wing president in history, considering that a postelection Gallup poll showed *conservatives* to be the largest ideological group in the nation? Fully 40 percent of Americans self-identified as "conservative," and another 35 percent as "moderate" (that's the three-quarters of the population who make up "center-right" America), while only 21 percent said they were "liberal."[7]

The answer, of course, is that besides an expertly run campaign, soaring oratory, staying on message ("hope," "change"), prodigious if questionable fund-raising, an ultrasophisticated online outreach, and other factors overseen by Axelrod, Obama also had an unprecedented advantage: the total, overt support of the establishment news media. So enchanted were they by the prospect of a young, eloquent, cool, liberal—and for the first time in history, *black*—president, they essentially picked Obama up, held him high overhead, and giddily raced together across the finish line.

Indeed, the media's election performance, admitted *Time* magazine editor Mark Halperin, was nothing short of "disgusting": "It was extreme bias, extreme pro-Obama coverage."[8] And *Washington Post* ombudsman Deborah Howell publicly confessed—as Halperin did, *after* the election, when it no longer mattered—that the paper's reporters and editors had grossly neglected to vet either Obama, who "deserved tougher scrutiny," or running mate Joe Biden—an omission she referred to as "one gaping hole in [the *Post*'s] coverage."[9]

But this is not about "gaping holes in coverage" or temporary abdication of professional journalism standards. This is about a shared worldview, namely, "Government is the solution to all problems." In fact, America's establishment press has come increasingly to resemble the state-directed media we see in China, with its gigantic Xinhua "News" Agency, in reality a mouthpiece for the Chinese Communist Party. Or maybe a more apt comparison would be with Russia, where despite the fact that criticism of the government can be found in some newspapers and especially on the Internet, the country's national television channels are essentially extensions of the state: "They are all either controlled by the Kremlin or run by editors who know what not to say," says Allison Gill, director of the Human Rights Watch office in Russia.[10]

In the United States, the media at least used to pretend to be objective, but that has changed. When I started in journalism in the early 1980s, the media behaved more or less professionally, but were biased leftward. Then throughout the 1990s the press experienced a huge influx of activists, including many homosexuals and pro-abortion feminists, intent on advancing their pet agendas by covering those beats for their journalism organizations—very *un-*

professional. Most recently, the "big media's" activism has evolved to the point of virtual abandonment of the charade of objectivity, with top national journalists openly praising Obama in almost messianic terms, like MSNBC's *Hardball* host, Chris Matthews, comparing him to Jesus and saying the candidate's oratory gave him "this thrill going up my leg." [11] Or *Newsweek* editor Evan Thomas declaring, "In a way, Obama's standing *above* the country, above—above the *world*, he's sort of *God*." [12]

It gets worse. Increasingly, the elite media display a completely different mind-set from that of regular citizens, regarding traditional American values as corny and stupid, but immorality and perversity as sophisticated. When six hundred thousand Americans participated in Tax Day "tea parties" to protest Obama's unprecedented deficit spending and nationalization of entire industries, two major cable TV news networks used the occasion not to report on the widespread protests, but rather mocked them by making on-air jokes about oral sex. In one report on the tea parties, MSNBC's David Shuster made a total of twenty-three sexual double entendres. [13] Not to be outdone, the same network's Rachel Maddow managed to pack thirty-six oral sex references into her segment on the tea parties. [14] CNN superstar Anderson Cooper had started off the media tea-party ridicule with his own deadpan reference to the homosexual act—"It's hard to talk when you're tea-bagging," a term with which most Americans were heretofore unaware—while interviewing veteran presidential adviser David Gergen. [15] (Maybe this is why Fox News dominates cable ratings; I've never seen their hosts degrade and ridicule normal patriotic Americans as occurs regularly on CNN and MSNBC.)

Can you just imagine, during America's Revolutionary War days, the press covering the Boston Tea Party by contemptuously mocking it and turning every sentence into a lewd sexual joke?

This polluted media mind-set goes way beyond just a few cable news personalities. A normally well-concealed side of the "mainstream press" was on display at the 2008 celebrity roast of NBC's *Today* co-anchor Matt Lauer in New York City. With cameras and recording devices turned off, news icons ranging from Lauer and *Today* colleagues Al Roker and Meredith Vieira to *CBS Evening News* anchor Katie Couric to *NBC Nightly News* anchor Brian Williams to NBC Universal CEO Jeff Zucker competed to see who could tell the raunchiest, filthiest sexual jokes about each other to a crowd of 1,900. I won't quote any of it verbatim—it's way too graphic— but the *Village Voice*'s lengthy eyewitness report started off like this: "Just got back from the Hilton in midtown after three hours of dick and pussy jokes from some of the biggest stars of TV and film." [16]

During the event, these immensely talented, charismatic media personalities, whom millions of Americans trust to tell them the truth about world events and their implications, demonstrated that they live in an alternate reality, light-years away from middle-class America. For instance—and I'll highlight this as modestly and non-graphically as possible—veteran network newswoman Meredith Vieira joked about Lauer and Roker having anal sex, CBS anchor Couric jested about having sex with Lauer, NBC chief executive Zucker joked about Lauer masturbating, Lauer joked about conservative author Ann Coulter having a man's private parts, NBC anchor Williams made a joking reference to Roker's "female" private parts, Lauer joked about Couric's colon in a sexual way, and one comedian even made a sexual reference to human feces and a woman's private parts. Believe me, I'm sanitizing madly and omitting the worst stuff. The word *perverse* doesn't begin to do the event justice.

Now, why do I take the time to focus on the gutter mentality of some in the big media? Because when people become this warped, when they fall so far away from modesty and common decency that they actually revel in the kind of depraved behavior I'm describing, they tend also to be cynical, even hostile, toward people and values that are genuinely virtuous.

Don't believe me? Haven't you ever wondered why, when someone on the public stage radiates noble character, common sense, and natural grace—as Ronald Reagan did, or more recently Sarah

Palin—he or she is regarded by the "big media" with an inexplicable revulsion? *Hatred* is almost too soft a word. It's because they manifest the very qualities of character that the jaded media elite lost long ago, and since being thus reminded of their lost innocence is painful and unwelcome, they feel compelled to attack the "reminder."

As the famous rabbinic saying goes, "Those who are kind to the cruel will end up being cruel to the kind." Before you know it, the "mainstream media" are tearing down the innocent and raising up the guilty. No wonder radicalism is on the rise.

"THE VERY FIRST RADICAL"

So, now we've established the key partnership opposing traditional America: big media cheerleading the liberal-left agenda and maligning those who oppose it, as well as corporate, cultural, and political marketers employing highly manipulative methods to influence all of us. Quite a team!

Now consider how they use their huge marketing advantage. They go on offense, and stay there, overwhelming Americans with a never-ending barrage of crises, emergencies, and unworkable "solutions" that just exacerbate the problems—all for the purpose of capturing and consolidating power. Let's take a closer look.

Since the rise of Barack Obama, most Americans have heard of Saul Alinsky, the Chicago Marxist and father of "community organizing" who had such a profound effect on the current president.[17] Indeed, while campaigning for the presidency, Obama said of his years steeped in Alinsky's revolutionary "community organizing" methods, "It was that education that was seared into my brain. It was the best education I ever had, better than anything I got at Harvard Law School."[18]

Alinsky's last and most famous book, *Rules for Radicals*, lays out his system for seizing power—tactics that are basically amoral, just as one would expect from a Marxist thinker for whom any method, no matter how unscrupulous, is "moral" if it accomplishes the intended goal.

The single most important operating principle behind Alinsky's methods, the one that makes the rest of them work—namely, *intimidation*—is increasingly the modus operandi of today's government. To put it bluntly, for Alinsky's "community organizing" rules, which Obama says were "seared into my brain," to really work, the general public must be made to feel intimidated, upset, frustrated, and hopeless. Alinsky explained why:

> Any revolutionary change must be preceded by a passive, affirmative, non-challenging attitude toward change among the mass of our people. They must feel so frustrated, so defeated, so lost, so futureless in the prevailing system that they are willing to let go of the past and change the future. This acceptance is the reformation essential to any revolution.[19]

That's you: *you* are supposed to feel "defeated" and "lost," and the radicals' efforts are directed at making you feel that way.

But what if you're a fighter and stand up to the would-be revolutionaries' abuses and usurpations of power? Then you are to be attacked. Here's Alinsky rule number five: "Ridicule is man's most potent weapon. It is almost impossible to counterattack ridicule. Also it infuriates the opposition, who then react to your advantage."[20]

What's the purpose behind making people "infuriated" so they'll "react to your advantage"? According to Alinsky, "The enemy properly goaded and guided in his reaction will be your major strength."[21] This statement capsulizes a major operating principle of evil we keep bumping into throughout this book. It's the reason little children can be turned into jihadists, and why jihadists in turn can cause Westerners to become submissive, and why dictatorships so easily take hold of a country, and why so many of us take legal and illegal drugs to feel better, and why government continues to grow out of control: when we're intimidated and upset, when we emotionally overreact, we're losing the battle.

Since we're focused on how evil works, you'll undoubtedly be interested in knowing to whom Alinsky dedicated *Rules for Radicals*. Here's the guy he honors as "the first radical" on the dedication page of the first edition:

> Lest we forget at least an over-the-shoulder acknowledgment to the very first radical: from all our legends, mythology, and history (and who is to know where mythology leaves off and history begins—or which is which), the first radical known to man who rebelled against the establishment and did it so effectively that he at least won his own kingdom—Lucifer.[22]

It seems Alinsky, just like the "very first radical" who inspired him, knew that if you can make people upset and frightened, you gain powerful and mysterious leverage in implementing your agenda.

The name of the game is intimidation. Consider what happens when government constantly upsets citizens by bombarding them with rapid-fire crises and "solutions" that just make the problems worse: Some people become so overwhelmed, they just give in and stop fighting so as to relieve the pressure. Others try to fight back, but become so frustrated that their efforts are misdirected and ineffective, and before long they burn out. A very few, in their rage, might become so unhinged they resort to violence, like Timothy McVeigh, who decided that blowing up a government building in Oklahoma City in 1995 was an acceptable way to fight back against a corrupt government. In reality, he succeeded only in murdering 168 of his countrymen, including a day-care center full of toddlers (which he later coldly termed "collateral damage"). Leftist leaders then capitalize handsomely on such "right-wing terrorism" as justification for their attempts to demonize and suppress conservative groups and voices across the board.

That's why those who are addicted to power are intent on keeping us off balance. Don't fall for it. There's a world of difference between righteous indignation and seething hatred. One is based on a strong sense of justice, the other is self-destructive, out-of-control rage. If we can rise above the temptation to hate, we're left with a truly righteous passion to right the wrongs in our beloved country. Then, whatever we do to reclaim America—whether we march in huge numbers on the nation's capital and elsewhere, recall or impeach activist judges, take over local government starting at the precinct level, run for Congress, encourage state legislators to defy the federal government when it usurps the states' constitutional Tenth Amendment powers, take our children out of government schools, or participate in peaceful civil disobedience—our efforts will be blessed.

Now let's see how it's done.

We're going to explore some brilliant examples of "the marketing of truth." And mind you, these people do it without resorting to lying, so they have a distinct disadvantage compared to those who defend the indefensible for a living and are unconstrained by any requirement to be truthful. For deceivers, "spin" is how their mind works 24/7. Their ability to instantly conjure up plausible-sounding rationalizations, to twist the narrative to make their side sound credible with cherry-picked facts and half-truths, and (very important) to smear their accusers becomes second nature. Regular folks, on the other hand, tend not to see any reason to "spin" or "present" their cause in any special way.

Nevertheless, with so much confusion everywhere today, America's traditional values need to be championed at least as powerfully and creatively as the seductions of socialism and cultural corruption are. To succeed, we need to understand something about the field of battle, namely, the public mind. Buried in that battlefield are all the mines the other side has planted: if you step on this one you're a "bigot," if you step on that one you're a "warmonger," or a "racist," or "greedy." Good strategizing anticipates this and skillfully crosses the battlefield—zigzagging past all the buried mines—to victory. For far too long, conservatives have, in effect, clumsily chanted the truth while marching in a straight line across the public's mental battlefield, stepped on mines, and gotten blown up.

SECRET WEAPONS

Each side in this battle has a secret weapon that creates tremendous leverage.

For those promoting statism and moral anarchy, their secret weapon, already discussed at length, is our universal human imperfection, which tends to make us vulnerable to their seductions.

But for those defending individual liberty rooted in a transcendent moral code, the secret weapon is *conscience*—literally the convicting power of inner truth, inside all of us. Whether someone is our ally, our adversary, or one of the millions caught in the web of destructive marketing messages, their conscience represents their vulnerability to truth.

To show how this works, let's immediately bring the entire discussion down to the level of street-level "combat." As we'll see from the following examples, sometimes defenders of traditional values get it exactly right.

First, we'll focus on one of America's most contentious issues: abortion. Although many pro-lifers fret over whether the Supreme Court will ever reverse *Roe v. Wade,* they have the ability to win the abortion war with or without the courts. There are plenty of weak points in the abortion "supply chain" that are vulnerable to intervention. Here's one.

THE ANTI-ABORTION CLINIC

Every day all across America, women and girls with an unwanted pregnancy, full of conflict and fear, drive to an abortion clinic, get out of their cars, and walk nervously toward their appointment with death. Often, just before the point of no return, they encounter a "sidewalk counselor"—a regular person, armed only with a little love, and with information the abortion clinic absolutely does not want that customer to have.

As a tactical matter, the sidewalk counselor doesn't necessarily talk to the expectant mother about the humanity of her unborn baby, since the woman is probably already in denial about that, having decided to abort. Rather, the conversation zeroes in immediately on the health of the mother.

"Excuse me," says the sidewalk counselor. "Are you aware of all the lawsuits against this clinic? Two women actually died here last year. I have all the info from the Cook County Courthouse right here. Would you like to see it?"

Many do. Once a dialogue is started and a rapport established, the sidewalk counselor offers to walk the mother around the corner—or perhaps even within the same building as the abortion clinic—to a crisis pregnancy center, "a clinic that doesn't have any lawsuits against it," where the mother-to-be can get help, advice, love, and a free ultrasound. "Then, if you still want to have the abortion, you can always come back here."

Hundreds of these pregnancy centers—springing up all over the United States just as fast as abortion clinics are closing (a few years ago there were approximately 2,000 abortion clinics; today there are about 700)[23]—feature the latest-generation "4-D" ultrasound machines. When the would-be abortion customer beholds, for the first time, the reality of her unborn baby—not a grainy, difficult-to-decipher, old-fashioned sonogram, but a modern, crystal-clear image of her own moving, kicking, thumb-sucking baby—in the great majority of cases she does not go through with the planned abortion.

"There's absolutely no joy in the world," says Chicago-area sidewalk counselor Cathy Mieding, "that can measure up to walking a girl over to the place where you know she's going to find help, and she's going to have love waiting for her there. And in some very small way, you're going to be responsible for this baby being born."[24] Mieding is one of several sidewalk counselors profiled in the video documentary *No Greater Joy*, produced by the Pro-Life Action League.[25]

The growth of crisis pregnancy centers with ultrasound capability was turbocharged in 2004 when Colorado-based Focus on the Family launched its Option Ultrasound Program, dedicated to placing ultrasound services in pro-life clinics across the country. Amazingly, Focus's research has shown that up to 87 percent of abortion-minded women who receive crisis pregnancy center services including ultrasound decide against having the abortion.[26] The organization's Shana Schutte tells a typical story of the effect ultrasound has on women headed for abortion:

> "Sue," 33 and drug-addicted, is one of those women. When she visited LifeChoices Medical Clinic in Joplin, Mo. . . . she thought it was just another stop on her way to a Tulsa, Okla., abortion clinic.
>
> God had other plans.
>
> At the suggestion of the LifeChoices staff, Sue had an ultrasound exam. Both she and her boyfriend were stunned. The test revealed what would not have been shared by an abortionist—an active, kicking, three-month-old fetus. Sue canceled her appointment at the abortion clinic and instead started discussing baby names.[27]

As of mid-2009, Focus had funded 338 grants for ultrasound machines in forty-nine states.[28]

Now, here's the "big-picture" point: The woman intent on aborting her baby is under the sway of lies (*It's not a baby*) and pressures (*You'll wreck your life if you don't have an abortion*). What could possibly overcome all of that "persuasion?" A personal experience of undeniable truth. When the pregnant mom sees her own child via ultrasound—kicking, thumb-sucking, and all—words cease, arguments ring hollow, excuses evaporate. Now that there is absolutely no question this is a real baby—*her* baby—she is simply not going to have the abortion.

This is a fine example of effective "marketing of truth." The "marketer" (sidewalk counselor) didn't confront the mother and hysterically plead, "Please don't kill your baby!" That would have amounted to marching straight across the battlefield clumsily chanting the truth. Rather, she wisely took a more circuitous route to avoid all the mental mines planted by the enemy. Thus she approached the woman with something she already cared about—staying alive. That got her attention and led ultimately to her having the free ultrasound and meeting her baby. Once that point was reached, *the mother's own conscience kicked in.* Game over.

AN END RUN AROUND THE MEDIA

Another highly effective "marketing of truth" campaign was that of the Swift Boat Veterans for Truth (later renamed Swift Vets and POWs for Truth), targeting the 2004 presidential candidacy of Senator John Kerry. The book, *Unfit for Command: Swift Boat Veterans Speak Out Against John Kerry,* by John E. O'Neill and Jerome R. Corsi, my friend and WorldNetDaily colleague, became the number-one *New York Times* bestseller, and the television ads featuring decorated Vietnam vets and POWs who served with Kerry were, in a word, devastating. There was simply no way for the Kerry campaign to recover.

Recall that when Kerry made his four-month stint in Vietnam a centerpiece of his campaign, many soldiers who had served with him came forward to protest what they considered Kerry's self-serving behavior in Vietnam and near-treasonous congressional testimony upon returning to America. To refresh your memory, here's what the young Kerry told the Senate Foreign Relations Committee on April 22, 1971. Speaking of his fellow soldiers, Kerry claimed they "had personally raped, cut off ears, cut off heads, taped wires from portable telephones to human genitals and turned up the power, cut off limbs, blown up bodies, randomly shot at civilians, razed villages in a fashion reminiscent of Genghis Khan, shot cattle and dogs for fun, poisoned food stocks, and generally ravaged the countryside of South Vietnam. . . ."[29]

Kerry's atrocity charges were utterly unsubstantiated. The 2008 public release of reports of the Army's Criminal Investigation Division[30] showed that the official investigation three decades earlier proved those soldiers who had made the charges spread by Kerry couldn't support their claims in any way, some either backtracking or totally disavowing their stories.[31]

The Swift Boat veterans knew the truth. But what could they do about it? The Kerry campaign marketing machinery, including the admiring media, was in full gear honoring this "hero" of Vietnam now seeking the presidency.

The Swift Boat vets released four TV spots. One of them, titled "Sellout," featured Kerry's 1971 testimony interspersed with decorated POWs saying Kerry's treachery back then hurt them far more than anything the enemy did:

KERRY: They had personally raped, cut off ears, cut off heads . . .

(Onscreen) JOE PONDER, WOUNDED IN VIETNAM NOVEMBER 1968: The accusations that John Kerry made against the veterans who served in Vietnam was just devastating.

KERRY: . . . randomly shot at civilians . . .

PONDER: . . . and it hurt me more than any physical wounds I had.

KERRY: . . . cut off limbs, blown up bodies . . .

(Onscreen) KEN CORDIER, POW DECEMBER 1966–
MARCH 1973: That was part of the torture, was to sign a
statement that you had committed war crimes.

KERRY: . . . razed villages in a fashion reminiscent of Ghengis
Khan . . .

(Onscreen) PAUL GALANTI, POW JANUARY 1966–
FEBRUARY 1973: John Kerry gave the enemy for free what
I and many of my comrades in North Vietnam in the prison
camps took torture to avoid saying. It demoralized us.

KERRY: . . . crimes committed on a day-to-day basis . . .

(Onscreen) CORDIER: He betrayed us in the past. How could
we be loyal to him now?

KERRY: . . . ravaged the countryside of South Vietnam . . .

(Onscreen) GALANTI: He dishonored his country, but more
importantly, the people he served with. He just sold them
out.[32]

Of course, Kerry tried to counteract the Swift Boat vets' efforts
by assembling a few Vietnam veterans loyal to him and carting them
around to campaign stops, and by relying on a sympathetic press to
ignore or discredit his accusers. However, the Swift Boat vets' multi-
pronged campaign, consisting of the bestselling book, a fund-raising
website, TV ads, and thousands of talk radio interviews, succeeded
in pulling off an effective end run around the establishment press.
And Kerry's small "band of brothers" was no match for the 245
members of the Swift Boat vets, many highly decorated—including
virtually the entire chain of command above Kerry—all of whom
agreed he was "unfit for command." The prospect of electing, during wartime, someone who had so egregiously given aid and comfort
to America's enemies while maligning and demoralizing our own
soldiers, proved intolerable to most Americans, thanks to the Swift
Boat vets' campaign. Game over.

Of course, there was a price to be paid—there often is. The establishment press, true to form, has continually maligned the Swift

Boat Veterans for Truth ever since 2004. Accustomed to defining reality for Americans, the media resented the veterans' impertinence in upstaging them with the truth, powerfully delivered—and they're still smearing the vets to this day.

LETTING EVIL SPEAK FOR ITSELF

Another effective way to confront evil with truth was demonstrated by the late Charlton Heston, long a champion of civil rights and individual liberty. In a speech at Harvard Law School in 1999, Heston showed his youthful audience exactly what it means to stand up for what's right, often referring to the civil disobedience tactics of Mahatma Gandhi and Martin Luther King, Jr.

"A few years ago," said the famous actor, "I heard about a rapper named Ice-T who was selling a CD called 'Cop Killer,' celebrating the ambushing and murdering of police officers." Heston proceeded to unfold a memorable story:

> It was being marketed by none other than Time Warner, the biggest entertainment conglomerate in the country, in the *world*. Police across the country were outraged—and rightfully so. At least one of them had been murdered. But Time Warner was stonewalling because the CD was a cash cow for them, and the media were tiptoeing around because the rapper was black. I heard Time Warner had a stockholders meeting scheduled in Beverly Hills, and I owned some shares of Time Warner at the time, so I decided to attend the meeting.
>
> What I did was against the advice of my family and my colleagues. I asked for the floor. To a hushed room of a thousand average American stockholders, I simply read the full lyrics of "Cop Killer"—every vicious, vulgar, instructional word:
>
> "I got my 12-gauge sawed-off. I got my headlights turned off. I'm about to bust some shots off. I'm about to dust some cops off."

It got worse, a lot worse. Now, I won't read the rest of it to you. But trust me, the room was a sea of shocked, frozen, blanched faces. Time Warner executives squirmed in their chairs and stared at their shoes. They hated me for that. Then I delivered another volley of sick lyrics brimming with racist filth, where Ice-T fantasizes about sodomizing the two 12-year-old nieces of Al and Tipper Gore:

"She pushed her butt against my . . ."

No. No, I won't do to you here what I did to them. Let's just say I left the room in stunned silence. When I read the lyrics to the waiting press corps outside, one of them said, "We can't print that, you know." "I know," I said, "but Time Warner is still selling it."

Two months later, Time Warner terminated Ice-T's contract. I'll never be offered another film by Warner Brothers, or get a good review from Time magazine. But disobedience means you have to be willing to act, not just talk.[33]

Notice that all three of these examples—the ultrasound intervention, the Swift Boat vets' campaign, and Charlton Heston's rap "performance"—resulted in a direct and convicting experience of truth on the part of the "audience." No persuasion or arguing was necessary. The message was devastating and the objective accomplished.

THE POWER OF ONE

But what happens if the truth is not sufficient, if, as is so often the case, those on the receiving end are so disconnected from their conscience that incontrovertible truth doesn't compel them to do the right thing? Then you help them out by applying so much pressure that it becomes too painful for them *not* to do the right thing. That's what happened in mid-2007 when President Bush, along with the leadership of both political parties and the mainstream press, all favored passage of the Kennedy-Kyl immigration bill, which would have resulted in amnesty for 12 to 20 million illegal aliens.

Though the entire Washington establishment was pushing for amnesty, a tsunami of opposition from across the country, urged on by the nation's radio talk show hosts, literally shut down the Senate switchboard with hundreds of thousands, perhaps millions, of phone calls, faxes, and e-mails reportedly running 9 to 1 against the bill. The sheer size and intensity of the popular uprising struck fear in the hearts of lawmakers and the bill went down in flames. This is what good people in America should be doing *all the time.*

Another problem: What happens when you've done everything right, you've championed the truth effectively, you've brought tremendous public pressure to bear—but those in power still remain unmoved?

Such was the dilemma of William Wilberforce in his decades-long campaign to end the slave trade in late-eighteenth-century Britain. Wilberforce tirelessly and eloquently led the abolition movement in Parliament, yet failed to muster the requisite votes *eleven different times* over the course of sixteen years. It seems that too many of his fellow parliamentarians had ties to slave-dependent industries and, while agreeing with Wilberforce in principle, argued that ending slavery would decimate the British economy.

Neither nationwide protests nor powerful testimonies before Parliament of the savagely inhumane treatment of Africans while at sea proved sufficient to persuade a majority to end slavery. Wilberforce's abolition campaign, popularly supported throughout Britain, failed year after year in Parliament.

Then one day Wilberforce's brother-in-law, a sharp maritime lawyer named James Stephen, came up with a brilliant idea. Britain was at war with France. Realizing that many of the British slave ships were sailing under a neutral flag—most often American—to avoid being bothered during the war, Stephen hatched a scheme to have a patriotic, anti-French bill introduced that no one in Parliament would dare oppose during wartime. The bill would prohibit British ships, even under a neutral flag, from transporting goods *or slaves* to non-British countries or colonies, including French colonies.

With Wilberforce and his small abolitionist cadre remaining tight-lipped as to their real intentions, the neutral-flag law sailed through Parliament, and ultimately brought about exactly the secondary effect the abolitionists anticipated—namely, ruining many of the English slavers by preventing their ships from sailing. Then, a few years later, with the trade seriously weakened and the time finally ripe, Wilberforce once again brought the issue before Parliament and this time they outlawed slavery in Great Britain outright. His radical change of tactics, thanks to some inspired, outside-the-box thinking, succeeded where the "straight across the battlefield" approach had repeatedly failed.[34]

By the way, the technique of using intentionally complicated and indirect means to accomplish something while masking one's true intentions is employed all day, every day by those advancing agendas inimical to freedom. It is literally their standard operating procedure. For example, after the aforementioned anti-amnesty citizen revolt led by talk radio, some incensed congressional Democrats were eager to reinstate the controversial "Fairness Doctrine" as a means of "regulating" those troublesome conservative talk hosts by requiring "equal time for liberals." However, they knew they didn't have the votes to reimpose such blatant, anti–First Amendment censorship. So, Democrats and like-minded advocacy groups such as the Center for American Progress "abandoned" the Fairness Doctrine in favor of other means—considerably more convoluted, decentralized, and indirect, and thus harder for the average person to understand, or care about—to accomplish exactly the same result: to throttle conservative radio talkers.

Some of their sneaky "reforms" designed to remedy what they call "the structural imbalance of talk radio": "Strengthened limits on how many radio stations one firm can own, locally and nationally"; "Shortening broadcast license terms"; "Requiring radio broadcasters to regularly show they are operating in the 'public interest'"; and "Imposing a fee on broadcasters who fail to meet these 'public interest obligations' with the funding to go to the Corporation for Public Broadcasting." [35]

Translation: *We can't pass the Fairness Doctrine because it too obviously violates the Constitution, so we'll attack Rush Limbaugh and other conservative talkers by gradually chipping away at them, over a period of time, out of the public view, at the local level, one station at a time.*

As you can see, in many ways this war for America's body and soul is a chess game. Elitists—those who believe they're ordained to rule over you, spend your money, and tell you how to live—think way ahead and develop strategies and tactics in a highly intelligent way, an expertise born of their naturally manipulative nature and fueled by their lust for power. To champion genuine freedom we need to be even more sophisticated—but a sophistication arising not from a deceitful nature or desire for power, but rather, as Sun Tzu wisely advised, because we deeply understand both our enemy and ourselves.

REVOLUTION

When it comes to fighting back against the elitist transformation of America, who or what can possibly counteract the ruinous influence of today's news media? After all, a nation's press establishment is undoubtedly the strongest "influencer" of all, since it has an unparalleled ability to shine a thousand-watt spotlight of truth on every area of life, which includes exposing the deceptions of all the other "influencers." Alternatively, as we see in America today, it can become society's preeminent manipulator and twister of reality.

Fortunately, the press happens to be in the midst of a revolution. While fewer and fewer people rely on the "Old Media"—the establishment daily newspapers (many of them struggling and some going bankrupt) and network news broadcasts with their low public credibility and ever-dwindling market share—millions are gravitating to the "New Media."

The New Media started with talk radio, which really began with Rush Limbaugh, thanks to the repeal of the Fairness Doctrine. "Ronald Reagan tore down this wall [the Fairness Doctrine] in 1987," wrote Daniel Henninger in the *Wall Street Journal*, "and Rush Limbaugh was the first man to proclaim himself liberated from the East Germany of liberal media domination." [36]

Limbaugh was, and still is, a great "marketer of truth." Before him, conservatives were widely stereotyped as humorless, uptight curmudgeons. But Rush was just the opposite—funny and confident, devastatingly on-target, not taking himself too seriously and yet seriously influencing tens of millions. He redefined what a conservative was while creating a new paradigm for talk radio.

Today, the airways are bursting with vibrant national voices such as Limbaugh, Sean Hannity, Michael Savage, Glenn Beck, G. Gordon Liddy, Mark Levin, Laura Ingraham, and many others, as well as thousands of local talkers broadcasting daily from every hill and valley in America. With America awash in propaganda, it's a salve on the nation's troubled soul for truth and common sense to be so unapologetically trumpeted on the public airways.

As novelist George Orwell is often quoted as saying, "In a time of universal deceit, telling the truth is a revolutionary act." [37]

Then there's the Internet, where I make my journalistic home at WorldNetDaily, founded by veteran newsman Joseph Farah. Just as the printing press Johannes Gutenberg invented five centuries ago paved the way for the Renaissance, the Protestant Reformation, and the scientific revolution of the sixteenth and seventeenth centuries, the Internet has provided the technological basis for a revolution just as radical and far-reaching, propelling communications, commerce, education, recreation, and information—including news—into a new universe.

It's hard to imagine now, but a generation ago middle-class Americans stared at their TV sets every night at dinnertime as liberal network news anchors aristocratically handed down the day's slickly packaged "news." You could change the channel, but all you'd get were clones—the exact same stories presented with the exact same spin. That's all there was.

Those days are gone forever, thanks to talk radio, cable television, satellite, and other communications technologies—but especially the Internet. For a news organization, the wizardry of hyperlinking, the speed-of-light availability of data it took research assistants days or weeks to laboriously gather two decades ago, audio and video on demand, the ability to update news in real time 24/7 and deliver it to millions of people for free, all make the Internet the future of news.

It's happening already, according to a major poll by Zogby International: "As broadcast television network newscasts continue to lose viewers by the month, the Internet is by far the preferred source for information," and "it is considered the most reliable source as well." While 56 percent of American adults polled said "if they had to choose just one source for their news information, they would choose the Internet," only 21 percent said they would choose television news.[38]

Best of all, because the Internet is a mighty leveler of playing fields (Matt Drudge's one-man site gets more readers than CBS News's or *Newsweek*'s with their thousands of employees), the press is one area of American life where the moneyed elitists are *losing* ground, while an authentic, moral, pro-American news culture is *gaining* ground. Thus the New Media, including not only talk radio, the Internet, and some cable news, but in a larger sense, citizen journalists, from bloggers and online researchers to everyday Americans with cell-phone cameras videotaping breaking news—in other words, everyone and everything that counterbalances the entrenched, elite media—has tremendous potential to undo a great deal of evil in our country by finally exposing it to the light of day. As such, I consider the New Media one of the most positive and hopeful developments in modern America.

But I'm even more hopeful for the future because, despite the army of "influencers" trying to reshape our minds at every turn, there are still, miraculously, millions of regular, hardworking, God-fearing, straight-shooting Americans who aren't drinking the Kool-Aid. Unlike MSNBC's Chris Matthews, who gets a thrill going up his leg when listening to Obama, they get a thrill listening to the words of the *real* Messiah. Unlike Saul Alinsky, who said he was inspired by Lucifer, they are still inspired by the One who really did "turn the tables on evil"—who totally outflanked and outsmarted his adversary, broke evil's hold on the human race, and led the most radical and important revolution in human history.

One of my favorite biblical sayings is what Jesus said to Pontius Pilate: "To this end was I born, and for this cause came I into the world, that I should bear witness unto the truth" (John 18:37). Is there some reason we're supposed to be doing something different? I don't think so.

It's clear that people of conscience cannot advance the cause of liberty and morality by resorting to the intimidation tactics of Saul Alinsky, or deliberately creating crises like the government does, or committing criminal acts as some "community organizing" groups do, or telling outrageous lies like so many politicians. But that's okay. Truth is enough—because when properly honed and targeted, it is more than sufficient to annihilate all of their grand seductions.

+

NOTES

1. IN GOVERNMENT WE TRUST

1. "Iraq: A Population Silenced," Bureau of Democracy, Human Rights, and Labor, U.S. Department of State, December 2002, http://www.state.gov/documents/organization/16059.pdf.
2. Ibid.
3. Andrew S. Natsios, administrator, U.S. Agency for International Development, testifying on "Life Inside North Korea" before the Subcommittee on East Asian and Pacific Affairs, Senate Foreign Relations Committee, Washington, D.C., June 5, 2003, http://www.state.gov/p/eap/rls/rm/2003/21269.htm.
4. Doug Struck, "Opening a Window on North Korea's Horrors," *Washington Post*, Oct. 4, 2003, http://www.washingtonpost.com/ac2/wp-dyn/A41966 -2003Oct3?language=printer.
5. Nelson Banya, "Zimbabwe inflation hits 11 million percent as talks drag," Reuters, Aug. 19, 2008, http://uk.reuters.com/article/worldNews/idUKLJ35337020080819 ?feedType=RSS&feedName=worldNews.
6. "Zimbabweans have 'shortest lives,'" BBC News, April 8, 2006, http://news.bbc .co.uk/2/hi/africa/4890508.stm.
7. "China Human Rights," Amnesty International USA, http://www.amnestyusa.org/ our-priorities/china/page.do?id=1011134&n1=3&n2=884.
8. Andrei Illarionov, "Freedom in the World 2007: Is Freedom Under Threat?," Carnegie Council, Jan. 30, 2007, http://www.cceia.org/resources/transcripts/5422 .html.
9. Frederic Bastiat, *The Law*, 1850, Foundation for Economic Education, Inc. (FEE .org), pp. 5–6, http://bastiat.org/en/the_law.html.
10. Ibid., pp. 6–7.

11. Arthur B. Robinson, "The one and only solution to America's energy problem," Whistleblower, August 2008, http://www.wnd.com/index.php?fa=PAGE.view &pageId=73452.

12. Bob Unruh, "Majority now cosponsors Ron Paul's Fed audit," WorldNetDaily.com, June 11, 2009, http://www.wnd.com/index.php?pageId=100855.

13. Rep. Ron Paul, M.D., "Abolish the Fed," House of Representatives, Sept. 10, 2002, http://www.lewrockwell.com/paul/paul53.html.

14. "An Interview with Tom Schatz, President of Citizens Against Government Waste," BlogCritics.org, Dec. 4, 2007, http://blogcritics.org/archives/2007/12/04/222036.php.

15. Larry Margasak, "Sen. Coburn questions 100 stimulus projects," Associated Press, June 16, 2009, http://apnews.myway.com/article/20090616/D98RI8302.html.

16. "Top Nine Most Wasteful Stimulus Projects," FoxNews.com, June 1, 2009, http://www.foxnews.com/story/0,2933,523919,00.html.

17. Brian M. Riedl, "Top 10 Examples of Government Waste," Heritage Foundation, April 4, 2005, http://www.heritage.org/research/budget/bg1840.cfm.

18. James F. Cooper, "Art censors: A closer look at the NEA," *New Dimensions: The Psychology Behind the News*, June 1991.

19. Drew Zahn, "Will Edwards get to keep his 'Father of Year' award?," WorldNetDaily.com, Aug. 11, 2008, http://www.wnd.com/index.php?fa=PAGE .view&pageId=72134.

20. George F. Will, "Tincture of Lawlessness: Obama's Overreaching Economic Policies," *Washington Post*, May 14, 2009, http://www.washingtonpost.com/wp-dyn/content/article/2009/05/13/AR2009051303014.html?sub=AR.

21. "Hitler as his associates know him," Office of Strategic Services, http://www .nizkor.org/hweb/people/h/hitler-adolf/oss-papers/text/oss-profile-03-02 .html.

22. Adolf Hitler, *Mein Kampf,* 1925, translated by James Murphy, http://gutenberg .net.au/ebooks02/0200601.txt.

23. Jim Simpson, "The Cloward-Piven Strategy, Part I: Manufactured Crisis," American Daughter Media Center, Aug. 31, 2008, http://frontpage.american daughter.com/?p=1878.

24. Mark Finkelstein, "Scare-Mongering on Steroids: NBC Warns Oceans Could Rise 200 Feet," NewsBusters.org, Nov. 17, 2008, http://newsbusters.org/blogs/mark -finkelstein/2008/11/17/scare-mongering-steroids-nbc-warns-oceans-could-rise -200-feet.

25. "Global Warming Petition Project," http://petitionproject.org.

26. "Hyping Hate Crime Vs. Muslims," *Investor's Business Daily*, Dec. 3, 2007, http:// www.investors.com/editorial/editorialcontent.asp?secid=1501&status=article&id =281576932449479.

2. SEXUAL ANARCHY

1. "Teacher jailed over sex with 13-year-old boy," Associated Press, Sept. 6, 2002.

2. Roxana Hegeman, "Judge: No credible evidence underage sex always harmful," Associated Press, Feb. 10, 2006.

3. Chelsea J. Carter, "Teacher-Student Sex Goes Under Radar," Associated Press, June 10, 2002.

4. Nancy Grace and Diane Clehane, *Objection! How High-Priced Defense Attorneys, Celebrity Defendants, and a 24/7 Media Have Hijacked Our Criminal Justice System* (New York: Hyperion, 2005), p. 100, excerpt at http://www.cnn.com/2005/LAW/ 06/14/grace.excerpt.01/index.html.

5. Melanthia Mitchell, "Wedding of Mary Kay Letourneau and former student shrouded in secrecy," Associated Press, May 20, 2005.

6. Tara Bahrampour and Ian Shapira, "Sex at School Increasing, Some Educators Say," *Washington Post*, Nov. 6, 2005.

7. Charol Shakeshaft, "Educator Sexual Misconduct: A Synthesis of Existing Literature," June 2004, http://www.ed.gov/rschstat/research/pubs/misconduct review/report.pdf.

8. Laurie Goodstein, "Scandals in the Church: The Overview; Abuse Scandal has been Ended, Top Bishop Says," *New York Times*, Feb. 28, 2004, http://www .nytimes.com/2004/02/28/us/scandals-in-the-church-the-overview-abuse -scandal-has-been-ended-top-bishop-says.html?pagewanted=all.

9. Caroline Hendrie, "Sexual Abuse by Educators Is Scrutinized," *Education Week*, March 10, 2004, http://www.edweek.org/ew/articles/2004/03/10/26abuse.h23 .html.

10. Ibid.

11. Shakeshaft, "Educator Sexual Misconduct."

12. Ibid.

13. Maura Dolan, "Not Only Men Are Molesters," *Los Angeles Times*, Aug. 16, 2002.

14. Wendy Koch, "More Women Charged in Sex Cases," *USA Today*, Nov. 30, 2005.

15. Ibid.

16. Denise Noe, "Mary Kay Letourneau: The Romance That Was a Crime," TruTV Crime Library, http://www.trutv.com/library/crime/criminal_mind/psychology/ marykay_letourneau/1.html.

17. "Newborn corpses, fetuses found in sewer blockages in Zimbabwe," Associated Press, Feb. 17, 2006.

3. HOW TERRORISM REALLY WORKS

1. Tim Johnston, "Three Indonesian girls beheaded," BBC News, Oct. 29, 2005, http://news.bbc.co.uk/2/hi/asia-pacific/4387604.stm.

2. Joe Kovacs, "Bush shown kissing Cindy in family pix," WorldNetDaily.com, Aug. 16, 2005, http://www.wnd.com/index.php?fa=PAGE.view&pageId=31822.

3. "Milosevic, Saddam trials both flawed: U.S. lawyer," *Daily Times* (Pakistan), March 19, 2006, http://www.dailytimes.com.pk/default.asp?page=2006%5C03%5C19% 5Cstory_19-3-2006_pg4_11.

4. "Saddam trial judge ejects Ramsey Clark," Reuters, Nov. 5, 2006, http://www .signonsandiego.com/news/world/iraq/20061105-0225-iraq-saddam-clark .html.

5. Joseph M. Carver, Ph.D., "Love and Stockholm Syndrome: The Mystery of Loving

an Abuser (Part 1)," http://counsellingresource.com/quizzes/stockholm/index
.html.

6. William B. Saxbe and Peter D. Franklin, *I've Seen the Elephant: An Autobiography* (Kent, Ohio: Kent State University Press, 2000), p. 163.

7. Tom Mathews, William J. Cook, and Martin Kasindorf, "Patty: Guilty," *Newsweek*, March 29, 1976.

8. Anthony Bruno, "The Kidnapping of Elizabeth Smart," TruTV Crime Library, http://www.trutv.com/library/crime/criminal_mind/sexual_assault/elizabeth _smart/1_index.html.

9. Hannah Bayman, "Yvonne Ridley: From captive to convert," BBC News Online, Sept. 21, 2004, http://news.bbc.co.uk/2/hi/uk_news/england/3673730.stm.

10. Eloise Napier, "Articles of faith," *Guardian* (U.K.), Feb. 24, 2004, http://www .guardian.co.uk/politics/2004/feb/24/pressandpublishing.afghanistan.

11. Ibid.

12. Ariel Sharon and David Chanoff, *Warrior: An Autobiography* (New York: Simon & Schuster, 2001), p. 76.

13. Kenneth Levin, "The Psychology of Populations under Chronic Siege," Post-Holocaust and Anti-Semitism, No. 46 (Jerusalem Center for Public Affairs, July 2, 2006), http://www.jcpa.org/phas/phas-046-levin.htm.

14. Ibid.

15. Aharon Megged, "One-Way Trip on the Highway of Self-Destruction," *Jerusalem Post*, June 17, 1994, cited in Levin, "The Psychology of Populations under Chronic Siege."

16. "The Great Divide: How Westerners and Muslims View Each Other," Pew Global Attitudes Project, June 22, 2006, http://pewglobal.org/reports/display.php?Report ID=253.

17. Julian Borger, "Poll shows Muslims in Britain are the most anti-western in Europe," *Guardian* (U.K.), June 23, 2006, http://www.guardian.co.uk/world/2006/jun/23/ uk.religion.

18. John Thorne and Hannah Stuart, "Islam on Campus: A survey of UK student opinions," Centre for Social Cohesion, http://www.socialcohesion.co.uk/files/ 1231525079_2.pdf.

19. Stanley Kurtz, "Polygamy Versus Democracy: You can't have both," *Weekly Standard*, June 5, 2006, http://www.weeklystandard.com/Utilities/printer _preview.asp?idArticle=12266.

20. Sarah Harris, "Three Little Pigs CD' banned from Government-backed awards for offending Muslims and builders," *Daily Mail* (U.K.), Jan. 24, 2008, http://www .dailymail.co.uk/news/article-509975/Three-Little-Pigs-CD-banned-Government -backed-awards-offending-Muslims-builders.html.

21. "Muslim prisoners sue for millions over ham sandwiches," WorldNetDaily.com, Oct. 27, 2007, http://www.wnd.com/index.php?fa=PAGE.view&pageId=44230.

22. "Chertoff's 'Islam PC' rankles fed officials," WorldNetDaily.com, Feb. 10, 2007, http://www.wnd.com/index.php?fa=PAGE.view&pageId=40087.

23. "Nigeria's journalist on the run," BBC News, Nov. 27, 2002, http://news.bbc.co .uk/2/hi/africa/2518977.stm.

24. Evan Thomas, "How a Fire Broke Out: The story of a sensitive *Newsweek* report about alleged abuses at Guantánamo Bay and a surge of deadly unrest in the Islamic world," *Newsweek*, May 23, 2005, http://www.msnbc.msn.com/id/7857407/site/newsweek/print/1/displaymode/1098/.

25. "Editor: Mohammad cartoons provoked vital debate," Reuters, Jan. 18, 2007, http://www.ynetnews.com/articles/0,7340,L-3353845,00.html.

26. "Pope Says He's 'Deeply Sorry' for Reaction to Islam Speech," Associated Press, Sept. 18, 2006, http://www.foxnews.com/story/0,2933,214184,00.html.

27. Peter Schweizer, *Reagan's War: The Epic Story of His Forty-Year Struggle and Final Triumph Over Communism* (New York: Anchor, 2003) p. 1.

28. Ibid., p. 3.

29. John Fund, "Leave It to Deaver," *Wall Street Journal*, Aug. 20, 2007, http://www.opinionjournal.com/diary/?id=110010494.

30. Schweizer, *Reagan's War*, back cover.

31. Ibid., p. 148.

32. Peter Schweizer, "WWRD? How would President Reagan fight the war on terror?," National Review Online, Oct. 15, 2002, http://www.nationalreview.com/comment/comment-schweizer101502.asp.

33. Ibid.

4. THE SECRET CURSE OF CELEBRITY

1. Lisa Marie Presley, MySpace blog, June 26, 2009, http://blogs.myspace.com/index.cfm?fuseaction=blog.view&friendId=42291868&blogId=497035326.

2. Kathleen Doheny, "Accidental Overdose Killed Heath Ledger: Medical Examiner's Report Finds Actor Took Fatal Combination of 6 Medications," WebMD Health News, Feb. 6, 2008, http://www.webmd.com/news/20080206/accidental-overdose-killed-heath-ledger.

3. Jessica Reaves, "Will Robert Downey Jr.'s Case Spark a Change in Drug Sentencing?," *Time*, Feb. 7, 2001, http://www.time.com/time/nation/article/0,8599,98373,00.html.

4. Drew Pinsky and S. Mark Young, *The Mirror Effect: How Celebrity Narcissism Is Seducing America* (New York: Harper, 2009), p. 4.

5. Ibid., p. 3.

6. Andrew Breitbart and Mark Ebner, *Hollywood, Interrupted: Insanity Chic in Babylon—The Case Against Celebrity* (New York: Wiley, 2004), p. 4.

7. Pinsky and Young, *The Mirror Effect*, pp. 13–14.

8. Mayo Clinic Staff, "Narcissistic personality disorder," MayoClinic.com, Nov. 29, 2007, http://www.mayoclinic.com/health/narcissistic-personality-disorder/ds00652.

9. Dr. Keith Ablow, "Inside the Minds of Rod Blagojevich and Bernie Madoff," FoxNews.com, Dec. 17, 2008, http://health.blogs.foxnews.com/2008/12/17/inside-the-minds-of-rod-blagoyevich-and-bernie-madoff.

10. Charles Krauthammer, "The Corner," Fox News Channel, April 20, 2009, http://corner.nationalreview.com/post/?q=NjViOWE5OWU4NDY5NDE5OTA4YjgzMjdhYjB1ZGU2N2I=.

11. Jack Kelly, "Obama's Narcissism," Real Clear Politics, July 26, 2008, http://www
    .realclearpolitics.com/articles/2008/07/obamas_narcissism.html.

12. Rush Limbaugh, "Narcissistic Obama Can't Deal with Bush's Success Against
    Terrorism," *Rush Limbaugh Show*, April 21, 2009, http://www.rushlimbaugh.com/
    home/daily/site_042109/content/01125112.guest.html.

13. Jean M. Twenge, Ph.D., and W. Keith Campbell, Ph.D., *The Narcissism
    Epidemic: Living in the Age of Entitlement* (New York: Simon & Schuster, 2009),
    Introduction.

14. Ibid.

15. Holly Brubach, "Enough About You: A Little Narcissism Goes a Long Way," *New
    York Times*, March 12, 2009, http://www.nytimes.com/indexes/2009/02/22/
    style/t/index.html#pagewanted=0&pageName=22brubach&. ·

16. Jaya Narain, "Constant praising is turning children into narcissists, expert
    warns," *Daily Mail* (U.K.), March 16, 2009, http://www.dailymail.co.uk/news/
    article-1162134/Constant-praise-turning-children-narcissists-expert-warns.html.

17. Tweng and Campbell *The Narcissism Epidemic*, Introduction.

18. Brubach, "Enough About You."

19. Mayo Clinic Staff, "Narcissistic personality disorder."

20. Rudyard Kipling, "If," 1895, from *Rewards and Fairies* (Garden City, N.Y.:
    Doubleday, 1910).

21. Ibid.

22. Mayo Clinic Staff, "Narcissistic personality disorder."

23. Kipling, "If."

5. DOCTORS, DRUGS, AND DEMONS

1. Jeffrey Collins, "South Carolina teen with troubled background contends
   antidepressants drove him to kill," Associated Press, December 2, 2004.

2. Charles Gibson, "Chris Pittman, Anti-Depressants and Violence," *Good Morning
   America*, Sept. 3, 2004.

3. Peter R. Breggin, M.D., "Suicidality, violence and mania caused by selective
   serotonin reuptake inhibitors (SSRIs): A review and analysis," *International Journal
   of Risk & Safety in Medicine* (2003/2004), p. 33, http://www.breggin.com/31–49
   .pdf.

4. Angela K. Brown, "Yates jury told about mom's tormented past, love for kids,"
   Austin American-Statesman, July 12, 2006.

5. Angela K. Brown, "'Homicidal ideation' added to list of antidepressant Effexor's
   rare adverse events," Associated Press, July 10, 2006.

6. "Lupin reaches settlement with Wyeth on Venlafaxine," *Business Standard*,
   May 11, 2009, http://www.business-standard.com/india/news/lupin-reaches
   -settlementwyethvenlafaxine/61166/on.

7. Peter R. Breggin, M.D., "Fluvoxamine as a cause of stimulation, mania and
   aggression with a critical analysis of the FDA-approved label," *International Journal
   of Risk & Safety in Medicine*, 2001.

8. Manny Fernandez, Marc Santora, and Christine Hauser, "Gunman Showed Signs

of Anger," *New York Times*, April 18, 2007, http://www.nytimes.com/2007/04/18/
us/18gunman.html?pagewanted=1&_r=1&hp.

9. Jim Nolan and David Ress, "In 2 hours, Virginia Tech was forever changed,"
Richmond Times-Dispatch, April 21, 2007, http://www.timesdispatch.com/rtd/
news/special_report/virginia_tech/article/=RTD_2007_04_22_0181/88391/.

10. "Mental health history of Seung Hui Cho," Report of the Virginia Tech Review
Panel, p. 35, http://www.governor.virginia.gov/TempContent/techPanelReport-
docs/8%20CHAPTER%20IV%20LIFE%20AND%20MENTAL%20
HEALTH%20 HISTORY; pc20OF%20CHOpdf.

11. Kara M. Conners, "Antidepressants: Can They Turn Kids into Killers? New Cases,
Evidence to Test 'Prozac Defense,'" *Press & Sun-Bulletin* (Binghamton, N.Y.), Feb.
20, 2005.

12. Ron Gasbarro, "List Links Many Violent Acts to Medications' Side Effects; Some
Say the Drugs Create Insanity but Don't Fight It," *Washington Times*, Oct. 15, 1990.

13. Martin Kasindorf, "Parents Struggled to Control Their Son but Couple Gave In
and Bought Teen Rifle, 2 Guns," *USA Today*, May 26, 1998.

14. Ray Gibson and Stevenson Swanson, "State Probing How Dann Obtained Drug,"
Chicago Tribune, June 3, 1988.

15. Joseph A. Lieberman, *School Shootings: What Every Parent and Educator Needs to
Know to Protect Our Children* (New York: Citadel, 2008), p. 33.

16. "Mother of Jeff Weise seeks to be appointed trustee," Associated Press, Nov. 26,
2005.

17. Conners, "Antidepressants."

18. Ibid.

19. Kurt Danysh statement to police, Kurt Danysh Legal Aid Fund, http://www
.kurtdanysh.com/about.htm.

20. Ron Gasbarro, "List Links Many Violent Acts to Medications' Side Effects."

21. Class Suicidality Labeling Language for Antidepressants, Food and Drug
Administration, http://www.fda.gov/cder/foi/label/2005/20031s045,20936s
020lbl.pdf.

22. Charles Barber, "The Medicated Americans: Antidepressant Prescriptions on the
Rise," *Scientific American*, February 2008, http://www.sciam.com/article.cfm?id
=the-medicated-americans.

23. David Stipp, "Trouble in Prozac," *Fortune*, Nov. 28, 2005, http://money.cnn.com/
magazines/fortune/fortune_archive/2005/11/28/8361973/index.htm.

24. Mark Thompson, "America's Medicated Army," *Time*, June 5, 2008, http://www
.time.com/time/nation/article/0,8599,1811858,00.html.

25. "Patient Information Sheet," Paroxetine hydrochloride (marketed as Paxil), http://
www.fda.gov/Cder/drug/InfoSheets/patient/paroxetinePT.htm.

26. Rhonda Rowland and Dr. Steve Salvatore, "ADHD may be overdiagnosed, study
says," CNN, Sept. 1, 1999, online at http://www.cnn.com/HEALTH/9909/01/
adhd.overdiagnosis/index.html.

27. Jasper Hamill, "Tattoo link to personality disorder in criminals," *Scotland's Sunday
Herald*, July 26, 2008, http://www.sundayherald.com/news/heraldnews/display
.var.2410400.0.tattoo_link_to_personality_disorder_in_criminals.php.

28. Brooke Shields, "War of Words," *New York Times*, July 1, 2005.

29. "Taking the Edge Off," *Christian Worldview Network*, June 22, 2007, http://www
.christianworldviewnetwork.com/article.php/2191/Jim_Elliff.

30. Ibid.

31. Ibid.

32. "Second Book of Hermas," Command IV, *The Lost Books of the Bible and the
Forgotten Books of Eden* (New York: Meridian, 1926), pp. 218–19.

6. FALSE GODS

1. Neale Donald Walsch, *Conversations with God: An Uncommon Dialogue, Book 1*
(Charlottesville, Va.: Hampton Roads, 1995), p. 183.

2. Ibid., p. 119.

3. Ibid., p. 204.

4. Neale Donald Walsch, *Conversations with God: An Uncommon Dialogue, Book 2*
(Charlottesville, Va.: Hampton Roads, 1997), p. 2.

5. Walsch, *Conversations with God, Book 1,* p. 205.

6. Ibid., pp. 205, 207.

7. Ibid., p. 61.

8. *Larry King Live*, April 7, 2000, http://transcripts.cnn.com/
TRANSCRIPTS/0004/07/1kl.00.html.

9. U.S. Department of the Army, *Religious Requirements and Practices of Certain
Selected Groups: A Handbook for Chaplains* (Honolulu: University Press of the
Pacific, 2001).

10. Vivianne Crowley, *Wicca: The Old Religion in the New Age* (Wellingborough, U.K.:
Aquarian, 1989), p. 219.

11. Electa Draper, "Neopaganism growing quickly," *Denver Post*, June 26, 2008,
http://www.denverpost.com/commented/ci_9695062?source=commented-news.

12. Helen A. Berger, *A Community of Witches: Contemporary Neo-Paganism and
Witchcraft in the United States* (Columbia: University of South Carolina Press,
1998), p. 43.

13. Aleister Crowley, *Magick in Theory and Practice, Book 3* (Paris: Lecram Press,
1932).

14. Raymond Moody, *Life After Life: The Investigation of a Phenomenon—Survival of
Bodily Death* (New York: HarperOne, 1975), pp. 11–12.

15. Tal Brooke, *The Mystery of Death* (Berkeley, Calif.: End Run, 2007), pp. 28–29.

16. Ibid., p. 29.

17. Wen Smith, "Twice returned from the near-death experience," *Art Bell After Dark*,
September 1996, p. 10.

18. Tal Brooke, phone interview with author, June 18, 2009.

7. REJECTING GOD

1. Laurie Goodstein, "More Atheists Shout It From the Rooftops," *New York Times*,
April 26, 2009, http://www.nytimes.com/2009/04/27/us/27atheist.html.

2. Barry A. Kosmin and Ariela Keysar, "The American Religious Identification Survey," March 2009, http://livinginliminality.files.wordpress.com/2009/03/aris_report_2008.pdf.

3. Gallup Poll, "Some Americans Reluctant to Vote for Mormon, 72-Year-Old Presidential Candidates," Feb. 20, 2007, http://www.gallup.com/poll/26611/Some-Americans-Reluctant-Vote-Mormon-72YearOld-Presidential-Candidates.aspx.

4. Laura Meckler, "Obama Walks Religious Tightrope Spanning Faithful, Nonbelievers," *Wall Street Journal*, March 24, 2009, http://online.wsj.com/article/SB123785559998620329.html.

5. Barack Obama, Inaugural Address, White House Blog, Jan. 21, 2009, http://www.whitehouse.gov/blog/inaugural-address.

6. "Following atheist trend, Britons seek 'de-baptism,'" Agence France-Presse, March 29, 2008, http://www.breitbart.com/article.php?id=CNG.ae71a038e9b3b47af4f0e9eac9598fd8.2b1&show_article=1&catnum=0.

7. Richard Dawkins, at http://richarddawkins.net/store/index.php?main_page=index&cPath=1.

8. Paul Starobin, "The Godless rise as a political force: Secularist, humanist, freethinking nontheists and atheists are coalescing into a movement with a real agenda," *National Journal*, March 7, 2009, http://www.nationaljournal.com/njmagazine/cs_20090307_9763.php.

9. Ibid.

10. Ibid.

11. Goodstein, "More Atheists Shout It From the Rooftops."

12. Starobin, "The Godless rise as a political force."

13. Ibid.

14. Dennis Prager, "Why Atheist Books Are Bestsellers," WorldNetDaily.com, July 10, 2007, http://www.wnd.com/index.php/index.php?pageId=42486.

15. Ibid.

16. Ibid.

17. Christopher Hitchens, *God Is Not Great: How Religion Poisons Everything* (New York: Twelve, 2007), p. 56.

18. Richard Dawkins, *The God Delusion* (Boston: Houghton Mifflin Harcourt, 2006), p. 51.

19. Jeffrey A. Trachtenberg, "Hitchens Book Debunking The Deity Is Surprise Hit," *Wall Street Journal*, June 22, 2007.

20. Hitchens, *God Is Not Great*, p. 232.

21. Stephen Prothero, "The Unbeliever: Hitchens argues that religion is man-made and murderous," *Washington Post*, May 6, 2007, http://www.washingtonpost.com/wp-dyn/content/article/2007/05/03/AR2007050301907.html.

22. Christopher Hitchens, "God Bless Me, It's a Best-Seller!" *Vanity Fair*, September 2007, http://www.vanityfair.com/politics/features/2007/09/hitchens200709?currentPage=1.

23. Sam Harris, *Letter to a Christian Nation* (New York: Knopf, 2006), p. x.

24. David Kupelian, *The Marketing of Evil: How Radicals, Elitists, and Pseudo-Experts Sell Us Corruption Disguised as Freedom* (Nashville, Tenn.: WND, 2005), p. 173.

25. "Catholic Board Rebukes Bishops For Failing to Stop Abuse," Online NewsHour, Public Broadcasting System, Feb. 27, 2004, http://www.pbs.org/newshour/bb/religion/church_in_crisis.html.

26. Harris, *Letter to a Christian Nation*, pp. 50–51.

27. Ibid., p. 52.

28. C. S. Lewis, *A Grief Observed* (New York: HarperOne paperback, 2001), p. 29.

29. Ibid., pp. 29–30.

30. Ibid., p. 30.

31. Ibid.

32. Ibid., pp. 51–52.

33. Ibid., p. 52.

34. Ibid., pp. 37–38.

35. Robert Jastrow, "The Religion of Science," in *God and the Astronomers* (New York: Readers Library paperback, 2000), p. 105.

36. Ibid., p. 106.

37. Ibid., p. 107.

8. THE WAR ON FATHERS

1. Polly Leider, "Why Boys Are Falling Behind," CBS News, Jan. 23, 2006, http://www.cbsnews.com/stories/2006/01/23/earlyshow/leisure/books/main1231713.shtml.

2. Jeff Swicord, "Survey Finds Young Boys Failing in Schools Across the U.S.," Voice of America, April 13, 2006, http://www.voanews.com/english/archive/2006-04/2006-04-13-voa4.cfm?CFID=159700649&CFTOKEN=97185741&jsessionid=0030230b1f6cfd5363542b 2fc18b2a3c567b.

3. Laura Clark, "Working-class white British boys falling behind everyone else at school," *Daily Mail* (U.K.), Jan. 31, 2008, http://www.dailymail.co.uk/news/article-511615/Working-class-white-British-boys-falling-school.html.

4. Michael Gurian and Kathy Stevens, *The Minds of Boys: Saving Our Sons From Falling Behind in School and Life* (San Francisco: Jossey-Bass, 2005), p. 22.

5. John Whitson, "Boys in school: behind the curve," *Manchester Union Leader*, May 21, 2006.

6. Gurian and Stevens, *The Minds of Boys*, p. 24.

7. Swicord, "Survey Finds Young Boys Failing in Schools Across the U.S."

8. "Attention-Deficit/Hyperactivity Disorder: Symptoms of ADHD," WebMD, http://www.webmd.com/add-adhd/guide/adhd-symptoms.

9. "DEA Briefs & Background, Drugs and Drug Abuse, Drug Descriptions, Methylphenidate," U.S. Drug Enforcement Administration, http://www.usdoj.gov/dea/concern/methylphenidate.html.

10. "Security Outline of the Controlled Substances Act of 1970," Office of Diversion Control, U.S. Drug Enforcement Administration, http://www.deadiversion.usdoj.gov/pubs/manuals/sec/schedules.htm.

11. Gardiner Harris, "Warning Urged On Stimulants Like Ritalin," *New York Times*, Feb. 10, 2006.

12. Ibid.

13. Claudia Wallis, "Getting Hyper About Ritalin," *Time*, Feb. 10, 2006, http://www .time.com/time/health/article/0,8599,1158901,00.html.

14. M. D. Rapport, et al., "Hyperactivity in boys with attention-deficit/hyperactivity disorder (ADHD): A ubiquitous core symptom or manifestation of working memory deficits?," http://www.ncbi.nlm.nih.gov/pubmed/19083090.

15. John Cloud, "Kids with ADHD May Learn Better by Fidgeting," *Time*, March 25, 2009, http://www.time.com/time/health/article/0,8599,1887486,00.html?imw=Y.

16. Jane Clinton, "Churchill 'would've been on Ritalin,'" *Daily Express* (U.K.), March 29, 2009, http://www.express.co.uk/posts/view/91808/Churchill-would-ve-been -on-Ritalin-.

17. "Quiet Gender Gap Hits Collegiate Balance," editorial, *Denver Post*, April 23, 2006.

18. Jennifer Delahunty Britz, "To All the Girls I've Rejected," *New York Times*, March 23, 2006, http://www.nytimes.com/2006/03/23/opinion/23britz.html?_r=1.

19. Judith S. Wallerstein, Julia M. Lewis, and Sandra Blakeslee, *The Unexpected Legacy of Divorce: The 25 Year Landmark Study* (New York: Hyperion, 2000), p. 296.

20. "The Status of Men in New Hampshire," First Biennial Report of the New Hampshire Commission on the Status of Men, Nov. 1, 2005, http://www.nh.gov/ csm/downloads/nh_status_of_men_2005.pdf.

21. "Clinton Signs Deadbeat Parents Punishment Act," CNN, June 24, 1998, http:// www.cnn.com/ALLPOLITICS/1998/06/24/deadbeat.parents.bill.

22. James Hibberd, "Fox zeroes in on 'Bad Dads,'" Reuters, April 23, 2008, http:// www.reuters.com/article/televisionNews/idUSN2347335520080424.

23. Kathleen Parker, "The Father of All Bad Ideas: Fox defines fatherhood down," National Review Online, May 2, 2008, http://article.nationalreview.com/?q=NjIz NmI3MjI0Yzg5ZjU4NTZmOGI4NThjMzhhMzM5ZGQ=.

24. Ibid.

25. Stephen Baskerville, Ph.D., "The Myth of Deadbeat Dads," *Liberty*, 2002, http:// www.ejfi.org/family/family-54.htm.

26. Christina Hoff Sommers, *The War Against Boys: How Misguided Feminism Is Harming Our Young Men* (New York: Simon & Schuster, 2001), p. 13.

27. Ibid.

28. Ibid., p. 44.

29. Ibid., p. 15.

30. Camille Paglia, "It's a Jungle Out There," *Newsday*, 1991, http://users.ipfw.edu/ ruflethe/itsajungleoutthere.htm.

31. Steven D. Stark, *Meet the Beatles: A Cultural History of the Band That Shook Youth, Gender, and the World* (New York: Harper, 2005), p. 3.

32. Richard Luscombe Miami, "U.S. girls embrace gay passion fashion," *Observer* (U.K.), Jan. 4, 2004, http://www.guardian.co.uk/world/2004/jan/04/usa.gay rights.

33. Rene Rosechild, "President Obama declares June Gay and Lesbian Pride Month," Examiner.com, June 6, 2009, http://www.examiner.com/x-6190-Denver-Gay -Parenting-Examiner-y2009m6d6-President-Obama-declares-June-Gay-and -Lesbian-Pride-Month.

34. George Gilder, *Men and Marriage* (Gretna, La.: Pelican, 1986), p. 115.

35. Trayce Hansen, Ph.D., "A Review and Analysis of Research Studies Which Assessed Sexual Preference of Children Raised by Homosexuals," http://www.drtraycehansen.com/Pages/writings_sexpref.html.

36. Andrea Dworkin, *Letters From a War Zone* (New York: Dutton, 1989), p. 146.

9. THE MYSTERIOUS POWER OF HATE

1. Henry Morgenthau, *Ambassador Morgenthau's Story* (Garden City, N.Y.: Doubleday, 1919), p. 307, http://www.armenian-genocide.org/statement_morgenthau.html.

2. Rep. Brad Sherman, D-Calif., *Congressional Record*, April 12, 2000, http://bulk.resource.org/gpo.gov/record/2000/2000_H02181.pdf.

3. "Holy Curiosity," *Time*, March 21, 1949, http://www.time.com/time/magazine/article/0,9171,933806,00.html.

4. Daniel Pipes, "Suicide bombers: A father's pride and glory," *Jerusalem Post*, Aug. 15, 2001, http://www.danielpipes.org/390/suicide-bombers-a-fathers-pride-and-glory.

5. Yaakov Lappin, "Jihad bee buzzes Hamas TV," YnetNews.com, July 16, 2007, http://www.ynetnews.com/articles/0,7340,L-3426218,00.html.

6. Liz Hazelton, "Saudi judge sentences pregnant gang-rape victim to 100 lashes for committing adultery," *Daily Mail* (U.K.), Feb. 11, 2009, http://www.dailymail.co.uk/news/worldnews/article-1141267/Saudi-judge-sentences-pregnant-gang-rape-victim-100-lashes-committing-adultery.html.

7. "Fresh 'honour killing' in Jordan," BBC News, Sept. 10, 2003, http://news.bbc.co.uk/2/hi/middle_east/3097728.stm.

8. "Saudi police 'stopped' fire rescue," BBC News, March 15, 2002, http://news.bbc.co.uk/2/hi/middle_east/1874471.stm.

9. Itamar Marcus, "The genocide mechanism," *Jerusalem Post*, April 25, 2009, http://www.jpost.com/servlet/Satellite?cid=1239710784660&pagename=JPost%2FJPArticle%2FShowFull.

10. Anti-Semitism Documentation Project, Middle East Media Research Institute, May 27, 2008, http://memri.org/bin/articles.cgi?Page=subjects&Area=antisemitism&ID=IA44208.

11. Jessica Bennett, "Into The War Zone: A new documentary explores the history of Bloods-Crips gang violence," *Newsweek*, April 2, 2009, http://www.newsweek.com/id/192153/page/1.

12. "Gangsta Girls," Robert Walker's "Gangs OR Us," http://www.gangsorus.com/gangstagirls.html.

13. "Identity Church Movement: Aryan Nations," Anti-Defamation League, 2001, http://www.adl.org/poisoning_web/aryan_nations.asp.

14. American Nazi Party, http://www.americannaziparty.com/rockwell/materials/index.php.

15. "Spewing hate in Saviour's Day speech following world tour, Louis Farrakhan condemns America and the Jews," Anti-Defamation League, March 5, 1996, http://www.adl.org/presrele/NatIsl_81/2686_81.asp.

16. "Columnist for Egyptian Government Daily to Hitler: 'If Only You Had Done It,

Brother,'" translated by the Middle East Media Research Institute, May 3, 2002, http://www.memri.org/bin/articles.cgi?Area=sd&ID=SP37502.

17. Phyllis Chesler, *The New Anti-Semitism: The Current Crisis and What We Must Do About It* (San Francisco: Jossey-Bass, 2003), pp. 26–27.

18. Ibid., p. 27.

19. Ibid.

20. Ibid., pp. 27–28.

21. John R. Lott Jr., *More Guns, Less Crime: Understanding Crime and Gun Control Laws* (Chicago: University of Chicago Press, 1998), p. 20.

22. Iris Chang, *The Rape of Nanking: The Forgotten Holocaust of World War II* (New York: Penguin, 1997), p. 195.

23. "An Angry Heart Can Lead To Sudden Death," ScienceDaily, Feb. 25, 2009, http://www.sciencedaily.com/releases/2009/02/090223221235.htm.

24. Rabbi Daniel Lapin, *Thou Shall Prosper: Ten Commandments for Making Money* (Hoboken, N.J.: Wiley, 2002), pp. 120–22.

10. SO, WHERE ON EARTH IS GOD?

1. "Church doesn't think like Jesus," WorldNetDaily.com, Dec. 3, 2003, http://www.wnd.com/news/article.asp?ARTICLE_ID=35926.

2. "Parents Describe How They Raise Their Children," Barna Group, Feb. 28, 2005, http://www.barna.org/FlexPage.aspx?Page=BarnaUpdate&BarnaUpdateID=183.

3. George Barna, *Revolution* (Wheaton, Ill.: Tyndale House, 2006), publisher's description.

4. Michael Alison Chandler and Arianne Aryanpur, "Going to Church by Staying at Home: Clergy-Less Living Room Services Seen as a Growing Trend," *Washington Post*, June 4, 2006, http://www.washingtonpost.com/wp-dyn/content/article/2006/06/03/AR2006060300225_pf.html.

5. David Murrow, *Why Men Hate Going to Church* (Nashville, Tenn.: Thomas Nelson, 2004), p. 21.

6. William Penn, *William Penn's Advice to His Children*, 1699, chapter 2, http://www.qhpress.org/quakerpages/qwhp/advice2.htm.

7. Jeanne Guyon, Michael Molinos, and Francois Fenelon, *A Guide to True Peace, or The Excellency of Inward and Spiritual Prayer* (New York: Harper, 1839), pp. 58–60.

11. TURNING THE TABLES ON EVIL IN AMERICA

1. Edward L. Bernays, *Propaganda* (1928; rept. New York: Ig, 2005), pp. 37–38.

2. Ibid.

3. John Stauber and Sheldon Rampton, book review of *The Father of Spin: Edward L. Bernays & The Birth of PR* by Larry Tye, Center for Media and Democracy, http://www.prwatch.org/prwissues/1999Q2/bernays.html.

4. Ibid.

5. Vance Packard, *The Hidden Persuaders* (New York: Pocket, 1957), p. 3.

6. Brian Friel, Richard E. Cohen, and Kirk Victor, "Obama: Most Liberal Senator In

2007," *National Journal*, Jan. 31, 2008, http://news.nationaljournal.com/articles/voteratings.

7. Lydia Saad, " 'Conservatives' Are Single-Largest Ideological Group: Percentage of 'liberals' higher this decade than in early '90s," Gallup Poll, June 15, 2009, http://www.gallup.com/poll/120857/Conservatives-Single-Largest-Ideological-Group.aspx.

8. Alexander Burns, "Halperin at Politico/USC conf.: 'extreme pro-Obama' press bias," Politico.com, Nov. 22, 2008, http://www.politico.com/news/stories/1108/15885.html.

9. Deborah Howell, "An Obama Tilt in Campaign Coverage," *Washington Post*, Nov. 9, 2008, http://www.washingtonpost.com/wp-dyn/content/article/2008/11/07/AR2008110702895.html.

10. Jefferson Morley, "Putin's Russia—Case Study in Media Control," *Washington Post*, July 13, 2006, http://blog.washingtonpost.com/worldopinionroundup/2006/07/putins_russia_case_study_in_me.html.

11. "Chris Matthews: 'I Felt This Thrill Going Up My Leg' As Obama Spoke," Huffington Post, Feb. 13, 2008, http://www.huffingtonpost.com/2008/02/13/chris-matthews-i-felt-t_n_86449.html.

12. Kyle Drennen, "Newsweek's Evan Thomas: Obama Is 'Sort of God,' " NewsBusters, June 5, 2009, http://newsbusters.org/blogs/kyle-drennen/2009/06/05/newsweek-s-evan-thomas-obama-sort-god.

13. Jason Linkins, "David Shuster: GOP 'Going Nuts' For Teabagging, But They 'Need A Dick Armey,' " Huffington Post, April 15, 2009, http://www.huffingtonpost.com/2009/04/14/david-shuster-nationwide_n_186815.html.

14. Jason Linkins, " 'Tea Bagging' Rallies Ruthlessly Mocked On Maddow Show," Huffington Post, April 15, 2009, http://www.huffingtonpost.com/2009/04/09/rachel-maddow-ana-marie-c_n_185445.html.

15. Matthew Balan, "CNN's Anderson Cooper: 'It's Hard to Talk When You're Tea-Bagging,' " NewsBusters.org, April 15, 2009, http://newsbusters.org/blogs/matthew-balan/2009/04/15/cnns-anderson-cooper-its-hard-talk-when-youre-tea-bagging.

16. Tony Ortega, "Matt Lauer's Roast: Tom Cruise, Katie Couric, and 3 Hours of Dick Jokes," *Village Voice*, Oct. 24, 2008, http://blogs.villagevoice.com/runninscared/archives/2008/10/matt_lauers_roa.php.

17. John Perazzo, "Saul Alinsky," DiscoverTheNetworks.org, April 2008, http://www.discoverthenetworks.org/individualProfile.asp?indid=2314.

18. Beth Fouhy, "Obama tackles questions about his experience, touting background as Illinois lawmaker," Associated Press, April 22, 2007.

19. Saul Alinsky, *Rules for Radicals: A Practical Primer for Realistic Radicals* (New York: Random House, 1971), p. xix.

20. Ibid., p. 128.

21. Ibid., p. 136.

22. Ibid., dedication page.

23. American Death Camps, Life Dynamics, Denton, Texas, http://www.lifedynamics.com/deathcamps/DeathCamps.cfm.

24. "No Greater Joy," Pro-Life Action League, http://prolifeaction.org/sidewalk.

25. Ibid.

26. Chelsea Schilling, "New trend: Ultrasounds before abortion," WorldNetDaily.com, Feb. 10, 2009, http://www.wnd.com/index.php/index.php?pageId=88517.

27. Shana Schutte, "Focus Celebrates Option Ultrasound Success," Focus on the Family, http://www.heartlink.org/OUP/a000000422.cfm.

28. "Option Ultrasound: Revealing Life, to Save Life," Focus on the Family, June 30, 2009, http://www.heartlink.org/pdf/DonorOUPUpdate.pdf.

29. "Kerry's Testimony," National Review Online, April 23, 2004, http://www.national review.com/document/kerry200404231047.asp.

30. "Army CID Investigations of VVAW War Crimes Allegations," WinterSoldier.com, March 4, 2008, http://www.wintersoldier.com/staticpages/index.php?page=WSI _CID.

31. Scott Swett, "Media still lying about the Swift Boat Veterans," American Thinker, May 25, 2009, http://www.americanthinker.com/2009/05/media_still_lying _about_the_sw.html.

32. Gwen Glazer, Meg Kinnard, and Jennifer Koons, "Kerry Vietnam Record At Center Of Several TV Campaigns," *National Journal*, Aug. 24, 2004, http://www .nationaljournal.com/members/adspotlight/2004/08/0824wh1.htm.

33. Charlton Heston, "Winning the Cultural War," speech delivered at Austin Hall, Harvard Law School, Feb. 16, 1999, http://www.americanrhetoric.com/speeches/ charltonhestonculturalwar.htm.

34. Walter Hemmens, "Forgotten hero who plotted a route to abolition," *Times* (London), March 28, 2007, http://www.timesonline.co.uk/tol/news/uk/ article1577379.ece.

35. James L. Gattuso, "Fairness Doctrine, R.I.P.: Stay tuned for the real fight over media regulation," National Review Online, July 5, 2007, http://article.national review.com/?q=NmYzNGU0ZjAxNWFlOWE2NmUzYWFjMmEwNWM1OTgy ZjQ=.

36. Daniel Henninger, "Rush to Victory: Why is Harry Reid acting like David Koresh? Because conservatives are winning," *Wall Street Journal*, April 29, 2005, http:// www.opinionjournal.com/columnists/dhenninger/?id=110006626.

37. "George Orwell," Conservapedia, http://www.conservapedia.com/George_Orwell.

38. "Zogby Poll: Online News Sources Top All Other Outlets," Zogby International, June 15, 2009, http://www.zogby.com/news/ReadNews.cfm?ID=1710.

+

ACKNOWLEDGMENTS

Many thanks to my journalistic colleagues and friends at World-NetDaily, especially Joseph Farah and Jerome Corsi, for their inspiration, encouragement, and valuable feedback, and to my longtime friend Bob Just for his superb insights on the manuscript. Thanks also to my designer, Linda Daly, for creating another outstanding book cover.

I'm grateful also to Anthony Ziccardi for believing in this book, as well as editor Mitchell Ivers and the rest of the world-class team at Simon & Schuster.

I'd like to acknowledge also the many readers of *The Marketing of Evil* who have written to encourage and edify me, and who have, in so many ways, prodded me to write this sequel.

Finally, heartfelt thanks to my wife and soul mate, Jean, and my children, Joshua and Sarah, for helping to keep me real.

INDEX